The Musical Theatre

A Celebration

By the same author

THE STREET WHERE I LIVE

The Musical Theatre

A Celebration

Alan Jay Lerner

COLLINS, 8 Grafton Street, London W 1   1986

To Liz, who is all the music

William Collins Sons & Co Ltd
London · Glasgow · Sydney · Auckland
Toronto · Johannesburg

BRITISH LIBRARY CATALOGUING IN PUBLICATION DATA

Lerner, Alan Jay
The musical theatre: a celebration.
1. Musical revue, comedy, etc.—History
I. Title
782.81′09   ML1700

ISBN 0—00—217249—6

First published 1986
© Gilmount Ltd. 1986

Photoset in Linotron Sabon by
Ace Filmsetting Ltd, Frome

Made and printed in Great Britain
by William Collins Sons & Co. Ltd, Glasgow

CONTENTS

PERMISSIONS

COLOUR PLATES

CREDITS

The publishers gratefully acknowledge the following sources for illustrations used in this book:

COLOUR PLATES

Dewynters: PAGE FIFTEEN. Dominic Photography: PAGE ELEVEN. EMI Music Publishing: PAGE SIX (below left). Mander and Mitchenson Theatre Collection: PAGE FOUR (both); PAGE FIVE (both). Museum of the City of New York: PAGE EIGHT (below); PAGE TEN (all). Martin Phillips Collection: PAGE SIX (below right). Phototeque: PAGE EIGHT (above). Royal College of Music, London: PAGE ONE, PAGE TWO, PAGE THREE. Martha Swope: PAGE THIRTEEN (both); PAGE FOURTEEN (both); PAGE SIXTEEN (both). Reg Wilson: PAGE SEVEN, PAGE TWELVE.

BLACK AND WHITE ILLUSTRATIONS

Author's collection: p. 46 (above); p. 62 (left); p. 101; p. 161 (above); p. 173; p. 185; p. 205 (below). Baron: p. 153 (top). The Bettman Archive: p. 34; p. 81 (below). Cecil Beaton/Courtesy of Sothebys, London: p. 184 (both). Culver Pictures: p. 67 (all); p. 74 (above); p. 118 (above); p. 134 (both); p. 155 (below); p. 161 (below); p. 166; p. 180 (right); p. 189 (right); p. 191; p. 194; p. 208 (above right). Chappell/Intersong: p. 78 (both); p. 86. Donald Cooper: p. 232 (right). Dominic Photography: p. 229 (above). Dewynters Ltd: p. 232 (left). Fred Fehl: p. 189 (left). Valli V. Dreyfus Firth: p. 51 (left). George E. Joseph: p. 229 (below). Karsh: p. 136. Mander and Mitchenson Theatre Collection: p. 29 (left and below centre); p. 30 (both); p. 40; p. 42; p. 46 (below); p. 89; p. 97 (both); p. 108; p. 111 (both); p. 112 (all); p. 157 (above); p. 200; p. 201; p. 223 (above). Angus McBean: p. 153 (below). Museum of the City of New York: p. 127 (above); p. 179; p. 205 (above); p. 219. New York Public Library: p. 55 (top, left); p. 72 (left); p. 74 (left); p. 106 (both); p. 129; p. 142; p. 208 (below). Cole Porter Musical Literary Property Trusts: p. 95. Rodgers and Hammerstein Theatre Library: p. 174; p. 180 (left). Royal College of Music, London: p. 15; p. 18; p. 23. Martha Swope: p. 223 (below). Vandamm: p. 51 (right); p. 62 (above); p. 88; p. 118 (below); p. 127 (below); p. 132; p. 144/145 (all); p. 148; p. 149; p. 157 (below); p. 167; p. 188; p. 212. Victoria and Albert Museum: p. 12; p. 27 (all); p. 29 (above centre and right); p. 208 (above left). White Studio: p. 55 (right); p. 62 (below); p. 72 (above); p. 81 (above); p. 103.

The author would also like to thank Stephanie Sheahan for her part in the making of this book.

Introduction

It is highly unlikely that any spectator from the days of stone seats to the present has ever learned anything from the theatre. He may experience the entire lexicon of emotions; be tickled to laughter or moved to tears; be stimulated, mystified or exalted by the grandeur of language. But leave the theatre genuinely intellectually changed? Never.

One service, however, that the theatre is ably equipped to perform is to transport the ticket holder to a cloud of enjoyment so that when the curtain falls, he walks up the aisle and back into life refreshed from a brief holiday from himself. Returning to his own skin, he may even feel a little more comfortable in it – at least for a while. Vacations have always been therapeutic. Years ago, before the medical age of specialization, antibiotics, pills for all occasions and computerized diagnoses, doctors frequently recommended a visit to the mountains or the sea. Emotional escape is also splendid therapy although psychiatrically unappreciated, and one of the art forms that at its best can provide the itinerary for this happy excursion is the popular musical theatre – originally *opéra-bouffe*, then operetta, then musical comedy, then musical play – or simply 'musicals'.

That is the subject of this book. Musicals. How they happened, how they developed, how they changed, how they were shaped and reshaped, who created them and why, what was responsible, and why musicals are the way they are today in this last quarter of what we all hope will not be the last century.

1 The Founding Father

Only the pyramids appeared without any cultural preparation. There is no record of pre-pyramid architecture or thought that would account for the intellectual complexity and visual glory of the great pyramid of Cheops. So the popular musical theatre, along with all the other creative inventions of man – with the exception of the pyramids – while deprived of a birth, had a beginning, a transitional beginning in which the artistic flame was fanned by the winds of the historic and sociological changes that began to swirl at the end of the eighteenth century.

The first crude steam engine was built in Alexandria, Egypt, in the second century BC. However, it did not become a practical invention until James Watt developed it into a useful instrument in 1769. What he did was turn on the valve of the industrial era which hatched the industrial revolution, fill the skies with the grey clouds of the factory, create a new kind of working and middle class, and with men leaving home to go to work for the first time, probably did as much to upset the sexual balance of man and woman as any single event since the inception of marriage. It also created financial competition which changed the landscape of the world, and made greed and ruthlessness not only respectable but envied.

The American Constitution was written exactly twenty years after Watt's invention. It was an agrarian doctrine created as much for the protection of property as for the rights of the individual. One cannot help but muse what the content of that document might have been if the founding fathers could have foreseen the industrial age waiting over the horizon.

Revolution was in the air and in 1793 the French, weary of taxes and war and the extravagance of the aristocracy, proceeded to lop off the periwigged heads of their oppressors and a burgeoning middle class began to roam the streets of Paris in search of entertainment.

Whether art follows life or life follows art, as early as the 1780s Mozart anticipated the popularization of the musical theatre by frequently, and at times bitterly, complaining that theatre music should be for everybody and not for the manicured gardens and gilded opera houses reserved for the titled few. In fact he recorded in one of his letters his ecstatic pleasure that his opera

Figaro had become a genuine 'hit' in Prague, and his melodies and quadrilles were being played and sung all over the city.

But it was in Paris that the operatic revolution dug in its claws. In Italy, they had developed a form of opera called *opera-buffa*, which fundamentally meant opera with dialogue and usually with lighter music. In Paris it became known as *opéra-comique* (and later *opéra-bouffe*) – in fact the theatre that became known as the Opéra-Comique was originally called Le Théâtre Italien – and many well-trained musicians began to lighten their ways. Opera houses and music halls began to dot the city, playing the music of such composers as François Boieldieu, Daniel Auber, Ferdinand Herold and Adolphe Adam. The music halls featured a form of light opera-vaudeville, composed of a series of musical sketches that were satirical and humorous and readily digestible. In 1840, Donizetti brought Paris to its feet with his *opéra-comique*, *La Fille du Régiment*. It was filled with all the popular musical idioms of the day, as well as one or two melodies that led the imaginary charts.

Donizetti

There was no doubt that a popular musical theatre was evolving. One of the leading lights was a prolific and gifted composer called Florimond Ronger who economized on programme ink by calling himself Hervé. His *Don Quichotte and Sancho Panza* is considered by many to be the first genuine operetta. But talented as he was – he was a librettist and actor as well as composer – Hervé was not a giant, and the musical theatre hungered for one. An explosive creative innovator who would make operetta an enduring art form. He finally appeared, arriving in Paris in 1833. His name was Jacob Offenbach. He was thirteen years old and he came from Cologne, Germany.

Although at the beginning of the eighteenth century a man named Farina invented a skin tonic of pleasing aroma which became known as Eau de Cologne, Cologne was not a perfume factory if you were Jewish. Nor, for that matter, was any city or town in Germany. Even before the still inconceivable Hitlerian horror, the fatherland did not have a distinguished record for tolerance. To be fair about the unforgivable, Germany at the time was not unique. Anti-semitism flourished in varying degrees in all the countries of Europe. In France, however, due primarily to the propagandizing efforts of Voltaire and Montesquieu, there was a dramatic change in attitudes towards the minorities. In 1784, the tax levied against the Jewish population was removed and, after the revolution, all the courts that presided over matters pertaining to religious faith were sent home for good. Paris became a magnet for such men of genius as Meyerbeer, Heinrich Heine, as well as lesser luminaries and, eventually, thirteen-year-old Jacob Offenbach.

Jacob's father, Isaac, took his name from the place of his birth, Offenbach-am-Main. Not surprisingly, they were a wandering family until they finally settled in Cologne in 1802 where Jacob was born in 1819. He was the seventh child. Eventually there would be ten.

Isaac was a cantor by profession, a cantor being the leading singer in a synagogue choir. He made a few extra Marks book-binding, and was also sufficiently accomplished on the violin, flute and guitar to give lessons. Among his pupils were his children, the most talented being Jacob and his older brother and sister, Julius and Isabella. Jacob was playing the violin at the age of six and by the time he was eight years old had begun to compose. At the age of nine, for reasons unknown, Jacob developed a fascination for the cello which unfortunately was a little larger than he; but before the year was out he had grown enough to handle it and his father bought him one. It soon became apparent that the cello was indeed his instrument and his talent prodigious.

It was painfully obvious to Isaac that there was a limit to the successful future of any Jew in Cologne. He also knew that Paris was the cultural centre of Europe and the home of the one and only Paris Conservatoire. So, for both religious and artistic reasons, when Jacob was thirteen, Isaac scraped up enough money to take him and his brother Julius to Paris.

Being a man of singular determination, Isaac finally procured an audition

with the Director of the Conservatoire, Cherubini, for auditions for both his sons. When Cherubini heard that Jacob was thirteen, he immediately informed Isaac that the Conservatoire did not take children of that age. However, he consented to listen. Halfway through Jacob's first piece on the cello, Cherubini raised his hand, stopped him and told Isaac that his son was now a student at the Conservatoire.

Jacob only lasted a little over a year at the Conservatoire. By 1835 he had Frenchified his name to Jacques and decided he had learned all he could from the Conservatoire, departed its premises and threw himself into the commercial world of recitals and composing. He began his performing career rather inconspicuously in a music shop, but his talent as a cellist was undeniable and he was soon a popular performer on the salon circuit. While celloing for his supper, his professional composing career began with an occasional number in the *opéra-bouffe* vaudeville world of the music hall.

His virtuosity on the cello attracted the attention of an English concert manager named John Mitchell, which produced two delightful events. First, Mitchell arranged for a concert tour in England which featured a performance before Her Majesty the young Queen Victoria. Secondly, Jacques fell in love with Mitchell's French stepdaughter, Herminie d'Alcain. Love proved to be profitable because he wrote a song for her, 'A Toi' (To You), which became his first popular success. (Marital love, as an inspiration, seems to be more rare than one would imagine. To my knowledge, only two popular composers actually wrote love songs to their wives, Irving Berlin and Harold Rome.)

In 1844 Jacques proposed to Herminie and was accepted. Marriage necessitated a minor religious alteration. Jacques converted to Catholicism, they were married, had five children and lived happily ever after – despite an occasional wander by Jacques from the straight and narrow. Considering the immense volume of work he produced, it is a wonder he had time to stray at all.

In 1847 came his first major opportunity. He had written a one-act comic opera called *L'Alcove*, which was presented before a gala audience in one of the more fashionable concert halls. The success of it was such that he was commissioned to write a comic opera for the Théâtre Lyrique, a theatre owned and managed by the composer Adam. It was to be ready for production in the following year of 1848.

Alas, in the following year of 1848 also came the 'July Revolution', leaving France in a turmoil. France, a nation celebrated for its logic, first removed its king during the revolution of 1799 and replaced him in 1804 with Napoleon Bonaparte, an emperor. With the defeat of Napoleon and because of general disenchantment with emperors, France immediately returned to a king; then in the revolution of 1848 the French got rid of the king and established a republic. To complete this tale of progress in government, in 1852, following a coup d'état, Napoleon III, the nephew of Napoleon I, was elected emperor.

When the 1848 revolution came, Offenbach was suddenly seized by a spell of homesickness, and he and his wife and daughter returned to Cologne. When he arrived there he once again became Jacob Offenbach. He and his little family remained in Cologne for two years, where he kept the food on the table by the occasional recital and by writing two songs that became quite popular. By 1850, Paris had returned to some degree of normality and Jacob decided it was safe to pack his bags and become Jacques again.

After two years' absence from the boulevards, Offenbach viewed the Parisian theatrical scene with a fresh and critical eye – and he was not pleased. In his opinion, to quote from one of his letters, the Opéra-Comique was 'no longer the home of true comic opera, with really gay, bright, spirited music with real life in it'. Perhaps he was not aware of it himself, but what Offenbach was searching for was operetta, a term he did not use to describe his own work for another six years.

Now it so happened that in 1851 London presented a Great Exhibition, rather like the expositions that are presented from time to time in cities today. It was a roaring success and Napoleon III decided that Paris must not be outdone. The French have always regarded cultural achievement as their exclusive property, and therefore a Great Exhibition was planned for 1855. There was no doubt that Paris would be inundated with tourists, and Offen-

Offenbach

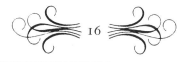

bach saw it as a propitious moment to relieve his artistic frustration in and for the theatre.

Off the Champs Élysées there stood a small wooden structure called the Théâtre Lacaze. It had a staggering capacity of fifty seats and had primarily been used for the presentation of magic shows. Offenbach rounded up a handful of backers, or 'angels' as we now refer to them, obtained a lease on the theatre, remodelled it, changed its name to the Théâtre des Bouffes-Parisiens, and sat down to provide the musical merchandise. The French licensing laws decreed that in a theatre of that size, only three speaking parts could appear on the stage at one time. Why such a law should have been in existence defies all logic. The restriction applied only to speaking parts. One could have as many characters on the stage as would fit, provided they remained mute. To compound the enigma, the law was later modified to allow four characters to speak.

On 5 July 1855, the Théâtre des Bouffes-Parisiens opened its doors to the public — well, fifty members of the public. Imagine, if you will, this minute theatre in which the seats were installed at a most precarious angle and the stage itself so raked that the actors had to be careful not to slide into the audience.

The bill of fare on that opening night consisted of a prologue, an assortment of miniature one-act *comiques* complete with pantomime (the fourth character), and, finally, a one-act *opéra-bouffe* entitled *Les Deux Aveugles* — literally 'The Two Blind Men', but later translated into English as 'The Two Beggars'. The plot of this revolutionary little piece was the work of the man who was to become one of Offenbach's most frequent collaborators, Ludovic Halévy. It concerned two impoverished street musicians who feigned blindness for sympathy, engaged in a bitter quarrel over who was entitled to a coin that had been thrown their way, until finally peace was restored by the appearance of another customer. Curtain.

Considering the cream-puff plots of the period, *Les Deux Aveugles* seemed from another planet. The goal of this bitter bit of life was fun. The music was light, melodic and dramatically skilful. And one song was soon hummed and whistled by 'tout Paris'.

In contemporary jargon, *Les Deux Aveugles* was a 'smash'. It became included in the repertoire of almost every fringe musical theatre in Paris. It was translated into English and German and reproduced in London and Vienna, where its success was repeated and its composer hailed.

Success, contrary to civilian belief, is not so much heady wine as it is a stimulant. When one writes something that one likes and then discovers others like it too, one is encouraged to do more. And no one did more than Offenbach. During the next six years, he composed over forty works for his little fifty-seat theatre. He satirized the styles of other composers, the social mores of his time and, above all, life at the Court.

Far from irritating the Emperor and his beautiful wife, the Empress Eugénie – she of the famous hats – the sovereigns were enchanted. Oddly enough, one of the principal sources of information about their enchantment with Offenbach was their dentist.

Dr Tom Evans, a Philadelphia dentist who lived in Paris for close to three dozen years, was probably the only qualified practitioner in the city. So far and wide was his reputation that his waiting room was constantly filled with the aching crowned heads of Europe, and he was a regular guest at the Palace. His memoirs mention Napoleon and Eugénie's enjoyment of Offenbach. They were, in fact, frequent first-nighters. Parisians were quite amazed because the disinterest of the 'royals' in music was well known.

It was inevitable that a composer of Offenbach's restless gifts would eventually find the parameters of the one-act musical too confining. Two years after the opening of the Théâtre des Bouffes-Parisiens, Offenbach decided to attempt a full-length work. The result was, and is, one of the landmarks of operetta. In 1859, the Théâtre des Bouffes-Parisiens presented its first full-scale operetta, *Orfée aux Enfers*, known in English as *Orpheus in the Under-world*.

Its birth was a reasonably smooth delivery. The press was good, not overwhelming but good, and the public seemed adequately entertained. Magnificently designed by Gustave Doré, the music was Offenbach at his captivating, melodic and 'spirited' best. Fresh in everyone's mind was the classical and much revered musical telling of the story of Orpheus by Gluck. In Offenbach's version, not only did he parody one of Gluck's melodies, but Orpheus and Eurydice are treated as a bitching married couple who speak in Parisian patois. Orpheus, instead of playing the lute, is a violinist and a wretched one at that. When Pluto ascends from the underworld and seduces Eurydice, she is delighted to escape from the arms of her husband. And so on. The run of *Orpheus in the Underworld* might have been limited had it not been for the invaluable assistance of one of the leading critics in Paris who, one day many months after the play had opened, took it upon himself to be portentously outraged by the work and blasted it in his column as a desecration of the beloved classics. The Parisians found this too enticing for words, and with whetted appetites flocked to the Théâtre des Bouffes-Parisiens in ever increasing numbers. (Ah, if only the theatre-going public of New York and London would react the same today to bad reviews, what a glorious, carefree life we authors would have! At least we can cheer ourselves by remembering an observation once made by Sibelius that on the entire face of the earth there is not one statue erected to a critic.)

With *Orpheus in the Underworld* and all that came thereafter, Offenbach established operetta as a genuine art form. To be precise, operetta means a musical with dialogue. It also implies a certain style of text and a specific dramatic level of characterization that forbids the tragic arias and high drama

Music sheet for *Les Brigands*

of opera. In Offenbach's case, he could not conceive of an operetta without wit, but the wit that later inspired Johann Strauss slowly faded into the sunset, until by the turn of the century operetta on the European side of the Channel became almost exclusively romantic, with the occasional heavy-handed comic interlude.

Interestingly enough, Offenbach is traditionally regarded as a French composer and what he created, French operetta. The truth is that his

influences were primarily Mozart, Rossini and Donizetti. Even the 'can-can', which he made his and which adorned so many of his works, is not of French origin but North African. No, what makes *Orpheus*, for example, French, is the libretto. It is true that the taste and inspiration for the style of the text may have been Offenbach and the manner of setting Offenbach. It is also true that had he not been in Paris where there was a public with an eager appetite, he may not have been encouraged to satisfy his own artistic instincts. But it was the frequently maligned and underestimated text which caught the attention of the audience whose sensitive ear heard the whispers of desire for change before they were even uttered. The works were French primarily because they were written in French and presented in Paris.

Offenbach's fame spread across Europe like a musical zephyr and his music became as well known in the major capital cities of Europe as it was in Paris. He also conducted in London, Paris and Berlin and legend has it that while conducting in Vienna, he met Johann Strauss (the younger) and suggested to him that he try his hand at operetta.

The influence of Offenbach's work is inestimable. At times it is startlingly specific. In 1869 he wrote a highly successful comic operetta called *The Brigands*. He sent it to W. S. Gilbert in London to see if he would be interested in translating and adapting it for the London stage. However, unknown to both of them, another management had asked another librettist to do the same work and that was the one eventually produced. But Gilbert's work was not a total loss, because the resemblance between *The Brigands* and *The Pirates of Penzance* exceeds all bounds of coincidence. Another of Offenbach's works, *La Périchole*, was of the fluffy, romantic stuff that later influenced Stolz, Kalman, Lehár, and all those who created the style of operetta at the turn of the century that endured until the end of operetta in the last days of the twenties.

When Offenbach died in 1880, he left behind over 100 operettas of various lengths and countless songs and orchestral works. At the time of his death, he was still at work on the last act of *The Tales of Hoffmann* and most of the orchestrations were still to be done. The work was completed by Ernest Guiraud. It was a wise choice because Guiraud, an expert craftsman, was able to accomplish the seemingly impossible task without destroying the style or fabric of the work.

To this day Offenbach remains one of the most performed composers who ever lived. *La Vie Parisienne* was revived in the 1960s in a brilliant production directed by Jean-Louis Barrault and took Paris by storm all over again. I am of the opinion that the text of *La Vie Parisienne* contains probably the best and wittiest lyrics France ever produced. Two of Offenbach's works, *La Belle Hélène* and *The Tales of Hoffmann*, found their way into the operatic repertoire of opera houses the world over. In the musical theatre he was indeed the father of us all.

2 The City that Danced

Beginning with the defeat of Napoleon in the early years of the nineteenth century, the Austro-Hungarian empire slowly, stitch by stitch, began to come apart at the seams. In Vienna, of which the rest of Austria is merely the suburbs, everybody knew it and everybody tried not to feel it. Through it all, the fountains still played exquisitely in the magnificent gardens of the summer palace of Schoenbrunn. And the people escaped. They ate (Viennese pastry was a triumph of epicurean art), they drank (over 400,000 barrels of wine and 380,000 barrels of beer a year), and they danced and danced and danced.

The traditional dance of the Austrian Tyrol was a three-quarter affair called the *Ländler*. It was not particularly graceful, but then how could it be with all the paraphernalia one wore to keep warm? It slowly found its way down the mountains to Vienna where it was reshaped and moulded by a young composer named Josef Lanner into that most irresistible, graceful and joyous of dances – the waltz.

The waltzes gushed from Lanner's pen to the delight of the Viennese and, in particular, his closest friend, the conductor and composer Johann Strauss. Although his music was a far cry from the melodic genius of his son, Johann Strauss II, Strauss's waltzes and polkas were satisfactory enough, and he became the Glenn Miller of his time, a conductor of wide renown and the favourite composer – until his son – of the Emperor Franz-Josef.

Johann Strauss II was born in 1825. Because of some bedroom activity of a highly irregular nature by his maternal grandmother, he grew up looking more Spanish than Viennese. Some say that his Latin looks stemmed from a Spanish nobleman. Others maintain the Spanish nobleman was an invention to give the tale a little style and that the original sire was a gypsy. But be it gypsy or hidalgo, Johann II was an extremely handsome man who took advantage of his talent and good looks at every possible feminine opportunity.

Life in the Strauss household was a tempestuous one, primarily due to Johann I who was a man of considerable temperament. As Johann II's talent began to emerge, he (Johann II) did everything in his power to prevent any competitive feeling with his father, and went out of his way to praise him on

every possible occasion. The truth is he had profound respect and admiration for his father, as the following quote will testify:

> My father was a musician by the grace of God ... he spread the fame of German dance music through the world and severe judges did not withhold acknowledgment ... that his sparkling rhythms stemmed from the pure spring of musical art. As a conductor he possessed that indefinable something which carried the players with him, implanted itself in the listeners, and made their hearts and pulses beat quicker. My father was a pure artist of the highest degree, but not for a moment was he presumptuous enough to put himself on the same pedestal with the heroes of great art. But his art made some sorrows vanish, smoothed furrows, raised life's courage, gave back the joys of life, comforted, rejoiced, elated ... and for this, humanity will preserve his memory.

As Hervé had been the predecessor of Offenbach, so the rightful father of Viennese operetta was Franz von Suppé. The evening of 24 November 1860 is considered by many to be when Viennese operetta began. The operetta was von Suppé's *The Boarding School*, and although it is long forgotten musically, historically it is not. His works may be little played today, but he was immensely successful in his time and his operettas were performed not only in Vienna, but in London, Paris and New York. He led a rich and luxurious life, but, with the exception of two overtures, the 'Light Cavalry' and 'Poet and Peasant', he was, alas, primarily a man who lived long after his operettas were forgotten.

In 1931 an attempt was made to resurrect von Suppé in the grand manner with a performance at the Metropolitan Opera of his most popular work, *Boccaccio*. In England when a play 'goes like a bomb', it is a howling success. In America when a play 'bombs', it is a screaming failure. The revival of *Boccaccio* was a New York 'bomb'. Nevertheless, von Suppé did indeed lay the road which Johann Strauss (from now on in this text Johann Strauss means Johann II) later paved so gloriously.

Whether Strauss was prompted by Offenbach's suggestion or by his own creative urge is of no consequence, but in 1870 he tried his hand at operetta, and in February of the following year his first effort, *Indigo and the Forty Thieves*, opened in Vienna. It was an English 'bomb' and even a rather inferior libretto could not dent the enthusiasm of the audience as wave after wave of melody came entrancingly from the pit and stage. Strauss was formally launched on a career that would see him become the emperor of Viennese operetta.

Like Offenbach, wit was the essential ingredient of the plot of all Strauss's operettas. He wrote eleven in all, but his triumph occurred on 5 April 1874 with the first performance of *Die Fledermaus*, which is unquestionably the greatest operetta ever written.

Although successful on the opening night, the reaction was far from the jubilation the work warranted. Part of it may be blamed on the social atmosphere of the moment. Vienna had just experienced an horrendous stock market crash and the financial life of the city was in chaos. The theatre in general suffered commercially and the mood of the people was far from high-spirited. The critics also failed to appreciate the glory of what they had seen and heard, and there was considerable nit-picking in the press.

Later that year *Die Fledermaus* opened in Berlin, where it was received with the enthusiasm it deserved, running over 200 performances compared to the mere 68 when it opened in Vienna. Two years later it went to London, where its reception was similar to that of Vienna. It reached New York in the early eighties. Slowly but surely its fame began to spread, and within a decade of its opening, Vienna and the world came to realize it was indeed a masterpiece. Besides being one of the most played works ever written, it is also performed in every opera house in the world. When it was revived on Broadway in 1931 and called *Champagne Sec*, the pit pianist was a struggling composer of Viennese birth named Frederick Loewe. The leading lady was Kitty Carlisle, who later married the great Moss Hart who directed the initial production of *My Fair Lady* in 1956, composed by Frederick Loewe. In 1950 the Metropolitan Opera presented *Die Fledermaus* in English with a text by one of the best lyric writers America has produced, Howard Dietz, and it was directed by Garson Kanin.

Die Fledermaus has a small cast for an operetta, only one or two more than the number of people responsible for the text. The libretto was by two gentlemen named Haffner and Genée, who based it on a French play by Meilhac and Halévy who had, in turn, based it on a German play by Roderich Bendix. There were four producers responsible for the original production, and with the addition of the five authors and Johann Strauss and the director, it made for quite a crowd. The plot of *Die Fledermaus* is considered one of the wittiest in operetta literature, although when one reads it in outline it hardly seems worthy of a chuckle. Plot-telling will not be a feature of this volume, but because it is the one and only *Fledermaus*, here it is, briefly.

Rosalind, married to Eisenstein, has a ubiquitous admirer named Alfred. Her husband is about to go to prison for insulting a tax collector. (Am I boring you?) Eisenstein's friend comes to take him to prison but suggests they make a brief detour en route to a party given by one Prince Orlofsky. When the two men have gone, the prison governor arrives, also to take Eisenstein to prison, and takes Alfred instead.

It so happens that Rosalind too is going to Orlofsky's party, for some reason as an Hungarian countess, mask and all. For some even more mysterious reason Adele, Rosalind's maid, is also a guest at the party. Eisenstein meets the 'countess' at the party and flirts with her scandalously.

Morning comes and Eisenstein appears in prison where Alfred has spent

Music sheet for *Die Fledermaus*

the night. Featured in this last act is the jailer, who does what has always seemed to me an endless comic turn which audiences find uproarious. (I suppose this scene is so successful because one so seldom laughs in an opera house.) Rosalind finally appears, the plot is unknotted and everyone lives happily ever after.

Needless to say, the success of Strauss and the popularity of his operettas inspired others to jump in 'the blue Danube'. Two of the less dim of the lesser lights were Karl Millocker and Karl Michael Ziehrer. Millocker's best known work was *Countess Dubarry*, which was a great success in Vienna and had numerous productions in numerous cities thereafter. In order not to violate the precious gaiety of the operetta style, the play did not end with Dubarry in two pieces. It actually made its way to Broadway, in English naturally, in the early thirties and Grace Moore played the lead. It became the stepping stone that led her eventually to the Metropolitan and a brilliant career.

Karl Michael Ziehrer achieved a fame far beyond his talent, not uncommon in the theatre, and one of his works, *The Kiss Waltz*, went to Broadway in 1911 where its most distinguished feature was the additional music provided by an unknown composer named Jerome Kern.

Johann Strauss died in 1899. He caught a chill while conducting a jubilee performance of *Die Fledermaus*. It developed into double pneumonia and he passed away a few days later. The joyous catalogue of operettas and waltzes that he left behind is unparalleled, and all composers of operettas thereafter owe him a considerable debt. Even Richard Strauss (no relation) incorporated (polite for pinched) one of his waltzes in *Der Rosenkavalier*.

Johann Strauss's funeral was that of an emperor's. More than 100,000 people lined the streets to bid him farewell. He was buried next to his father and his good friend, Josef Lanner, and, quite rightfully, close to Schubert and Brahms.

LA FILLE DU REGIMENT.

Music sheet for Donizetti's *La Fille du Regiment*

Music sheet for *Patience*

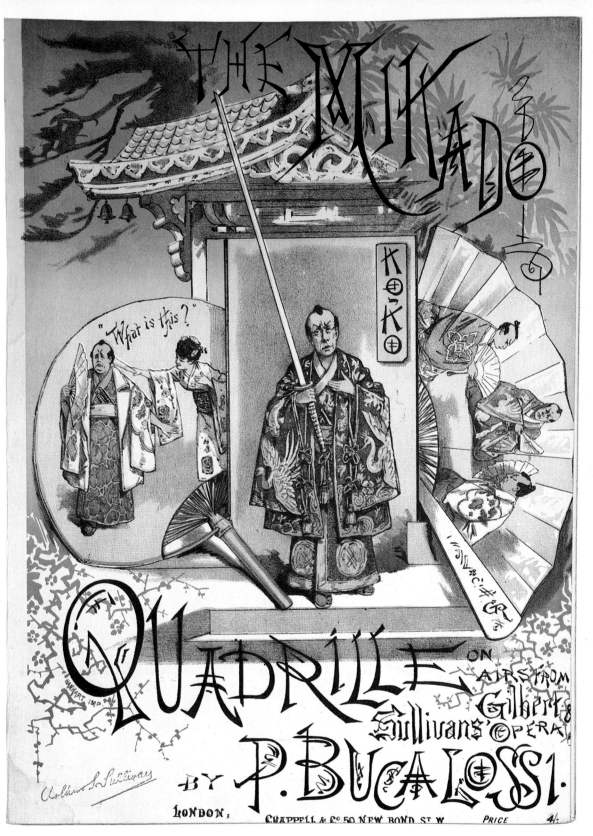

Music sheet for *The Mikado*

Programme cover for *The Pirates of Penzance*

Programme cover for *Iolanthe*

3 England

I have always thought that a civilization should be judged by the intelligence it has developed and the way it is used, the compassion it is capable of and the priority it receives, a never-ending effort to close the rift between rich and poor, the responsibility of man for his neighbour, and the magnitude of the art it produces. One of the anomalies of art and culture, enigmatic and inexplicable, is that the Germanic peoples who, with Bach, Beethoven, Brahms, Mozart and Wagner, have produced the world's great music, should also have the most dolorous record in barbaric militarism since the dawn of Christianity. Not only in this century, but as far back as Attila the Hun, it almost seems as if there has been an anti-Christ gene in the Germanic heritage. Then whence the music? A mere handful of poets dominated by Goethe; a meagre contribution – until this century – to painting; one novelist, Thomas Mann, great but not on the same shelf with Balzac, Tolstoy and Dostoevsky. But music, yes. Genocide, yes. I repeat, enigmatic and inexplicable.

By these standards, although I seriously doubt there is a civilized country, there can be a civilized society. And if I were to rate them, it is my biased opinion that the British society is the most civilized on the planet Earth. It is all the more astounding when one considers the incredibly large number of people who live on a relatively small piece of real estate. It is an accurate statistic that if all the people who live in the world today were moved to the United States of America, they would not live as closely together as do the British.

One of the most prominent reasons for the civility of the English is their possession of that most precious of all human traits – a sense of humour. The French may be witty, but there is no appreciation of civilized silliness. Lots of aphorisms but no giggles. George Bernard Shaw, for instance, who although born in Ireland spent more than seventy years of his creative life in England, is the only major humorist who ever lived who was not bitter.

Therefore, it was quite natural that when the middle class with its variety of levels turned to the theatre for entertainment, the theatrical invention they turned to should have been the music hall whose primary product was comedy. The type of vaudeville of the English music hall was entirely different

to that of the French. Whereas the French was, as I have said, mostly musical sketches, the English was burlesque, knockabout and Cockney songs. It was in 1860 that the music hall began to flourish, and by the turn of the century there were over two hundred dotting the landscape.

Furthermore, it seems all the more natural that when operetta emerged in England its main ingredient should have been lyrical humour. The two collaborators who created this musical theatre were William Schwenk Gilbert and Arthur Seymour Sullivan. Sullivan was the composer and Gilbert was the Adam of modern lyric writing. P. G. Wodehouse, Lorenz Hart, Cole Porter, Ira Gershwin, Oscar Hammerstein and their contemporaries and descendants all owe their lyrical, genetic beginning to W. S. Gilbert.

It is true that in the previous century John Gay had written a savagely humorous and celebrated musical called *The Beggar's Opera*. However, the humour lay not in the lyrics but in the subject. His only follower was himself when he wrote a sequel, *Polly*. *The Beggar's Opera*, oddly enough, reached the peak of its fame when it was adapted into German in 1927 by Brecht and Kurt Weill, and became the world famous *The Threepenny Opera*. (The French with their passionate devotion to money changed the title to *The Fourpenny Opera*.) Of no interest to anyone but me, in the late forties, two years before Kurt Weill died, he and I had been discussing returning to John Gay and adapting *Polly*.

Light verse had begun to proliferate in England in the early to mid-nineteenth century, principally in the magazine *Fun* and later *Punch*. The first light versifier who attained any prominence was, surprisingly enough, a vicar named the Reverend Richard Barham, who, before entering the church, had tried unsuccessfully to be a novelist. Years later, in 1840, using the pen name of Thomas Ingoldsby, he published a lengthy series of burlesque, metrical tales called *The Ingoldsby Legends*. The subject matter was inconsequential, but the rhyming was inventive, clever and highly original – and one of the first examples of what we call today trick rhyming. Byron had indulged from time to time in rhyming such things as 'history' with 'this to ye', but the Reverend Barham's work was exclusively an exercise in rhyme. Almost thirty years later, another volume of light verse was published called *Bab Ballads*. Many of them had previously been published in *Fun*, were laced with wit, and fired cannonballs at the seven deadly virtues. The author was a former barrister named W. S. Gilbert, who changed professions not only because he had a gift for writing but because he had none for the law.

Gilbert, a man of boundless energy which he retained throughout his life, had also turned his hand to writing plays. One of them, *Pygmalion and Galatea* (no similarity to Shaw's), which endeared him to his bank manager, he wrote in blank verse and in the satiric vein that later characterized his work with Sullivan, in which, for example, he mocked the aesthetes of the Mauve Decade in *Patience*, and Tennyson's 'The Princess' in *Princess Ida*. He also

LEFT: Studio portrait of Sir William Gilbert
CENTRE: Studio portrait of Sir Arthur Sullivan
RIGHT: Portrait of Richard D'Oyly Carte

wrote a play called *Rosencrantz and Guildenstern*, anticipating Tom Stoppard by almost a century.

While Gilbert was occupied with his light verse and plays, Sullivan, six years younger, had been busying himself writing songs, ballet music, a cantata and, most prominently, music for a production of *The Tempest*. It was primarily his contribution to *The Tempest* that brought him not only to public attention but caught the professional eye of the manager of the Royalty Theatre in London, Richard D'Oyly Carte, occasionally known by people who worked for him as Oily Carte. It was he who, in 1875, conceived the notion that the combination of Gilbert and Sullivan might be productive. He introduced them and proposed the collaboration.

All new collaborations invariably begin with two words: 'Any ideas?' It just so happened that Gilbert not only had one, but had written it. It was based

on a short story he had written for *Fun*, and one cold winter night he brought it to Sullivan's house for Sullivan to read. It was a one-act piece called *Trial by Jury*. Although Sullivan did not laugh as he read it, which annoyed Gilbert intensely, he did enjoy it and agreed to set it to music, which he did in two weeks. The influence of Offenbach was marked.

The disparity between the two men was marked. Sullivan was on the small side, soft-spoken, slightly effeminate in manner, courtly and reserved. Gilbert was precisely the opposite. He was tall, vociferous, never at a loss for words and admirably equipped with the caustic reply, which at times spilled over into plain insult. When a play was in rehearsal, he never left the theatre and remembered every piece of business, every light cue, even the number of ropes used in *Pinafore*. He badgered the actors unmercifully and on opening nights drove the cast to distraction, reminding them of every bit of direction they had been given. But once the opening night performance began, he left the theatre. He paced the streets, visited the pubs, even went to other plays – totally incapable of coping with the nervous exposure of an opening night. (I sympathize with him completely because, if I may intrude for a moment, I have never been able to sit down at any time at any play of mine, even if it has been running for three years. On opening nights I pace the rear of the theatre, happy to be near the exit in case, as I always expect, the entire audience turns on me.) Sullivan, on the other hand, would calmly walk down the aisle, seat himself comfortably, and become a member of the audience.

Much has been written of Gilbert and Sullivan's incompatibility, most of which is exaggerated. The embellished legend has even included the erroneous fact that they hardly ever spoke and collaborated mostly by post. They did indeed communicate a good deal by mail, but it is reasonable to assume that they did so because there were no telephones. They, of course, had the normal collaborative tiffs, and as their fame grew Sullivan did anguish that his music was merely the servant of Gilbert's brilliant lyrics. They may not have seen each other socially when they were not working, but once writing began, creativity overwhelmed all differences of character.

Trial by Jury had its premiere at the Royalty Theatre on 25 March 1875, to a thunderous ovation, an enthusiastic press, and created in all the spectators who came thereafter an eager desire for more of the same. Two years later they did indeed receive more. The next was *The Sorcerer* in 1877, which, though not as frequently played today as their other works, repeated the reception of *Trial by Jury*. Then in 1878 came *HMS Pinafore* which, to put it simply, was a sensation.

Offenbach and Strauss had swept the world, but the success of Gilbert and Sullivan was so dependent upon the lyrics that, with one exception, their fame was never equalled on the Continent. Translating English verse into a foreign language is never simple. It can be done with reasonable success in Germany and Scandinavia, but it is almost an impossibility in the romance languages.

Clara Dow as Phyllis in
Iolanthe, 1907

George Grossmith as
the Lord Chancellor in
Iolanthe

Rutland Barrington as
the Sergeant in
The Pirates of Penzance

'Three little maids from
school are we': *The Mikado*

First of all, English has almost double the number of words of any other language. That is one of the reasons it is the language of poetry. Secondly, in the case of Gilbert, the difficulty is compounded by his intricate, multiple, internal and original rhyming. It is rather interesting to note that although there have been authors who wrote brilliantly in a foreign language, i.e. Conrad (who was Polish but wrote in English), and Nabokov (who was Russian and also wrote in English), there has never been a poet who wrote in a foreign tongue. Thus, the acclaim of the world for the work of Gilbert and Sullivan was limited geographically by its very genius. When *Trial by Jury* opened in London, Offenbach's *La Périchole* was playing down the street, but when *The Tales of Hoffmann* opened in Vienna, there was no Gilbert and Sullivan playing down the street.

LEFT: Savoy Theatre programme cover
for *Princess Ida*, 1884
RIGHT: Programme illustration for *H.M.S. Pinafore*

The other major theatrical marketplace for Gilbert and Sullivan was America. But sadly enough there was no copyright law in existence at the time to protect them against theft. The first copyright law was not written until 1887, as a result of a multinational meeting in Berne, Switzerland, attended by fourteen countries, but not the United States. The US did not join in any sort of universal copyright agreement until 1910 when the Pan-American Convention took place in Buenos Aires. It was not, however, until 1955 that the Pan-American agreement and the Berne Convention became amalgamated into one universal copyright law. Even after the United States did subscribe, there was a variance between Europe and America. A European author and his family controlled the rights to his works for fifty years after the author's death.

In the United States, the author only had the rights to his works for twenty-eight years after their creation, but then had the option of renewing those rights for an additional twenty-eight years. Under these conditions, a healthy author could easily outlive his own copyright. Only in the last decade has the United States finally amended the fifty-six-year limit to coincide with the universal copyright convention of the author's life plus fifty years.

So Gilbert and Sullivan had to depend upon the integrity of American theatrical management, whose record for honesty was about as sturdy as a grass hut in a hurricane. Nevertheless, there was a handful of respectable producers and, on occasion, there would be two productions of a Gilbert and Sullivan operetta running on Broadway simultaneously. One would be the inaccurate, pilfered version, the other would be a replica of the London version for which the producer and the authors had signed a contract.

HMS Pinafore was followed by *The Pirates of Penzance* and *Patience*. It was in between *Pirates* and *Patience* that the first rumble of trouble between the two men occurred. During the period following *Pirates*, Sullivan had purchased a libretto based on Longfellow's poem, 'The Golden Legend'. Gilbert was anxious for them to start work on *Patience*, but Sullivan postponed it and composed *The Golden Legend* first. It was a tremendous success and a serious work, which appealed to Sullivan's concept of the definition of art. He found himself wanting more and more to become a 'grander' composer. However, he finally did agree to *Patience* and wrote the score ten days before rehearsals began. As usual it was one more smash hit.

Their next effort was *Iolanthe* which Gilbert based on one of his poems in *Bab Ballads*, but before the writing began Sullivan was knighted. Gilbert was not. Gilbert bore this with comparative good grace, but was not in the best of humour while directing *Iolanthe*. Biographer Hesketh Pearson quotes an example of Gilbert's humour in those days when, after berating one of the cast, the actor said: 'Look here, sir. I will not be bullied. I know my lines.' Gilbert replied: 'That may be so, but you don't know mine.'

Iolanthe was followed by *Princess Ida*, which was successful but not in the same league as their other plays. The principal reason was because Gilbert tried an experiment and wrote it in blank verse, and the audience obviously missed the scintillating rhyming that goes hand in hand with humour. Nevertheless, the critics hailed it as Sullivan's best score to date, an opinion that is often shared today.

In 1885 came their masterpiece and that one international exception, *The Mikado*. It was a biting satire on everything English but set in Japan, and the foreign public accepted it as Japanese. It ran for over two years in London and was translated – somehow – into a host of foreign languages where it was always received with great critical acclaim. It remains the most performed of all their plays.

They wrote five other operettas/operas before their partnership finally

dissolved: *Ruddigore*; *The Yeomen of the Guard*; *The Gondoliers*; *Utopia Limited*; and *The Grand Duke*. *Ruddigore* and *The Yeomen of the Guard* were more melodramatic than their predecessors but when *The Gondoliers* opened, which was more in their traditional, comedic vein, the audience literally cheered until they were hoarse. The press accorded them the greatest reviews they had ever received and the general reaction was that Gilbert and Sullivan were Gilbert and Sullivan again. They completed their extraordinary collaboration with *Utopia Limited* and *The Grand Duke*, two lesser works, making thirteen in all.

And there it ended. After eighteen years.

Sullivan who had suffered from kidney stones almost all of his life, died at the early age of fifty-eight in 1900. Gilbert lived on to be seventy-five and drowned in his own lake in 1911 trying to save a young girl. But he died Sir William Gilbert, having finally been knighted a few years previously.

Although one cannot underestimate the grace, skill and melodic invention of Arthur Sullivan, there is no doubt that Gilbert was the driving force. It was he and he alone who took operetta by the neck and raised lyric writing from a serviceable craft to a legitimate, popular art form.

The D'Oyly Carte company continued to function long after D'Oyly Carte himself had passed on, so the traditional presentation of Gilbert and Sullivan remained intact. There was even a D'Oyly Carte company in America which emulated to the last minute detail the English productions. It is only recently that the D'Oyly Carte companies on both sides of the ocean have been finally disbanded, but the performances of Gilbert and Sullivan continue throughout the English-speaking world without loss of pace. There have, of course, been changes in the style of production. There have been black versions of *The Mikado* and *Pinafore*, and a modern version of *The Pirates of Penzance* was presented in New York in the early eighties and became one of the highlights of the theatrical season. But there is no question that no matter how many varieties in production there may be in the future, Gilbert and Sullivan are for ever.

4 The Land of the Free

Since the creation of the Declaration of Independence in 1776 and the Constitution of the United States in 1789, America has lived with a shameful hypocrisy. The preamble of the Declaration of Independence states that all men are created equal. In the second paragraph of the Constitution it also states that a black man is equal to three-fifths of a white man. The reason for the second paragraph of the Constitution was because the South found itself impaled on the dilemma of Catch 22. The South insisted upon its right to the possession of slaves. Each state in the Union would have two senators, but the number of members of Congress would be determined by the population of each state. Since the blacks in the South far outnumbered the whites, the voting wishes of the whites would be endangered, and so they agreed to the hideous compromise of making a black man equal to three-fifths of a white man. (The bitter irony of it all was that the South made certain that the blacks never voted. For example, voting booths were placed in parks where blacks were forbidden, etc.) Each state would have the right to slavery if it so voted. The North never did.

As a codicil to slavery, America has always prided itself on being the melting pot which opened its doors to the downtrodden peoples of the world, and to those who sought the golden land of opportunity. Not true. As everyone knows, no black man before the mid-twentieth century came to America of his own free will. He was sold into slavery, often by his own black brothers in Africa, and brought to America in chains.

I cannot believe that almost three centuries of man's inhumanity to man, which reached a peak of organized violence with the Civil War, is worth a single bar of music. But without the presence of the black race in America, there never would have been the popular music or the popular musical theatre that we know today.

Nor did the American eagle flap its wings in joyous welcome to the other major contributors to the popular musical theatre, the Jews. Barred from all major industry well into the twentieth century, they turned their energies to unrestricted professions such as medicine and the law, shop-keeping and entertainment, both creative and interpretive. That social suppression was the father of artistic expression would be a hard case to prove, but, nevertheless, the overwhelming number of great composers and lyricists of the popular musical theatre of the twentieth century were Jewish. So were the theatre owners, so were the producers, and so were the visionaries who founded the motion picture industry.

In the theatre, what happened in Europe logically happened in America. As the industrial revolution expanded, the urban societies grew in proportion. Before the good old steam engine and the migration to the cities, small villages and towns found entertainment in community singing, folk dancing, storytelling around the fire and interesting ways to keep warm. Once they arrived in the cities, they, as had the French and English, began patrolling the streets in search of amusement. There was the occasional legitimate play, but they were more frequented by the landed gentry than the gentry who had just landed. A man named William Dunlop, who was a playwright, producer and director, tried for over twenty years at the beginning of the century to produce American plays and find actors who could achieve some degree of professionalism. But it was a losing battle. The majority of the public was simply not interested. An English actor who came to America in search of employment summed it up by reporting, when he returned home, that 'the rapid increase in population in newly formed cities produces a style of patrons whose habits and associations afford no opportunity for the cultivation of the arts'. Amen. What the public wanted was humour as broad as possible, ad libs as contemporary as possible, interspersed with the occasional overly-sentimental song. It took considerable courage to perform in those days because if the audience was displeased, its

Minstrels playing instruments, circa 1840

reaction was immediate. Criticism took the form of not only booing but the chucked missile. (This form of critical review is still alive and well in some corners of northern England.)

It was not long before this grab-bag form of entertainment began to evolve into what became known as the Minstrel Show. It began to grow in about the middle of the second decade of the century. Its form consisted of a group of entertainers, banjo players, singers, dancers, etc., who were held together in a frame comprised of two end men and an interlocutor who stood or sat in the centre. The interlocutor was the straight man and the two end men who, not surprisingly, stood or sat at each end, told the jokes. The two end men in time became known as Mr Tambo and Mr Bones. The humour consisted of a series of sketches and/or riddles, punctuated by music and dance. Here is a typical routine:

End Man

I lost a beautiful silk umbrella yesterday.

Interlocutor

Did you leave it anywhere?

End Man

No, the man that owned it came along and took it out of my hand. I hear that they are going to make *square* umbrellas.

Interlocutor

Umbrellas in square shape. What is that for?

End Man

So you won't leave them *round*. Did you ever notice how people carry umbrellas? Of course, you've heard of the handkerchief flirtation. Well, umbrellas tell the story of the people who carry them.

Interlocutor

Give me a simile.

End Man

For instance, if you see a man with an umbrella, and he's very careful of it, keeps his eye on it all the time; that's a sign he's just acquired it and is afraid of losing it himself. If you see a couple going along the street, and he carries the umbrella in such a way that she is thoroughly protected and *he* gets all the rain down his neck and over his new clothes; that's a sign that they are courting. They're in love!

Interlocutor

Yes?

End Man

And if he carries the umbrella so *she* gets soaking wet, and the umbrella covers him; why, they're *married*.

Interlocutor
Suppose it isn't his wife?

End Man
Then I'll bet ten dollars *it's his mother-in-law.*

One of the most famous turns was a satire on Mark Antony's oration from *Julius Caesar*. It began: 'Friends, Romans and countrymen. Lend me your ears. I'll return them next Saturday. I come to bury Caesar because times is hard and his folks can't afford to hire an undertaker. The evil that men do lives after them in the shape of progeny who reap the benefit of their life insurance ...' Etc.

In the beginning, the Minstrel Show was exclusively performed by white men. Travelling through the South, the performers and managers became fascinated with black humour, rhythm, song and dance. The hereditary black dance movement that was indigenous to the Africans had slowly, over the years, evolved into a shuffle which eventually became 'the soft shoe'.

Legend has it that somehow, in some manner, the blacks were influenced by the migrating Yorkshire and Lancashiremen of England with the clogs they wore and the tapping sound they made when they danced. The tribes in Africa sent signals by drums, but when the slave owners put an end to the drums, the slaves communicated to neighbouring plantations by a primitive form of tap dancing. It is a fascinating theory but certainly apocryphal.

What is cogent, however, is the influence the blacks had on the Minstrel Show. Bit by bit, not only did their rhythms and songs become incorporated in the Show, but the performers began appearing in black-face. By the late 1820s, black-faced white Minstrel Shows were touring the country. After the Civil War and Abraham Lincoln's Emancipation Declaration of 1863 had freed the slaves, black entertainers began to join the Minstrel Shows. But in order to preserve a unity of look, even they had to black up.

Of more importance to the history of the musical was the influence of black music. In the mid-century, America produced its first composer of talent, Stephen Foster. The songs he wrote include 'Ole Black Joe', 'My Old Kentucky Home' and the most black-influenced of them all, 'Camptown Races'. What distinguished black music from all other until that time, and what is fundamentally the definition of jazz, is the afterbeat. When you clap your hands or tap your feet on the second and fourth beat of the bar, that is jazz. The melody may be soaring, as, for example, 'If I Loved You' from *Carousel*, or 'Can't Help Lovin' That Man of Mine' from *Showboat*, and the tap may be soft or just a pulse, but nevertheless it is there. With Offenbach, if you clap at all during a can-can, you would clap *with* the beat.

The new music so prominently featured in the Minstrel Show was performed by the Minstrels not only across the land, but found its way to the

water where it was played by smaller groups on the luxurious steamboats that paddled up and down the Mississippi River. The Mississippi River ends in New Orleans, which was considered by the South and primarily the citizens of New Orleans as the Paris of the New World. First of all, it had been a French possession until Napoleon, fed up with the inability of the French army to hold even so small an island as Santa Domingo, one day in a pique of fury sold to the United States the tremendous tract of land that it owned on the American shore. Part of that land was Louisiana and Nouvelle Orléans. Proud of its French heritage and rich from plantations and shipping, it developed an aristocracy that was similar to all American aristocracies; that is, based on wealth at least two generations old. But the young blades sought more earthly pleasures and New Orleans soon boasted the largest number of brothels per square inch of any city in the country. But what is significant to us pure music lovers was the ragtime jazz that emanated from every bordello on the street. Make no mistake. Those bordellos were almost as plush as the mansions the customers lived in. The madams were characters extraordinaire, the women gay and salty, and the music joyous.

One day the hue and cry against the growing epidemic of pleasure finally reached the city government. There was a concerted effort by the church and the 'good people' of New Orleans to get those damned houses closed. It was not as simple a job as one may think because among the patrons were, naturally, members of the city council. But the oratory that ensued in the debate was passionate and, to say the least, florid. One minister, concluding his address, said: 'I speak of those houses of darkness and despair, the pitfalls in the way of virtue in this great city. There are over five hundred of these dark places that run the gamut of condition from palatial palaces of velvet and gilt down to the pestholes filled with foul hags and germ-ridden jezebels.'

How about that? But he was not finished.

'Do you know how many of these creatures bed down in our midst? Eighteen hundred and forty-two. Yes! Eighteen hundred and forty-two, according to the heroic and painstaking research of this unholy problem by city councillor, Sidney Story.'

At this point, a rather weary, but undoubtedly happy, Sidney Story rose to present his solution – or compromise.

Said Mr Story: 'Members of the city council, I propose the following ordinance be adopted by the city of New Orleans. From and after the first of October 1897, it shall be unlawful for any prostitute to occupy, inhabit, live or sleep in any house *not* situated within the following limits: from Custom House Street to St Louis Street; from Northern Basin Street to Robinson Street; from the riverside of Franklin to the woodside of Locust and from Upper Perdido to Lower Gravier.'

The motion was passed unanimously.

The citizens of bordello-land willingly co-operated and, after a certain

amount of relocation, there was indeed a precise area for the joys of life that became known as Storyville.

Storyville was like a little bit of paradise in the middle of New Orleans. As I have mentioned, the ladies who operated these glorious emporia were unique. One of the more illustrious was a creature named Queen Gertie Livingston. One day she fired one of her vassals, a Miss Cecile Torrence, because she had had a fight with one of the other girls and, according to Gertie, had bitten off her best finger. A lawyer soon appeared to demand Miss Torrence's trunk, on the grounds that it contained four dozen towels which Gertie had no right to withhold, as it transgressed the Act that a workman's tools cannot be retained.

There was another well known madam named Miss Josephine Claire, who was better known as Josephine Icebox. Storyville had its own little newspaper, and Miss Icebox was widely advertised as the coldest joy ever to fill a dress. A prize of $10 in trade and a loving cup was offered to any fellow who could 'wake her up'.

But our interest in these delicious females and their business associates lies in their deep sense of musical appreciation. Every house had either a jazz soloist or a jazz combo. The music was sometimes called ragtime, but its generic title was Dixieland. It was here that real Dixieland music began.

The performers were, of course, all black. The first genuine jazz combo was called the Spasm Band, later known as the Razzy Dazzy Spasm Band. They were six in all: Cajun; Stalebread Charlie; Chinee Whisky; Warm Gravy; and one musician with the peculiar name of Charlie Stein. All the latter day saints who came marchin' in owe a debt to the Razzy Dazzy Spasms.

Out of Storyville came such classics as 'Basin Street Blues' and, of course, the most famous of all, 'When the Saints Come Marchin' In'. That particular song started its career as a funeral march when a beloved lady or performer had passed on to green pastures. The coffin was held high and paraded around Storyville, surrounded by trumpet and trombone sending the deceased to heaven to a Dixieland beat.

'When the Saints Come Marchin' In' is one of those rare songs, like Kurt Weill's 'Mack the Knife', that one can listen to over and over again with ever increasing rapture. When I staged President Kennedy's last birthday party at the Waldorf, I arranged for the great Louis Armstrong to march into the room in the traditional Storyville fashion and parade around the hall playing 'When the Saints'. He played twenty-seven choruses of it and if the President had not had to return to Washington that evening, the audience would have been happy for the irreplaceable Satchmo to play it until dawn.

OPERETTA   Meanwhile, way up north on Manhattan Island, Broadway ignored the musical revolution that was happening in New Orleans and people continued flocking to the theatre to hear the good old traditional American music of Franz Lehár, Emmerich Kalman, Robert Stolz, Oscar Straus and Leo Fall, the

descendants of Offenbach and Johann Strauss. The major exception was George M. Cohan – he of 'I'm a Yankee Doodle Dandy' and 'Mary Is a Grand Old Name' fame – who was writing a musical comedy which he also composed, directed, starred and danced in, and which owed its musical origins to the gaslight music of the Gay Nineties.

There had been an attempt at a musical spectacular with musical sketches à la Offenbach and with ballet way back in 1866. It was called *The Black Crook* and it ran long. Five and a half hours to be precise. Although it influenced nothing, it was a primitive and primary example of American showbiz with all the 'hype' that goes with it.

When I mention Lehár and company being descendants of Johann Strauss, it is true but with a difference. The music of these men ushered in the romantic style of Viennese operetta, which later Sigmund Romberg, Victor Herbert and Rudolf Friml embellished with modified, contemporary rhythms.

In Vienna, Franz Lehár was the master. His greatest work, *The Merry Widow*, which opened in Vienna in 1905, has never stopped being performed. What was interesting about *The Merry Widow* was Lehár's use of the waltz. There were two kinds of waltzes: the Viennese waltz, which was distinguished by the hesitation; and the French, which was shorn of it and which the Viennese considered, rather contemptuously, as merely a song in three-quarter time. Nevertheless, *The Merry Widow* waltz that swept Vienna and the world was a pure and simple French waltz.

The debut of *The Merry Widow* is one of the mysteries of the musical theatre. It opened to acceptable but not hat-throwing reviews and a mild reception from the audience. It played several weeks to half-empty houses. The music was not performed in the cafés and, as far as one knows, there was no particular ecstatic word of mouth. However, one day, for reasons that will never be deciphered, there suddenly appeared a line at the box office and within two days the house was filled to capacity, and remained so for over a year. When it opened in Berlin, the leading male character, Prince Danilo, was played by a celebrated figure from the Viennese light opera named Edmund Loewe – the father of Frederick Loewe. It is also the one operetta of the romantic school possessed of a comedic turn in the plot. That it was there at all is astounding, because Lehár's primary interest was in the sweeping melody of songs of love. The lyrics, of course, were something else. The English wit of Gilbert's lyrics was not only far beyond the mentality of the Viennese librettists, but the music predominated so overwhelmingly that there was no room or musical accommodation for lyrical humour or the well-turned rhyme.

As an example of the platitudinous lyrical heights that even *The Merry Widow* scaled, a line from one of the loveliest melodies in the score, translated into English, is: 'Come where the leafy bower lies.' Not a lyric for a tenor with bridge-work.

Lehár, the quintessential Viennese composer, was actually born in Hun-

gary, but he migrated at an early age. His output was not prolific but his financial success was probably the greatest of any composer up until that time. Within a few years of the opening of *The Merry Widow*, he was far north of a millionaire.

Before *The Merry Widow*, having been impressed with the success in Vienna of *Cavalliera Rusticana* and *I Pagliacci*, Lehár wrote a one-act opera, which is difficult to judge because it was never produced. What brought him to public attention was an orchestral work he had composed for a royal 'Gold and Silver' ball in 1902, which, not illogically, became known as 'The Gold and Silver Waltz'. It was an apt title, because if Strauss was the golden period of Viennese operetta, Lehár and his contemporaries were the silver.

His most popular works after *The Merry Widow* were *The Count of Luxembourg*, *Frederika* and *The Land of Smiles*. Both *Frederika* and *The Land of Smiles* were vehicles for that most remarkable Viennese tenor, Richard Tauber, and were both written in the twenties.

Lilly Elsie in *The Merry Widow*

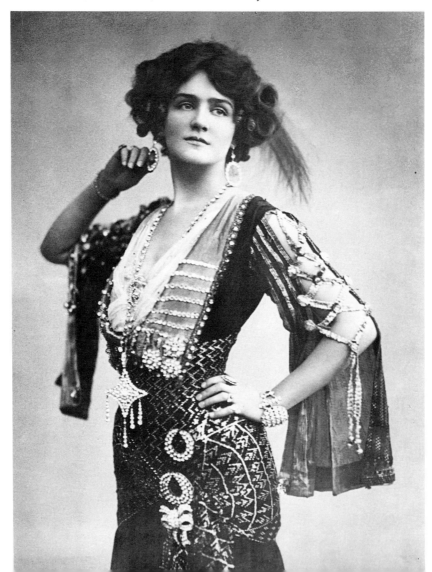

When the Nazis invaded Austria, Lehár and his wife chose not to leave, as had so many other artistes. The reasons given were age and poor health. One views this bit of information with a raised eyebrow. Lehár was still only in his sixties and his health was good enough for him to accept numerous Nazi awards, including the Ring of Honour from the Nazi-occupied city of Vienna and Hitler's Goethe-Medallion. His works continued to be played in Germany all through the war, but the names of any of his Jewish collaborators were dropped while his royalties continued to pour in from Germany and all over the world. The world forgets easily, but when I recall the long evenings I spent with Kurt Weill hearing of the tragedy that befell German writers of Jewish origin, and the hair's-breadth escapes from Hitler's Nazis — let alone the constant reminder of the Holocaust — to this day when I am transported by the music of Franz Lehár, my glass of champagne is rimmed with aloes.

Emmerich Kalman, like Lehár, was also born in Hungary. His first operetta, *Tatarjardas*, was produced in Budapest with modest success, but enough for him to be enticed by Viennese managers to go to Vienna, where he eventually made his career. His principal works were *The Countess Mariza*, which contained one of the most famous songs to emerge from all the operettas of the period, *Play Gypsy, Laugh Gypsy, The Gypsy Princess* and *The Circus Princess*. But it was *The Countess Mariza* that gave him an international reputation. In 1927 he visited New York for the American production of *The Circus Princess* and stayed on for a year, partially collaborating with Oscar Hammerstein II and Otto Harbach on the score for an operetta called *Golden Dawn*. Robert Stolz and an American composer, Herbert Stothart, also contributed. He returned again to the United States in the thirties and there he spent the remaining years of his life.

After Rodgers and Hart separated, Kalman began collaborating with Lorenz Hart, but the collaboration was interrupted for ever by Hart's untimely death in 1943. Kalman's last work came two years later. It was called *Marinka*, which enjoyed a less than modest run on Broadway. I shudder to do so, but I am compelled to summarize the plot. It was based on the tragic story of Mayerling, which ends with the double suicide of Prince Rudolph and his mistress in the hunting lodge outside Vienna. This had been made into an unforgettable film by Anatole Litvak in the 1930s and it was the picture that brought Charles Boyer to public attention. In *Marinka*, and my face is straight, they did not commit suicide but retired peacefully to a New England farmhouse.

Before passing on to Oscar Straus, who was certainly the most celebrated composer, and justifiably so, after Lehár, one must pause for a word or two about a man of enormous talent, who died at a very early age, named Leo Fall. Unlike the two great Viennese composers, Lehár and Kalman, who were born in Hungary, Leo Fall was a Viennese composer born in Czechoslovakia. His melodic gift was unique and I remember my old partner, Frederick Loewe,

often saying that he considered him potentially the most talented of them all. His most popular work was *The Dollar Princess*, which made the usual circuit of Paris, Berlin, London and New York.

The last of the great Viennese was Oscar Straus – who was born in Germany. Besides being a melodist of rare virtue, he was the only one of them all with an appreciation of comedy. Perhaps it was because he was Jewish, and for the Jewish people humour has always been a defence. One of his earliest works was a satire on Richard Wagner. He was also one of the few Viennese who worshipped Gilbert and Sullivan.

The success of *The Merry Widow* made a considerable impression upon everyone, not excluding Oscar Straus, who proceeded to stifle his natural comedic strain and concentrate on the lush, romantic operetta. His first great success was *The Waltz Dream*, which was so popular that it even ran longer in Vienna than *The Merry Widow*. There were about five hundred musical theatres in German-speaking countries, and at one time or another most of them played *The Waltz Dream*. The London production starred the most famous leading lady of her day, Gertie Millar, who later married the Earl of

The Chocolate Soldier, 1910: The Finale of Act II

Dudley. (The members of Debrett's frequently found their mates on the entertainment pages. One remembers that Fred Astaire's famous sister, Adele, married Lord Cavendish.) Believe it or not, *The Waltz Dream* was made into a silent film in the mid-twenties; later it appeared as a talking picture with Maurice Chevalier. But Straus's most celebrated work was *The Chocolate Soldier*. It was based upon George Bernard Shaw's splendid comedy *Arms and the Man*.

Shaw had made a habit of presenting his plays first in Germany before they reached the London stage. His reason was that if the English critics, whom he irritated constantly, did not give him the press he felt his due, then the life of his plays would end in London. So, for good and sound financial reasons, his plays were first translated into German and performed there where they were invariably hailed, and he was therefore not denied a healthy source of revenue. *Pygmalion* was not only presented in Germany before it reached London, but then played the German-speaking Irving Place Theatre in New York City. So London saw it third-hand.

After much persuasion, Shaw allowed the plot of *Arms and the Man* to be used by Straus and his collaborators. What Shaw failed to understand, however, was that according to German copyright law the adapters, because they wrote the dialogue, automatically owned the rights. So the Irish Pope outsmarted himself and received no royalties.

The score of *The Chocolate Soldier* contains one of the most famous of all waltzes, 'My Hero'. Richard Rodgers once told me that he thought it the most perfectly constructed song in modern musical literature.

The most celebrated composer of all is thought of by most Americans as theirs alone. Actually he was born in Dublin in 1859 and studied in Europe; his instrument, like Offenbach's, was the cello. He came to America in the early 1890s and his first operetta was produced on Broadway in 1894. The programme read: 'Prince Ananias' – Music by Victor Herbert.

In 1898 he became a household name with the production of *The Fortune Teller*, which included such famous songs as 'Slumber On My Little Gypsy Sweetheart' and 'The Gypsy Love Song'. (I have never quite understood the fascination the operetta composers had for gypsies. Their population was relatively small, their contribution to society nil, their antecedents were Himalayans, and as far as I know their main talent was swirling around and card-reading. But they were a never-ending source of subject matter, even starring in James Barrie's enchanting novel, *The Little Minister*.)

In 1903 came *Babes in Toyland* with 'The March of the Toys'. It swept not only America but Europe as well. In 1905 he wrote *Mademoiselle Modiste*, which many Herbert aficionados consider his greatest score. Certainly he created one of the most original of all waltzes, 'Kiss Me Again'. It was a slow waltz, almost a chanson, but requiring more voice than a chansonier.

As far as song hits are concerned, however, he reached his peak in 1910

with *Naughty Marietta*, which not only reached the far corners of the earth but became a staple of Jeanette MacDonald and Nelson Eddy. The score was quite extraordinary, including 'I'm Falling in Love with Someone', ''Neath the Summer Moon', 'Tramp, Tramp, Tramp' and 'Ah Sweet Mystery of Life'.

One of my personal favourites appeared in 1917 called *Eileen*. There were always hints of his Irish heritage in his music, which frequently gave his melodies a wistful tenderness. But *Eileen* was an Irish operetta and featured the beautiful song, 'Thine Alone'.

Although he wrote many other operettas, these were his most famous. He was also a kind and caring man, generous with his praise for those whose work he admired. Every songwriter who has lived since Victor Herbert owes the financial fruits of his labours, be they small or great, to him because it was he, aided by Jerome Kern, who was the driving force in creating the American Society of Composers Authors and Publishers, better known as ASCAP. Until the creation of ASCAP in the early twenties, a composer's work was sung or played everywhere in the world without the composer, lyricist or publisher receiving any recompense for the performance. ASCAP created the machinery for a collection agency which corrected the free usage of material.

The music of these men and others less famous provided the musical fare on Broadway until the beginning of the First World War – and after. (Music by German composers was verboten during the war.) During those first fourteen years of the century, the New York theatre remained untouched by Storyville; deaf even to Scott Joplin, whose works for the piano gave a heightened form to ragtime music. In 1907 he went as far as to write a ragtime opera called *Treemonisha*, which did not reach Broadway until 1975, after Marvin Hamlisch had brought Joplin into vogue by using one of his pieces as background music for the Academy Award-winning film *The Sting*.

How long the theatre might have slumbered is no longer of consequence, because we know exactly when and by whom it was awakened. The when was 1911 and the by whom was Irving Berlin. The alarm clock was 'Alexander's Ragtime Band'.

5 'America's Franz Schubert'

'A lexander's Ragtime Band' caught the scattered winds of ragtime and created a storm that swept the world. It profoundly influenced popular music and the popular musical theatre. It also changed the social life of the country by making people want to dance. They pulled up their carpets and danced at home, hotels added ballrooms, and nightclubs began to flourish. The world of entertainment was never the same again, and all because of one song. Thirty-two bars of music and lyrics written by a 23-year-old Russian immigrant, who could neither write music nor read it, and whose formal education ceased before he was ten years old. If one wonders how it was possible, for once there is a simple answer. Irving Berlin is a genius. Genius is a word that suffers from metal fatigue. Some people have it but few are. Irving Berlin is.

He was born in a diminutive town in Siberia where, periodically, the Cossacks would spend a rollicking evening wreaking havoc on the Jewish community. His father, like Offenbach's, was a cantor. The family name was Baline and Irving's was Israel. When he was four, his father, to escape Russia, bundled up his wife and eight children and made the long journey to the Baltic Sea, where they found space on a freighter bound for the land of opportunity. Arriving in America, they joined their brethren in the crowded and impoverished Lower East Side of New York City.

When Izzy was in the second grade his father died, and he abandoned school to deliver newspapers and do any odd job he could find that would earn a few pennies to bring home to his mother in the evening. Like his father he had a lyrical singing voice, but instead of devoting it to services in the synagogue, as his mother wished, he became a singing waiter in a Bowery beer hall, which was more profitable. He sang and sang until, one day, words and ideas of his own began to crowd his mind.

He started picking out melodies on the piano. He used only the black notes. All his life he has used only the black notes. Later, when he became more affluent, he found a piano that had been invented in England almost one hundred years earlier that had a lever which changed the key. Wherever he went he took the piano with him.

In 1907, at the age of nineteen, his first song was published. It was called

Portrait of Irving Berlin, 1916

Song sheet for
'Alexander's Rag-Time Band'

'Marie from Sunny Italy' and he wrote only the lyric. Deciding he needed a new name for his new profession, he became Irving Berlin. His share of the royalties from 'Marie from Sunny Italy' was thirty-seven cents. Not a hit, but not a loss. In 1909 came his first total composition, 'That Mesmerizing Mendelssohn Tune'. But it was as a lyric writer that he first tasted the fruits of fame. Until 1911. In 1911 he added a lyric to a ragtime piece he had written the previous year. Without lyrics it was called 'Alexander and His Clarinet'. With lyrics its title was changed.

He first sang it at a gala night of a theatrical club in New York City. It was well received, but there was not a hint of the revolution it was to cause. That began later in the year in Chicago when a popular vaudevillian of the day included it in her act. Within two months it was a universal anthem. The illustrious American drama critic and essayist of the twenties and thirties, Alexander Woollcott, describing it years later wrote: '... [it] wore out the pianos in New Orleans' dives and filled the night air under countless campus elms. They played it in Moscow and along the Riviera. You heard it in every corner of Shanghai and it came in brass across the harbour of Singapore from the boats riding at anchor there. It was called "Alexander's Ragtime Band".'

Berlin entered the theatrical arena that same year of 1911 with a revue, *Jardin de Paris*. His melodies and his lyrics were so strong and so individual that they suited the proscenium arch no less than the sheet music racks. His style, once it had matured, never aged, nor did it ever become out of date. Not even a half-century later.

In 1914 he followed *Jardin de Paris* with another revue, *Watch Your Step*. Before the end of the twenties he had written eight more revues. Only once did he apply his talent to the growing development of the musical comedy theatre. That was in 1925 when he did the score for *The Cocoanuts* starring the Marx Brothers. He did not write a second show with a book until the thirties.

Berlin's genius is as a songwriter. When Jerome Kern was asked what place Berlin had in American popular music, he replied: 'No place. Irving Berlin *is* American popular music.' George Gershwin thought of him as 'America's Franz Schubert'. Popular songs differ from show music, although show music can produce songs as popular as popular songs. To clarify and confuse even more, songwriters can write good musicals, but composers of scores as a rule cannot write popular songs, albeit songs from their scores can become popular. Further, there is no ceiling to musical and lyrical literacy and aspiration in the theatre. Popular songs live in a one-storey house. Beautifully furnished, perhaps, but one storey. But not the songs of Irving Berlin. He defies generality and is above definition. His songs have a musicianship equal to those of the most trained composer. His lyrics touch the centre of every emotion, always pure, always simple, always direct, but never banal. What he wrote said it for everyone.

In 1969 he prepared a handful of volumes which contained the sheet music

of all his songs from 1907 to 1969. He sent me one as a present. To study his lyrics and examine the musical structure of his songs is a constant source of consternation, bewilderment, awe and admiration. 'Oh, How I Hate to Get Up in the Morning' (the Army show of the First World War), 'A Pretty Girl Is Like a Melody' (the Ziegfeld Follies of 1919), 'Say It with Music' (Music Box Revue 1921), 'Lady of the Evening' (Music Box Revue 1922), 'What'll I Do?' (Music Box Revue 1923); and between 1923 and 1929, 'Lazy', in which the melody meanders from idea to idea without repetition, 'All Alone', 'Always', 'Blue Skies', 'Puttin' on the Ritz', etcetera, etcetera, etcetera. The melodies, the originality, the rhyming, the singing use of the language ... It is explainable only by the occult, the meaning of which is simply 'secret knowledge'.

Historically, what Berlin did for the modern musical theatre was to make it possible. Whether he breathed in the air of New Orleans and then breathed it out or merely breathed it out because he was alive in 1911 belongs to the perennial creative enigma. But because of him jazz became unavoidable in the big city.

Three years later a musical opened on Broadway called *The Girl from Utah*. One of its songs was 'They Didn't Believe Me', which became the model for all modern show music. The composer was Jerome Kern.

Song sheets for four Jerome Kern musicals: *Roberta*,
Very Good Eddie, *The Cat and the Fiddle* and *Sunny*

6 The Master

On Monday morning, 5 November 1945, an elegant gentleman of sixty years of age was browsing through the antique shops along East 57th Street in New York City. He reached the corner of 57th Street and Park Avenue, and while waiting for the light to change he suddenly fell to the pavement unconscious. A small crowd gathered and a policeman arrived on the scene. The man was still alive. The policeman searched his pockets for identification, but all he could find was an unsigned card indicating membership of ASCAP. An ambulance was called and he was taken to the City Hospital on Welfare Island, the hospital for the poor, the derelict and the unknown.

ASCAP was called and somehow, someone had the presentiment to call the office of Oscar Hammerstein. Hammerstein was not there but he was reached, and he, too, had the instinct to rush to the City Hospital. By three o'clock the news was abroad that Jerome Kern had had a cerebral haemorrhage. Later that afternoon he regained consciousness long enough to recognize those at his bedside, and then lapsed back into a coma. Three days later he was moved to the Doctors' Hospital on Fifth Avenue where he died, on 11 November.

The following day, at a cemetery about an hour from New York City, Irving Berlin, Otto Harbach, Richard Rodgers, Edna Ferber, Dorothy Fields, Mary Martin, Cole Porter, Sigmund Romberg, Louis Dreyfus and a host of producers, friends and associates gathered in a chapel to say farewell. Oscar Hammerstein rose to deliver the final eulogy. His first words were: 'I have promised myself not to play upon your emotions – or on mine . . .' But he never completed the eulogy because in spite of his intentions, he became too overcome with grief to finish.

The nation, led by President Harry Truman, eulogized him from coast to coast. People the world over mourned the loss of this extraordinary man who had lightened the lives of millions with the joy and beauty of his unique gift of melody. Only a few, however, realized his importance in the history of the modern musical theatre. He had, in fact, laid the cornerstone.

Curiously enough, he had come to New York from his home in California to collaborate with Dorothy Fields on the score for a new musical, *Annie Get Your Gun.* They were replaced by Irving Berlin.

Unlike Irving Berlin, Jerome Kern never knew the Lower East Side and never knew a day's poverty in his life. His father, Henry Kern, born in Germany, had come to America when still a boy and proved himself to be a breadwinner of considerable propensity. He was, in fact, the president of a company which had a contract with the city of New York to keep the streets clean. (Oh, Henry Kern! Where are you now?) From this hygienic enterprise he amassed a more than considerable fortune. Henry and his wife Fanny desperately wanted a family and they eventually had one, after much pain. She lost six children, all boys, at birth, but finally in 1885 produced one who survived.

The Kern residence was in the then posh district of the Upper Bronx in an area called Jerome Park. The house they lived in had previously belonged to the Jerome family, whose daughter, Jenny, later became the mother of Winston Churchill. Because they lived in Jerome Park in the Jerome House, the Kerns named their son Jerome.

It soon became apparent that Jerome was not interested in keeping the streets of New York clean. From the beginning he showed a joyous aptitude for the piano. Mrs Kern encouraged this with piano lessons when he was still a boy and frequent visits to Carnegie Hall. In his early teens he was dispatched to the Heidelberg Conservatory in Germany and in 1902, at the improbable age of seventeen, his first song, 'At the Casino', was published in New York. But his career truly began in 1904 when he ascended the steps of a rather shabby-looking brownstone on East 22nd Street, which was the office of the music publishing firm of T. B. Harms. His objective, of course, was to play his songs for the president of the company, Mr Max Dreyfus.

Max Dreyfus was the dean of Tin Pan Alley. Starting in 1880, music publishers began moving uptown, almost in a phalanx. They eventually arrived in the theatrical neighbourhood. One composer/publisher, Harry von Tilzer, used to place strips of paper behind the piano strings in order to approximate the sound of a guitar. In 1903 a journalist, writing an article about the growing publishing industry, likened its sound to a tin pan and titled his article 'Tin Pan Alley'. Tin Pan Alley became the colloquial name for the world of popular music, and time made it official.

Max Dreyfus, more than any other publisher on the beat, had the taste to recognize genuine talent when he heard it, with an admiration for that talent and the dedication to ensure its propagation. The only mistake he made was with Richard Rodgers. In 1922, Rodgers, who already had contributed to the Broadway theatre, played his wares to Mr Max who said: 'There's nothing of value here. I don't hear any music and I think you would be making a great mistake.' Three years later he was the first to admit his error and Richard Rodgers forgave him. Rodgers' association with T. B. Harms, which later became Chappell Music, was to last throughout his lifetime.

When nineteen-year-old Jerome Kern played for him, Dreyfus made no

LEFT: Max and Louis Dreyfus at the
original Chappell office in New York
RIGHT: Jerome Kern

mistake. As Kern was ushered into Max Dreyfus's office, he was profoundly
impressed to be greeted by a publisher wearing striped trousers and a morning
coat. (He did not know that Max was going to a funeral.) Max Dreyfus was
equally impressed by Kern's music, and in that year of 1904 two of Kern's
songs made their way into a Broadway show called *An English Daisy*.

Many years later Dreyfus said: 'I decided to take him on and start him off
by giving him the toughest job I had – selling music.' Every music publisher in
those days had demonstrators: pianists who would play the latest additions to
a publisher's catalogue, not only for artistes looking for material but to
producers in search of songs for their shows. Often the 'pluggers', as they were
commonly known, would even visit the local stores and give a free concert for
the passing customers. One of the first songs Dreyfus bought from Kern was
called 'How Would You Like to Spoon with Me?' (When it appeared in a
show, it was sung by a group of beauties who sang it while on swings, which
soared out over the heads of the first few rows in the audience and embellished
the song with a splendid view.)

Mr Max was a slender reed of a man, of chalky-white complexion, barren
of hair, and who seemed terminal at the age of fifty and lived to be ninety. He
was soft-spoken, but his eyes were tinselled with humour. When the life of
Rodgers and Hart was to be made into a film, the producer (Arthur Freed)

went to see Mr Max to get his permission for someone to play him on the screen. Mr Max gave it. When Freed asked him if he had any suggestions for an actor, Mr Max thought for a moment and replied: 'Clark Gable.' His philosophy was pure. Periodically he would assemble the members of his staff and remind them: 'The writers. The writers. Always take care of your writers. Without them you are nothing.' (Alas, music publishing as Max Dreyfus knew it and practised it is a lost art. Music publishers today are mere accountants and book-keepers. Songs are usually published by the people who perform them on records, and there is no creative continuity. In the publishing house there is no one with the ability to sense genuine talent and fight for it and develop it. As a result, the supply of standard music in which Max Dreyfus played such a part dwindles daily, and all that is left is a record business primarily aimed at teenagers, the overwhelming proportion of which is cacophonous, illiterate rubbish that comes and goes like a shooting star leaving nothing in its wake. In fairness, show music, which traditionally created the standards which are still played today, for the most part has also declined in value, aided and abetted by disinterested publishers.) But, as I say, Max Dreyfus was something else. Although many of the names I will mention now will naturally be explored as this book progresses, it was Max who first put Gershwin under contract, who told Richard Rodgers in 1925: 'If you ever need anything, any money, anything, you come to me.' It was Max who, in 1912, discovered an unknown Bohemian concert pianist and teacher called Rudolf Friml who had never written a note in his life, and encouraged him to write the score for an operetta called *The Firefly*. It was Max who, when 22-year-old Vincent Youmans played him one song, immediately signed him. As late as the forties, when I began my career, I, too, with my partner Frederick Loewe, found myself at the office of the famous Mr Dreyfus. He immediately took us on. When the lawyers were drawing up contracts there were several stumbling blocks. At lunch one day Max said to me, with that twinkle that never left his eyes: 'Let the lawyers fight, Alan. It doesn't matter as long as you know you can have whatever you want.'

Max was later joined by his younger brother Louis, younger by less than two years. Louis became head of Chappell of London and Max was head of Chappell of New York. They were to me a pair of surrogate fathers. One time in 1965 I was writing and producing a musical called *On a Clear Day*. My co-producers, who were first-rate men in their field and for whom I had and have a great affection, had had at some time or other a contretemps with Louis, who immediately decided that one of them was a crook. (Not true.) He was not one for subtlety. Louis was to have lunch with me in New York and on his way ran into 'the crook' on Park Avenue. 'What are you doing on Park Avenue?' he roared. 'You are a crook and belong over on Third. What are you doing anyhow?' The producer said he was presenting a play with me. Louis was outraged. He stormed into the Drake Hotel where we were to lunch, and in no uncertain terms said that he did not want me associating with this producer.

'What's he giving you?' he demanded.

'Two hundred thousand dollars to begin with,' said I.

'Is that right?' said Louis. 'Well, you come over to the office after lunch.'

We went back to Chappell after lunch, where Louis sat down and wrote me out a cheque for two hundred thousand dollars. 'Now,' he said, 'you get rid of that crook!'

To return to Jerome Kern. In 1904, undoubtedly at Max Dreyfus's suggestion, Kern journeyed to London and presented himself to London's number one musical impresario, Charles Frohman. It began for Kern a love of London which lasted his whole life. It was personified by his falling in love with and marrying an eighteen-year-old English girl, Eva Leale, which also lasted his whole life.

Musical scores with interpolated songs were the fashion of the day, both in London and New York. Kern not only contributed to several Frohman productions, but between 1905 and 1912 almost one hundred Kern melodies found their way into thirty Broadway musicals. Thirty musicals for a man who had not yet reached thirty years of age!

Besides the occasional Viennese import, most were English. There was a group of minor composers in England, among them Ivan Caryll, Lionel Monckton, Paul Rubens and Leslie Stuart, who were responsible for the musical theatre in London and whose plays frequently made the journey to Broadway. Invariably, once they reached American shores, songs were added to bolster the frequent sags. Kern's music was a principal source of transfusion. For one American show called *La Belle Paree* he added seven songs. *La Belle Paree* was the first show of Al Jolson, who became one of the greatest entertainers and song-sellers of all time.

The Shubert brothers, Sam, Lee and J.J., were collectively the Charles Frohman of Broadway. But more than producers, they also founded a theatre chain which to this day is still the largest in America. Sam died early, but Lee and J.J., producing separately because of total incompatibility, continued well into the forties. It was the Shuberts who were among the major importers of the musicals that featured Kern's music.

In 1914 an event of singular significance to the musical theatre occurred on Broadway. It was a show called *The Girl from Utah*. It had begun its career in London with a score by Paul Rubens. To prepare it for Broadway, Kern added eight songs. The one that belongs to history was called 'They Didn't Believe Me'. Richard Rodgers once said that Jerome Kern had one foot in Europe and one foot in America. It is true that his German training and his admiration for the great Viennese composers contributed to his musical expression. Before *The Girl from Utah*, his songs had covered a wide range of influences in which frequently both America and Europe figured. With 'They Didn't Believe Me',

all the ingredients were digested and the Kern style was born. When Victor Herbert heard Kern's songs for *The Girl from Utah*, he told Max Dreyfus there was no doubt that Jerome Kern would inherit his mantle in the musical theatre. He was not quite accurate. Kern did indeed acquire his fame, but 'They Didn't Believe Me' was the definitive beginning of the popular musical theatre that has existed ever since. It was a refined, beautiful melody with a built-in, unobtrusive afterbeat. Were Kern alive and writing today, it would not be an inappropriate part of the score.

I think it necessary here to lay to rest for ever a tale which has found its way into many biographies of Jerome Kern and which is totally false. The fiction is that he was booked that year, 1915, to accompany Charles Frohman to England on the *Lusitania*, overslept and missed the sailing. (The *Lusitania* was sunk by a German torpedo off the British coast and Charles Frohman and Alfred Vanderbilt were among the eleven hundred passengers who perished.) Not a word of truth in it. Kern had no plans to sail on the *Lusitania*. No one knows the source of the story, but I should not be surprised that if one had the time to search through the newspapers that wrote of the tragedy, one would find it to be the invention of some imaginative journalist. The press has a long and, at times, injurious record for publishing calculated misinformation concerning those related to the performing arts.

Three years earlier, in 1912, the Shuberts and two associates had built a theatre on 39th Street which they called the Princess Theatre. It was quite a distance from Broadway which officially began at 42nd Street. It was a small theatre with a capacity of only 299 seats and a balcony of but two rows. Having built the theatre, no one was quite sure what to do with it. It started presenting one-act plays by aspiring young dramatists. Hardly a commercial zinger.

But there was one agent and producer who had a startling idea. Her name was Elizabeth Marbury, the only lady agent and producer in the theatre. She conceived the notion of presenting small musicals that would fit into this very small house. In March 1915, it was announced in the newspapers that a musical adapted from an English original by Paul Rubens, with additional songs by Jerome Kern, would open at the Princess Theatre. The title was not indicated, but it was a revised version of an English confection from 1905 with the frightfully English title of *Mr Popple of Ippleton*.

A year and a half before, the imaginative Bessie Marbury, as she was known, had decided that an ideal collaborator for Jerome Kern would be a young architect turned playwright named Guy Bolton. Bolton was English bred, but his parents were American. She introduced them and they both agreed the collaboration was a good idea. In January of 1915, their first effort reached Broadway and it was called *Ninety in the Shade*. Bolton not only provided the play but the lyrics as well. He was a skilful playwright but his lyrics left much to be desired, and the play was somewhat less than a success.

TOP: *Nobody Home*
LEFT: Georgia Harvey and Dane Ferguson
in *Very Good Eddie*
RIGHT: Marilyn Miller in *Sally*

But the two men got along famously and sat down together to work on *Mr Popple of Ippleton*. By the time Bolton had finished with the play, there was very little of 'Mr Popple' left and it was retitled *Nobody Home*. It received a mixed press. Perhaps because it had been oversold as something new – which indeed it was. It nevertheless enjoyed a good run and from it Kern learned a

great deal about the marriage of music, lyrics and text. After two more shows to which he merely contributed, he sat down again with Bolton to work on a Princess Theatre show. The one they wrote was a vast improvement on *Nobody Home*; it was called *Very Good Eddie*. Richard Rodgers saw the show at the age of fourteen and claims it was that show which convinced him the musical theatre would be his life. The effect on him, he said, was 'startling'.

During the opening night, as Bolton and Kern paced the rear of the theatre, Bolton drew Kern's attention to a man sitting in the audience wearing very large spectacles who seemed to be enjoying the show immensely.

'Wodehouse,' said Bolton.

'I suppose it is,' said Kern. 'But that's only to be expected on an opening night.'

Bolton looked at him curiously. 'What are you talking about?'

Replied Kern: 'You said it was a good house.'

'No, I didn't,' said Bolton. 'I said Wodehouse.'

And it was on that night that Jerome Kern met P. G. Wodehouse. After the show, Kern asked Wodehouse how he had liked it. 'Not bad at all,' said Wodehouse. 'But the lyrics could be a lot better.' True, true, true. Nevertheless, *Very Good Eddie* was an unqualified hit both with the critics and the audience.

In his memoirs, Wodehouse, who was always known as Plum, wrote the following:

> Went to the opening of 'Very Good Eddie'. Enjoyed it in spite of lamentable lyrics. Bolton, evidently conscious of his weakness, offered partnership. Tried to hold back and weigh the suggestion, but his eagerness so pathetic that consented.
>
> Mem: Am I too impulsive? Fight against this tendency.

There is no doubt where the Jeeves literature came from.

Very Good Eddie was a much more integrated effort then *Nobody Home*. Kern was more and more determined that songs should not be added for entertainment's sake, but flow out of action and character. What a far cry from operetta! In that same year of 1915, he nevertheless contributed two songs to a show called *A Modern Eve*; the following year he added a song to a musical called *Go To It*; and in the same year, he added four songs to *The Ziegfeld Follies of 1916*.

In 1916 and 1917, Kern seemed to have been writing three shows at the same time: a musical called *Have a Heart*, with book and lyrics by Bolton and Wodehouse – not for the Princess Theatre; *Love o' Mike*, with lyrics by Harry B. Smith, a popular journeyman lyricist of the time – not for the Princess Theatre; and finally, *for* the Princess Theatre, *Oh, Boy!* With *Oh, Boy!* the trio became firmly attached and entrenched. As Kern had become the first modern composer in the musical theatre, Wodehouse was the forerunner of Lorenz

Hart, Ira Gershwin and all who toiled thereafter in the lyrical vineyards. He was indeed, in his own way and a different atmosphere, the descendant of Gilbert, and brought charm, literacy and rhyming ingenuity to the theatre.

Oh, Boy! was a more than worthy successor to *Very Good Eddie*, critically acclaimed and ran over one hundred performances longer. 'Till the Clouds Roll By', to this day one of Kern's perennially-played songs, came from *Oh, Boy!* It bore out the prophecy made by one of the leading critics, Alan Dale, a few years earlier when he wrote in his column: 'Who is this man Jerome Kern with music that towers in an Eiffel way above the average hurdy-gurdy accompaniment of our present day musical comedy?' (You can imagine my chagrin and eventual uproarious laughter when my father told me, after *Brigadoon*, that I had been named after Alan Dale – a drama critic, no less. I was un-named for weeks until one day my father had a drink with Mr Dale, whom he knew casually, and decided that Alan would be the perfect first name. It was as if Napoleon had a son and named him after Wellington.)

Oh, Boy! was followed by *Leave It to Jane*, with music, book and lyrics by the illustrious trio. *Oh, Boy!* continued to fill the Princess Theatre, so it was presented elsewhere. The score contained one of Kern's and Wodehouse's most delicious songs, 'The Siren Song'. In the same year came *Miss 1917*, which was a review presented by Florenz Ziegfeld at still another theatre and, surprisingly enough, with additional music by Victor Herbert.

In 1918 *Oh, Boy!* finally closed at the Princess, but the theatre did not stay dark for long. Kern, Wodehouse and Bolton had *Oh Lady, Lady* ready to replace it. *Oh Lady, Lady* was so successful that at one time there were two companies of it playing simultaneously on Broadway.

The future spokeswoman of the twenties, Dorothy Parker, who was then a critic, wrote in her review:

> Well, Bolton and Wodehouse have done it again. If you ask me, I will look you fearlessly in the eye and tell you in low, throbbing tones that it has it over any other musical comedy in town. I like the way the action slides casually into the songs. I like the deft rhyming of the song that is always sung in the last act by the two comedians and the comedienne. And, oh how I do like Jerome Kern's music!

There was one song in *Oh Lady, Lady* that all three collaborators were fond of, but because of the demands of the book they painfully decided it had to go. The song was 'Bill', but as history knows, it was not lost for ever. It reappeared in 1927 in Kern's masterpiece, *Show Boat*, and is not only a classic, but one of the rare examples of an American chanson. A chanson, for purposes of definition, is sung freely with minimum regard for tempo and maximum attention to the emotion expressed in the lyric. For example, the song 'My Man', made famous by Fanny Brice and more recently in the film *Funny Girl* by Barbra Streisand, was originally French and is a typical chanson. The lines

at the end of 'Bill', '. . . because he's – I don't know – because he's just my Bill', are among the most touching few words on the lyrical shelf.

Dorothy Parker's review of *Oh Lady, Lady* was, in effect, a summing up of the Princess Theatre shows. They were genuine little musical plays, elegantly caparisoned with featured players of the day who were responsible for all the singing and movement, and with a few smaller parts supplying the function of the larger choruses and ensembles of the ordinary, extravagant musicals. This required a book with a beginning, a middle and an end, light but legitimate comedic situations, all of which were swept along, as opposed to halted by, Wodehouse's integrated lyrics and Kern's music. In recent times, Sandy Wilson's *The Boy Friend* was a more elaborate, less genuine because it was tongue-in-cheek, and, in general, pastiche version of the Princess style. Even its music was a conscious echo which was faint but amusing.

Oh Lady, Lady marked the end of the constant stream of Princess Theatre shows by Kern, Bolton and Wodehouse. Not because of disagreement, but simply because Wodehouse's yearning to turn his hand to the novel became irresistible and he returned to England to fulfil his ambition. He did come back in 1924 for one last fling, but the interruption of continuity paid its price. Although the score was pure Kern–Wodehouse, the show, called *Sitting Pretty*, was not a success.

After the Princess Theatre shows, Kern continued pouring out his seemingly inexhaustible talent. Three more shows the same year as *Oh Lady, Lady*. One in 1919. Three in 1920, of which the most famous was *Sally*. The book was by Guy Bolton and the lyrics by Clifford Grey and B. G. De Sylva, who later became part of the exuberant collaboration of De Sylva, Brown and Henderson who produced two razzmatazz musicals of enormous success, *Good News* and *Follow Through*.

Sally starred one of the great leading ladies of the twenties, Marilyn Miller, and the score included – and I say the title on bended knee with my head bowed low – 'Look for the Silver Lining'.

The success of *Sally* inspired a well-known producer of the time, Charles Dillingham, to try and repeat it with a show of the same frothy style and mood. To begin the project he called upon Otto Harbach for the book and lyrics. Harbach had no ideas – he thought – but in a taxi on the way to tell Dillingham, he suddenly remembered two ideas he had had for musicals, and by the time the cab arrived he had put them together into one plot. The show was to be titled *Sunny*, and to assist him Harbach engaged his young and talented friend, Oscar Hammerstein, to collaborate on the book and lyrics. (The work of both men will be discussed in more detail in the next two chapters.) It was the first time Hammerstein collaborated with Jerome Kern. The following is the way he later described his meeting with Kern.

I had been told Kern was a hard man to get along with, a tough guy. He certainly didn't seem so at first meeting. A man ... with keen eyes and a quick smile, he bounced nimbly from one subject to another giving me the feeling that I would have to be very alert to keep pace with him. He and Otto and I discussed a plot they had already hit upon before my entrance into the collaboration. Jerry stuck to the high spots of the show. He didn't care what came in between. Otto and I could worry about that. He wanted to talk only about the big stuff and his talk developed it and made it bigger. He didn't play any music. It was all story and showmanship that day. But there were interludes when we didn't talk show. We skimmed over other topics and it seemed that Jerry knew something about everything. I felt stimulated and a little dazzled by him as I left his home that afternoon.

Sunny opened on Broadway in September 1925 and proved to be as successful as *Sally*. Its score contained one of Kern's great standards, 'Who?' In the same year, he followed *Sunny* with a show called *The City Chap*, which did not fare well despite the presence of Irene Dunne in the cast. In 1926 he collaborated again with Otto Harbach on *Criss-Cross* and yet again in 1927 on *Lucky*, for which Harbach only wrote the book. Finally, in 1927, Kern wrote the immortal *Show Boat*. His last show of the Jazz Age was *Sweet Adeline* which opened a month before they started jumping out of the windows on Wall Street.

Starting with *They Didn't Believe Me* and continuing through the Princess Theatre shows and thereafter, what Kern had done was for ever to cut the ties that had previously linked the American musical theatre – and eventually all musical theatre – to the European tradition that had begun with Offenbach. In fact it was during the First World War that not only the musical theatre but, with the production of Eugene O'Neill's first play, *Beyond the Horizon*, America at long last found its own artistic soul. Up until then the theatre had been dominated by the plays and musicals that had migrated from the Old Country. With the publication in 1920 of *This Side of Paradise* by F. Scott Fitzgerald, American musicals, American theatre and now American literature were prepared for the fundamentally dolorous hysteria of the 1920s which became known as the Jazz Age: that era when, primarily because of Coco Chanel in Paris, the bustle disappeared and skirts went up – and morals went down; the cloche hat prevailed; and, because of the American law prohibiting the sale of liquor which had been passed soon after the First World War, speakeasies were the favourite rendezvous of the country, and, parenthetically, the foundation of the fortune of that future hero of countless motion pictures, Al Capone. To paraphrase Heywood Broun, the celebrated journalist of the time, it was the age when people discovered there was a lot of sex around if only they knew where to find it; that adolescents led very amorous lives (*This Side of Paradise*); that there were a lot of neglected

Anglo-Saxon words (James Joyce's *Ulysses* 1921); that girls were sometimes seduced without being ruined and that even rape could turn out well (*The Sheik* 1924); that glamorous English ladies were often promiscuous (Michael Arlen's *The Green Hat* 1924); that in fact they devoted most of their time to it (Noel Coward's *The Vortex* 1924); and that on the whole it was a damn good thing, too (*Lady Chatterley's Lover* 1928).

Despite the Jazz Age, operetta did not suffer a violent death. Even though jazz and the accompanying appropriate lyrics and musical comedy reigned on Broadway, an American version of operetta continued to flourish, dominated by Victor Herbert, Sigmund Romberg and Rudolf Friml. The revue, which was also in vogue, usually fell on the jazz side of the street. In other words, operetta and the new musical comedy ran side by side on Broadway and in London.

The talents of the composers and lyricists were such that during the twenties there were sixty-three theatres in operation on Broadway, and at various times half of them were filled with operetta and musical comedy. (More than a dozen shows opened the same night as *Show Boat*.) In contrast, there are less than thirty theatres on Broadway today and it is not uncommon for almost half of them to be dark.

To clarify the roles played by the book writers, lyric writers and composers, let me state that the outstanding operetta composers were, as I have said, Herbert, Romberg and Friml, and the leading operetta lyricists were Otto Harbach and Oscar Hammerstein II. In the world of musical comedy the leaders were, of course, Kern, the Gershwins, Rodgers and Hart, Vincent Youmans and, later in the twenties, Cole Porter, Howard Dietz and Arthur Schwartz.

7 *Lyrics by…*

The most unappreciated and yet one of the most influential lyric writers of the first third of the twentieth century was a man called Otto Harbach. The chances are that it you were to ask current citizens of the theatre about him, their knowledge would run the gamut from miniscule to nothing. A few may recall that he was a co-author of a group of shows in the twenties. (There was one year when Harbach had five plays running simultaneously on Broadway, a feat never equalled before or since.) The little that has been written about him by the musical theatre's historians has either been incomplete or incorrect, which seems to be an occupational disease of chroniclers, and his contribution, which was considerable, totally ignored. In most books his name suddenly appears as the lyric writer of numerous shows, without a word about how he happened to become the lyric writer of those shows. So, let me tell you a little about Otto Harbach, who he was, and what he did.

The first common inaccuracy that one reads about him is that he was German-born and that his real name was Hauerbach, which he changed to Harbach. The truth is he was of Danish descent, his family came to America in the 1830s and settled in Salt Lake City, where he was born in 1873. Secondly, the family name was Christiansen, but during the 1800s, when Danish men were conscripted into the army, especially from the farm country, many were given the name of the farm upon which they worked in order to simplify the book-keeping. The Christiansen men worked on the Hauerbach farm. During the First World War, when anti-German feeling began to soar, Otto Hauerbach shortened his name to Harbach as a concession to the anti-Bosch sentiment. It still sounded German, but with a question mark.

Salt Lake City is the centre of the Mormon church and has been since the days of Brigham Young. But Mr Hauerbach Senior, of a rebellious nature, withdrew from the church. Those who did so became known as Jack Mormons. Despite the fact the family barely had two copper pennies to rub together, Otto worked his way through college and eventually became a teacher at Whitman College in the state of Washington. Seeing little future in his underpaid job at Whitman, he made his way to New York to take a graduate course at Columbia University. (The number of composers and

Roberta

LEFT: Otto Harbach

Rose-Marie

lyricists who began at Columbia University reads like the roll call of the American musical theatre.)

In 1906, while struggling through Columbia, Otto was riding a street car uptown and passed a billboard advertising a new Webber and Fields show starring Fay Templeton. For reasons unknown to logic, Otto looked at the sign and said to himself: 'I wonder what it would be like to write a musical.' If historians query the source of my information, it was Otto Harbach. Two years later, one of the most popular songs of the day was called 'Cuddle Up a Little Closer'. On the cover of the sheet music it said: 'Lyrics by Otto Hauer-bach.'

Following the usual route of the day, Otto began to contribute to shows through the war years until, like Kern and, later, Oscar Hammerstein II, George and Ira Gershwin, Rodgers and Hart, and almost all those who followed Kern, he found himself in the office of Max Dreyfus.

With the burst of talent that exploded on Broadway in the twenties – a period that Oscar Levant called 'the classical period of American popular music' – it became more and more difficult to follow a straight line; but if there was one at all, it led to the publishing firm of T. B. Harms and the office of Mr Max Dreyfus. In the early twenties, as Irving Caesar, the lyricist of 'Tea for Two' among scores of other songs, recalls: 'To get into the orbit of Harms was every composer's dream.'

In the Dreyfus office was a parlour of sorts with a piano, naturally. Jerome Kern, Richard Rodgers, George Gershwin, Vincent Youmans and, a little later, Arthur Schwartz, Harold Arlen and Cole Porter would drop in several times a week to talk shop and play their latest. You would also find lyricists there such as Oscar Hammerstein II, Lorenz Hart, B. G. De Sylva, occasionally Howard Dietz – and Otto Harbach.

No finer tribute can be paid to Harbach and no clearer definition of his talents than that written of him by Oscar Hammerstein II:

> The field of libretto writing was filled with hacks and gagmen who extended the tradition of ignominy attached to musical comedy books. There were, on the other hand, a few patient authors who kept on writing well-constructed musical plays, most of which were successful, and they continued to give their best with very little chance of being praised for their efforts. Among these was my dear friend and erstwhile tutor, Otto Harbach. Over a long period of years he was the author or co-author of such musical successes as *The Three Twins, Madam Cherry, The Firefly, Wild Flower, Mary, Rose-Marie, No! No! Nanette!, Sunny, The Desert Song, The Cat and the Fiddle* and *Roberta*. These plays were written with many composers: Hoschner, Friml, Kern, Hirsch, Romberg and Youmans.

It is almost unbelievable that a man with this record of achievement received so little recognition. I feel this perhaps more than anyone because I know so well his unusual attainments as an artist, and because I am so indebted to him. I was born into the theatrical world with two gold spoons in my mouth. One was my uncle, Arthur Hammerstein, who took me into his producing organization after I left law school and gave me wise guidance. It was he, too, who supplied the second gold spoon. Otto Harbach. Otto Harbach, at my uncle's persuasion, accepted me as a collaborator. It is true that this was not entirely a gesture of friendship on Otto's part. I know that he felt well of my talents at the time and saw promise in me. From the very start, our relationship was that of two collaborators on equal footing. Although he was twenty years older than I and had written many successes while I had been going to school and college, his generosity in dividing credits and royalties equally with me was the least of his favours. Much more important were the things he taught me about writing for the theatre. Otto was the best play analyst I have ever met. He was also a patient man and a born tutor. Like most young writers, I had a great eagerness to get words down on paper. He taught me to think a long time before actually writing. He taught me never to stop work on anything if you could think of one small improvement to make.

Skipping forward a bit, there were two operettas Hammerstein mentioned that Kern wrote in the beginning of the thirties for which Otto Harbach alone supplied the book and lyrics. One, in 1931, was a conscious attempt to blend the book, music and lyrics into a unified form. It was, however, operetta and far removed from the Princess Theatre. It was called *The Cat and the Fiddle*. One critic (not my namesake; he was gone by then) summed it up by saying that it was 'one of the more painless of the light operas, having many of the blessings and few of the blights that accompany the drama's occasional interferences with music. As a concert, it is Jerome Kern in his most orchestral mood, and as a play it is Otto Harbach rapt in utterances of some of the softest love bleats that he has ever murmured.'

In 1933 Harbach and Kern wrote *Roberta* which received a mixed press and might have had a limited future had it not been for the advent of the Variety Show on radio. The first Variety Show that caught the public was hosted by one of the popular crooners of the day, Rudy Vallee, who had come down from Yale with an orchestra called Rudy Vallee and his Connecticut Yankees, and in which Mr Vallee bewitched the public by singing through a megaphone. A short time after *Roberta* opened, Vallee sang one of the songs from the play, 'Smoke Gets In Your Eyes', on his radio programme. Within three days there was a line at the box office and *Roberta* was a hit. Incidentally, the cast included Fay Templeton whose name it was Otto Harbach had seen on the billboard back in 1906. To complete life's never-ending coincidental circle, that play with Fay Templeton was the last successful musical Harbach

Show Boat – the 1971 revival in rehearsal

Oklahoma! – the original Broadway cast
performing the title song.

Mary Martin and Theodore Bikel in the Wedding Scene
from *The Sound of Music*

wrote. The comedian in the play was a young, recent vaudevillian named Bob Hope, and one of the smaller parts was played by Fred MacMurray.

I cannot leave *Roberta* without quoting what is to me one of the most touching and typical Harbach lyrics he ever wrote. It was called 'The Touch of Your Hand' and it was only six lines. They were these:

> When you shall see flowers that lie on the plain,
> Lying there sighing for one drop of rain;
> Then you may borrow
> Some glimpse of my sorrow,
> And you'll understand
> How I long for the touch of your hand.

Otto Harbach lived to be almost ninety. I met him two or three times during his declining years because his son Bill and I grew up together, went to school together and have remained chums ever since. One day when Otto was in his late eighties and confined to a chair, I happened to ask Bill how his father was feeling. Bill said he had seen him the day before and that when he had asked him the same question, his father replied that he had not slept well the night before. When Bill asked him why, Otto Harbach replied that he had not been able to sleep because he had suddenly realized what was wrong with the lyric of 'Smoke Gets In Your Eyes'. The fact that time had already decided there was nothing wrong with the lyric of 'Smoke Gets In Your Eyes' had nothing to do with it. Otto was a perfectionist to his last breath.

8 Oscar Hammerstein II
The Early Days

Oscar Greeley Clendenning Hammerstein was born on 12 July 1895, on 135th Street in New York City. When he was four his parents moved downtown near Central Park. In that same year, he was taken by his father to the Victoria Theatre on 42nd Street which was the mecca of pre-war vaudeville. During one of the songs, Oscar suddenly broke out into a cold sweat and felt dizzy. When he was taken home he was put to bed, his family assuming it was something he had eaten. It was not. The cause of his malaise was the sickness of excitement, an excitement that remained with him throughout his life. As he was to say repeatedly during the sixty-five years he lived: 'I am almost foolishly in love with the stage.' His contribution to that stage he loved so was greater than any dramatic lyricist of the twentieth century. He may not have had the wit of Lorenz Hart, Cole Porter, Ira Gershwin or Howard Dietz, but no other lyric writer altered the course of the musical theatre as did Oscar Hammerstein.

Unlike all his compatriots, he came from a theatrical family. His grandfather, the first Oscar Hammerstein, an imposing, bewhiskered gentleman, arrived in America from Germany during the Civil War. His first occupation was cigar-making. But although he loved cigars, he discovered he loved the theatre more and devoted his entire post-cigar-making life to building theatres and opera houses and producing the appropriate merchandise to fill them. He built ten theatres in New York City, the most successful of which was that very Victoria Theatre four-year-old Oscar II visited that exciting day.

Oscar I even decided to compete with the Metropolitan Opera House and built his own Manhattan Opera House on West 34th Street, in which he presented some of the more modern operas, such as *Louise, Thais* and *Le Jongleur de Notre Dame,* that the Metropolitan found too avant garde for its culturally timid Fifth Avenue patrons. Eventually, the competition of the Manhattan Opera House became too hot for the Metropolitan and they proceeded to pay Mr Hammerstein $1,000,000 to shut up – operatically

ABOVE LEFT: Evelyn Herbert in *The New Moon*

ABOVE RIGHT: Jules Bledsoe in 'Ol' Man River' from *Show Boat*

ABOVE CENTRE: Norma Terris and Howard Marsh in *Show Boat*, 1938

speaking. To be precise, he was to produce no more operas in New York for at least ten years. With the one million dollars he decided to build an opera house in London. When this failed, he tried to build another in New York City, but the Metropolitan took him to court and prevented it.

His son, William, produced two more standard-bearers of the Hammerstein name, Oscar and Reginald. Oscar called himself Oscar Hammerstein II because it was simpler than writing out his four given names to distinguish him from his grandfather. Because of his grandfather's financial ups and downs, Oscar's parents did not regard the theatre as a reliable profession and Oscar was induced to study law at Columbia University. At Columbia he began his creative career, as did so many other future professionals – myself included, at Harvard – by writing the college show. That Columbia roll call I mentioned earlier included, besides Oscar, Rodgers and Hart, Arthur Schwartz, Howard Dietz and Morrie Ryskind, who collaborated on the Pulitzer Prize-winning Gershwin musical *Of Thee I Sing*. Oscar's first collegiate effort was a satiric item called *The Peace Pirates*. During the First World War, Henry Ford took it upon himself to finance a 'peace ship' to Europe to try to bring the war to an end, which as a venture was as ludicrous as it was unsuccessful. *The Peace Pirates* was a satire on that farcical effort.

As Oscar mentioned in his memoirs of Otto Harbach, it was his Uncle Arthur who first launched him in the theatre – as assistant stage manager. The following year Oscar was promoted to stage manager in Friml's *Sometime*, the show that featured Mae West as the vamp. The story goes that Mae West took a fancy to Oscar – professionally – and one day gave him a bit of advice. Said she: 'Kid, get out of the theatre and be a lawyer. As long as you've studied law, be one. The theatre isn't for you. You've got too much class.' Fortunately, Oscar did not take her advice.

In 1919 he tried his hand at writing a play which, to put it delicately, was a cataclysmic disaster. It was called *The Light*, and the light went out after five performances. The day after it closed, Oscar was sitting in the park and had another idea. It was for a musical. His uncle produced it, Herbert Stothart wrote the music and Oscar the book and lyrics. It began its career on the road with the whimsical title of *Joan of Arkansas*. The times being what they were, the title had to be changed because of church censorship and the show arrived in New York innocuously entitled *Always You*.

The reviews were above average and although the play only ran a short time, Oscar was left with the feeling that he had found his home. In 1920 he finally scored handsomely with a musical called *Tickle Me*. The critics, with one exception (not Alan Dale), were all on the good side and the show not only enjoyed an extremely felicitous run but did wonders for Oscar's solvency. It was also the first show in which he collaborated with Otto Harbach, a fact that obviously influenced its success.

From 1920 until 1927 Hammerstein wrote thirteen musicals, nine in

collaboration with Otto Harbach. The most successful of that magic number thirteen were *Rose-Marie, Sunny* and *The Desert Song*.

In October 1926, Jerome Kern happened to read a novel by Edna Ferber, one of America's most popular novelists, called *Show Boat*. Edna Ferber had a knack, similar to James Michener today, of taking a period or a locale, such as *Cimarron* (the opening up of the West) or *Ice Palace* (the story of a family in Alaska) and exploring and dramatizing it through the eyes of her characters. The show boats that sailed up and down the Mississippi River provided an ideal springboard for her, and she wrote an engrossing story of a show boat family that spanned the decades. When Kern read it he was instantly convinced it could be converted into a musical.

The majority of operas are based on former plays or, occasionally, a novel, such as *La Bohème*, but the idea of basing a musical on a book with dimensional characters living out a human story was unknown to the Broadway theatre. Kern approached Hammerstein with the project, who, upon reading the book, was as swept away with it as was Kern, but at a temporary loss how to scale down so sprawling a novel to the parameters of a musical. But Kern had other ideas. It was not to be the conventional musical, but a true musical play in which the songs would dramatize, illuminate character and provide local colour. Without either of them realizing it, the inspiration of the book would cause them to leap into the future of the musical theatre and still preserve the idiom of the period in which they were writing.

The more Hammerstein explored Ferber's book, the more he realized that the dramatic centre of the story was the Mississippi itself and that there must be a song to dramatize it. The song they wrote was 'Ol' Man River' which I believe to be the greatest folk lyric ever written in the musical theatre. (I say folk lyric to distinguish it from the light verse lyrics of Hart, Porter and Ira Gershwin.) 'Ol' Man River' is probably the profoundest lyric ever to emerge on the musical stage. I am sure that not even Hammerstein realized what a work of art he had wrought when he wrote it.

The entire score was studded with both brilliance and depth, almost as if each man had suddenly opened a door in his creative soul behind which a greater artist had been waiting to see the sunlight.

There are times in the theatre when plays and musicals are wildly overpraised. There are times when imperfect plays of quality do not receive their due. But one who writes for the theatre must live by the belief that when something truly good or great comes along, everybody will know it. When *Show Boat* opened, everybody knew it. Brooks Atkinson of the *New York Times* said simply that 'it was the greatest American musical ever written'.

Hammerstein successfully dramatized Edna Ferber's huge book without the loss of a value. The lyrics and music grow more familiar as time goes on. 'Fish gotta swim/Birds gotta fly/I gotta love/One man till I die' is probably as stunningly simple a quatrain as anyone has ever written.

In short, Kern and Hammerstein had written a masterpiece which will endure as long as there is a musical theatre. It was the only musical of the entire decade whose book was sturdy enough and emotionally true enough to survive the period and remain a permanent musical experience.

Hammerstein followed *Show Boat* almost immediately with *The New Moon*, which, although successful, reverted to the pre-*Show Boat* operetta. Then came *Rainbow* which only ran twenty-nine performances. In 1929, he and Kern joined forces again to write *Sweet Adeline*, with a story that took place at the turn of the century and featured two of their most beautiful songs, 'Why Was I Born?' and 'Don't Ever Leave Me'. After another three musicals without Kern, none of which succeeded, they collaborated in 1932 on *Music in the Air*. Although the tide had turned for operetta, the score for *Music in the Air* which featured 'I've Told Ev'ry Little Star' and 'The Song Is You' was enchanting enough for the show to achieve a successful run.

Hammerstein's career following *Music in the Air* was not a happy one, being a mixture of unsuccessful musicals and songs for films, albeit some of those film songs were out of his top drawer. Certainly 'The Folks Who Live on the Hill', written with Jerome Kern, is one of the loveliest in his catalogue. In 1939 he wrote his last musical with Kern, 'Very Warm for May', which, although it featured that most ecstatic song 'All the Things You Are', lasted only fifty-nine performances on Broadway.

There is a definite 'Part Two' to the work of Oscar Hammerstein II, that began in 1943 with Richard Rodgers. But had there never been a Part Two, for all the musicals he wrote for the theatre during the twenties and early thirties, and with *Show Boat* rising like an obelisk, for all that alone Hammerstein would remain a major figure in the musical theatre.

9 The Composers

Sigmund Romberg was born in Hungary and Rudolf Friml emerged from the womb in Prague. They both went to America before the assassination of Archduke Ferdinand at Sarajevo. Romberg, during the war years, was a regular contributor to both revues and operettas. In 1917 he established himself firmly on the Broadway scene with *May Time*, which featured one of the most glorious of operetta songs, 'Will You Remember?' Its fame was re-established in the thirties by Jeanette MacDonald and Nelson Eddy. In 1921 came *Blossom Time*, based primarily on melodies by Franz Schubert, and in 1924 Romberg wrote the most successful of all his operettas, *The Student Prince*, featuring, among others, the perennial 'Serenade'. 'Serenade' became part of the score only after a threatened law suit with the Shubert brothers who were producing the show. They felt it was too sad a song with which to end a play. Romberg dug in his heels, sought legal assistance, and eventually 'Serenade' won out – or should I say Franz Schubert won out?

It is worth mentioning at this point a fact of Romberg's creative life which is unique in the annals of popular music. He had assembled over the years a library of all the great operas, operettas, *lieders* and orchestral works that had ever been written. He read them all carefully and made notes next to hundreds and hundreds of orchestral and vocal parts. Perhaps it would only be four bars, but next to it he would write 'good baritone solo', or 'soprano'. He then kept a catalogue of all his notes. When the time came to sit down to write a score, if he were about to write a baritone solo, he would check his files for 'good baritone solo', etcetera. Perhaps he would not use it verbatim, but it would give him a start. The wheeze around Broadway during the war was that Romberg's music was suffering because there were no German scores being shipped in. Of course it was all in jest because, as I mentioned, *May Time* was written in 1917. Had he lived in the day of the computer he might have written a score every month. But there was no denying his talent, which was prodigious, and there was no argument about his theatrical acumen. In 1926, inspired by the hysterical popularity of Rudolf Valentino, he wrote *The Desert Song*, with lyrics, you may remember, by Otto Harbach and Oscar Hammerstein II. It was unfortunate for Harbach and Hammerstein, as was the case in early operettas, that the lyrics were overwhelmed by the music.

The Student Prince

LEFT: Sigmund Romberg

Oscar told a famous story about struggling for days to write a lyric for one of Romberg's melodies. When it was finally completed, he brought it to Romberg who placed it on his piano, played and sang it through. Oscar waited breathlessly for approval, and when Romberg finished he looked up at Oscar and said: 'It fits.'

Although *The Desert Song* was unquestionably a hit, the critics thought the plot was absurd and one famous critic wrote: 'With so many pleasant people in the cast and so much music, colour and romance, I am perhaps ungrateful in regretting that, with the exception of one song called "It", the lyrics gave indication that W. S. Gilbert lived and died in vain.'

In 1928, Florenz Ziegfeld produced *Rosalie*, with the score not only by Romberg but George Gershwin, too. The most popular song in the score, however, was written by Cole Porter when *Rosalie* was made into a film in the thirties and Porter added the title song.

Despite his extraordinary string of successes, Romberg was not finished. In 1928 he wrote another hit, *The New Moon*, which included such memorable songs as 'Softly as in a Morning Sunrise', 'Stouthearted Men' and 'Lover, Come Back to Me'.

During the Depression years he added three more operettas to his catalogue which, although of musical value, failed. However, in 1945 he ended his career with two more efforts, one of which was successful – *Up in Central Park* – but hardly reaching the heights he had attained during the twenties.

Of all the operetta composers who carried on after Victor Herbert, none was as prolific as Romberg. With or without his library, he was an extraordinary melodist and left an enduring musical shelf.

Rudolf Friml studied music at the Conservatory in Prague and one of his teachers was none less than Antonin Dvořák. Between 1902 and 1906 he made two or three visits to the US as accompanist to the great violinist, Jan Kubelik, and in 1906 he settled permanently in New York. He staked his claim on Broadway with his first operetta, *The Firefly*, which contained the lovely song 'Sympathy'. For the next ten years he contributed to and wrote a handful of operettas, including *Sometime* in which, as already mentioned, Mae West played the vamp, but somehow none of them measured up to *The Firefly*. Finally, in 1924, he found his bearings and produced the world famous *Rose-Marie*, which featured the equally famous 'Indian Love Call'. (When *Rose-Marie* was presented in London, a young soprano appeared on stage to audition 'Indian Love Call' and sang: 'When I'm calling you – Double O, Double O/Will you answer too – Double O, Double O.' When she had finished, the casting director said: 'Thank you, Miss Levine.' She looked at him and replied. 'It's LeVine.') Needless to say, *Rose-Marie* returned in all its glory on the silver screen starring the inevitable pair, Jeanette MacDonald and Nelson Eddy.

Although Friml's output could hardly compare in volume to that of Romberg's, to many operetta devotees his best was the best. By the best I mean *The Vagabond King*, which featured such songs as 'Only a Rose', the 'Huguette Waltz' (one of my personal favourites in the Friml litany), 'Some Day', 'Song of the Vagabonds' and 'Love Me Tonight'. 'Love Me Tonight' is one of those titles that probably has been used by more composers and lyricists than I can remember, Rodgers and Romberg among them. In fact, when written by Rodgers it became the title song of one of Maurice Chevalier's earliest and most famous films.

(I keep using the word lyricist, but I think it worth noting that although it has been for years the colloquial appellation for my profession, it is a bastardized word. The true word was lyrist, and only in recent years, when the

Dennis King and Carolyn Thomson in
The Vagabond King

LEFT: Rudolf Friml

Oxford and Webster Dictionaries finally threw up their hands in despair, was lyricist admitted to the hallowed pages.)

Friml's other most celebrated work was *The Three Musketeers* which opened in 1928 under the auspices of the great Florenz Ziegfeld. In the score were such Friml anthems as 'Ma Belle' and 'March of the Musketeers'. For unfathomable reasons, *The Three Musketeers* did not enjoy the run it deserved, but over the years its fame grew and its songs became an indelible part of musical literature. Friml's collaborators were Clifford Grey, a popular

English lyric writer of the time and – surprisingly enough – 'Plum' Wode-house, who must have been on holiday from a novel.

Friml wrote several other operettas which were not at all up to his standards, and so I shall pass them over. The world is filled with would-be artistes who are capable of being incapable. All that matters are those with the capacity for glory, and their hiccups are of little consequence. Friml was a superb and inspired composer and *The Three Musketeers*, *Rose-Marie* and *The Vagabond King* are quite enough to justify any man's existence.

I met Friml only once, in 1971, when the songwriters of America decided to establish a Songwriters' Hall of Fame. Naturally it was for living songwrit-ers or the list would have been encyclopaedic. Ten were to be chosen, elected by all the songwriters in the country, and who the first ten would be was a nail-biting moment for all those present. In the audience was Rudolf Friml, accompanied, as he invariably was, by two Chinese ladies who took care of all his needs. He was then over ninety but as tall and erect as a flagpole. Before I could express my awe at meeting him, he extended his compliments to me.

Mohammed Ali was fighting that night and I am a great fight fan. I was standing at the rear of the hall waiting to make a quick exit when the festivities were over and dash to the boxing ring. Next to me was Duke Ellington, whom I discovered was also going to the fight. Rudolf Friml's name was announced, then Irving Berlin, Richard Rodgers, Ira Gershwin, Johnny Mercer, until finally number eight was reached. The Duke looked at me and said: 'Kiddo, we're not going to be nine and ten, so let's go.' And we left. Well, Duke Ellington was nine and I was ten, and we were both in a car on the way to Madison Square Garden. The tragedy is that of the ten who were elected, only two are still alive: Irving Berlin and I. And Irving Berlin, as of this writing, is ninety-eight.

10 *G.G.*

Of the composers who followed Kern there is little doubt that one of them was the greatest musical genius America has ever produced. He was born in Brooklyn in 1898 and grew up on the East Side of New York. His family, though not rich, was comfortable, enabling him to study the piano when still a boy. His mother was a driving, dominating lady, ambitious for her son. Although he always professed deep affection for her, which was undoubtedly true, he was secretly more attached to his gentler father. He began working for a music publishing house as a song-plugger.

The influence of 'Alexander's Ragtime Band' on him was enormous. In later years he wrote: 'Irving Berlin is the greatest American song composer . . . America's Franz Schubert.'

In 1916 the first piece of music bearing his name appeared. It was called 'When You Want 'Em, You Can't Get 'Em'.

He was instinctively drawn to jazz and ragtime and published two ragtime pieces for the piano in 1916. He literally absorbed and assimilated the music of his growing years and applied them to his own music. He was a brilliant pianist and during the war years made a living as a rehearsal pianist in the theatre.

Offered a job by Irving Berlin as a sort of musical secretary, he turned it down and a short time later was put under contract by Max Dreyfus for $35 a week. When asked what his job would be, Max Dreyfus replied: 'Write.' He did not have to check in, he did not have to demonstrate, he did not have to arrange. His only job was to write music and bring it to Mr Dreyfus.

And so began the career of George Gershwin.

Max Dreyfus always refused to accept credit for 'discovering' George Gershwin or even assisting in his development. 'A man with Gershwin's talent,' said Max, 'didn't need anybody to push him ahead. His talent did all the pushing.' But there is no doubt that Max Dreyfus's guidance was incalculable.

(I know I have said this before in the book so I beg your indulgence for repeating it. But every time I write the name Max Dreyfus and record his life, my eyes blur. Not only because of what he was, but because I, who am still

writing, realize there is no one to turn to now, as writers of that age could turn to Mr Max.)

The twenties were filled with a variety of musicals running the gamut from operetta to musical comedy to revue. The most famous of all revues was, of course, the annual Ziegfeld Follies. But there were also 'George White's Scandals' and 'Earl Carroll's Vanities'. They all provided opportunities for the interpolated song and, perhaps, the discovery of an unknown.

So in 1918, when a producer came to Max Dreyfus in desperate need of five songs for a revue he was planning for Joe Cook, Dreyfus immediately said, 'George Gershwin.' The revue was not a success, but Gershwin had cut his eye teeth.

The following year he wrote his first complete score called *La'La Lucille.* Not a smash hit but nothing to be ashamed of. It enjoyed a modest run. The following year came his first, genuine, eighteen-carat, no-argument-about-it hit. But it did not start off as one. The lyrics were by Irving Caesar and the song was called 'Swanee'.

In those days, there were theatres on Broadway which were primarily motion picture theatres in which the feature film was prefaced by a sumptuous stage show. That tradition, incidentally, lasted until the 1960s, the last of which being the Radio City Music Hall which featured the famous Rockettes. One of the theatres was The Capitol and it was there that 'Swanee' first appeared – and disappeared. When *La'La Lucille* was trying out in Atlantic City – a famous trying-out town of the day as well as a weekend retreat where one seldom took one's wife – Gershwin met Al Jolson. They were introduced by the conductor, Charles Previn, uncle of André. Some time later Jolson gave a party in New York and invited George. Now when George Gershwin went to a party, any party, throughout his life, he headed straight for the piano the way an alcoholic heads for the bar. Going through his repertoire that night he eventually came to 'Swanee', and Jolson seized it the way an alcoholic seizes a glass. At his next appearance on Broadway, Jolson sang 'Swanee' and within a year the country was singing 'Swanee'. It sold over two million records and one million copies of sheet music.

For a decade preceding and during the war years, one of the leading 'hoofers' in the annual Ziegfeld Follies was a man named George White. In 1917 he left Ziegfeld and decided to become a producer in his own right. Thus began a series of revues that lasted into the thirties called 'George White's Scandals'. Although they never approached the lavishness of Ziegfeld's Follies, they achieved considerable success. With Max Dreyfus's inevitable assistance White acquired some first-rate composers to contribute, among them George Gershwin. From 1917 to 1922 Gershwin's music appeared regularly in the 'Scandals'. One of the most famous was 'I'll Build a Stairway to Paradise'. 'Paradise' is of historical importance because it was the first major Gershwin song in which his brother Ira was co-author of the lyrics.

LEFT: George Gershwin
AND RIGHT: Ira Gershwin

In 1922 an unsuccessful but significant event occurred in George's life. He was working on the 'Scandals' and collaborating with B. G. De Sylva, known as Buddy De Sylva. Buddy suggested they do a one-act jazz opera. They went to George White, presented him with the idea, and to their astonishment White accepted it. So they wrote a twenty-five-minute, one-act piece called *Blue Monday*. Looking back, it was quite adventuresome of White to allow it in the show. Unfortunately it only lasted one night. But all was not lost. Far from it. One of America's most popular band leaders of the era was Paul Whiteman. By chance, he happened to conduct that one performance of *Blue Monday* and he became imbued with the idea of demonstrating to the world the potential of jazz as a serious form of musical expression. So he decided to give a jazz concert, an event of fascinating originality, and invited Gershwin to compose a piece for the occasion.

The concert took place in New York at the Aeolian Hall on 12 February 1924. In the audience were John Philip Sousa, Jascha Heifetz, Leopold Stokowsky (who, incidentally, was born Leon Stokes in south London and because it did not sound imposing enough for the podium changed his name to Stokowsky), Rachmaninoff, John McCormack, Mischa Elman and Stravinsky, to name but a few. To perform before an assembly such as that I cannot conceive of the state of Gershwin's nervous system. His composition

was called, of course, the 'Rhapsody in Blue'. Written for two pianos, it had been orchestrated by a well-known arranger and composer in his own right, Ferde Grofe.

At the conclusion there was little doubt that George Gershwin, at the age of twenty-five, had written the finest piece of music America had thus far produced. Some believed it to be the greatest concerto for piano and orchestra since Tschaikowsky's 'B Flat Minor'. Ernest Newman, the most celebrated music critic of his time and the author of the definitive work on Wagner, wrote: 'Mr Gershwin's Rhapsody is by far the most interesting thing of its kind I have yet met with; it really has ideas and they work themselves out in a way that interests the musical hearer. Perhaps it is better not to prophesy. What is at present certain is that Mr Gershwin has written something for a jazz orchestra that is really musical, not a mechanical box of tricks – such as the dull clowning of Rimsky-Korsakov's Hymn To The Sun . . .' The 'Rhapsody' became the cornerstone of Gershwin's serious jazz compositions: 'Concerto in F', the 'Cuban Rhapsody' and 'An American in Paris', which culminated in the theatre with his monumental *Porgy and Bess*.

When one hears the 'Rhapsody' as it was originally performed – there is a record of it made about that time – there is an astonishing difference between the way Gershwin wrote it and the way it is customarily performed today. The difference is in the tempo. It was far brisker and the emotional passages had far less emotional sweep.

Later in that same year, on 1 December, *Lady Be Good* opened. It was the first complete score the Gershwin brothers wrote together and it starred Fred and Adele Astaire. (I find it impossible not to mention that Fred and Adele Astaire began dancing professionally in 1908. It is now 1986, and if you include the rare occasions when Fred Astaire is interviewed on television, it means that he has been a performer for seventy-eight years. Seventy-eight years!)

Lady Be Good was the first, unqualified Gershwin smash. The book was lightweight, as were all the books of the twenties – written, incidentally, by Fred Thompson and none other than Guy Bolton. Bolton on the subject of Gershwin was quoted as saying: 'He is beginning to look uncommonly like a genius.' The only critic to quibble was – wouldn't you know? – Alan Dale. The score was a sunburst of musical invention which included the uniquely Gershwin 'Fascinating Rhythm'. How lyrics were ever written for that I will never know. They not only made sense but they sang. Two qualities, I might add, that only appear spasmodically today. The most famous song in the score did not appear in the show. It was 'The Man I Love', which echoed the last theme of the 'Rhapsody'. 'The Man I Love' was one of those songs that journeyed from score to score and was invariably dropped because directors and producers thought it too slow. As in the case of the 'Rhapsody', all Gershwin ballads were played at almost twice the tempo we are accustomed to hearing them

today. 'Embraceable You', which I happened to hear myself at an early age, was sung almost as if it were an opening chorus. Finally, 'The Man I Love' found a home in 1930 in *Strike Up the Band*. It remains to this day one of his most performed songs.

Tell Me More was Gershwin's next production on Broadway, opening in April 1925, with lyrics by Buddy De Sylva and Ira Gershwin. It enjoyed a moderate run, but the title song was Gershwin at his best. It opened in Atlantic City with a different title which the collaborators decided would not do. It was called *My Fair Lady* and there was even a song in it by that name.

In the fifties I spent a good deal of time in Hollywood and there was hardly an evening when I did not drop in to see the Gershwins – Ira and his dear wife Lee. They ran an open house for a handful of Hollywoodites, such as producer Arthur Freed, concert pianist and wit Oscar Levant, Dorothy Parker when she was in town, Vincente Minnelli and any and all misplaced New Yorkers who were temporarily in Hollywood on assignment, such as I. We became good friends and I loved Ira dearly. But when *My Fair Lady* opened, he never mentioned to me that he had once written a show with the same title. I found out about it several years later, and when I asked him why he had not told me, he simply shrugged and said: 'I didn't think it mattered.'

George Gershwin's music and personality were so electric that frequently the brilliance of Ira's lyrics was overlooked. Of all the lyric writers of the twenties, his lyrics were in a way the most indigenous to the period. Aside from his ingenious and never-forced rhyming skill, his lyrics, with their wonderful, slangy sentimentality and use of the popular idioms of the day, were more redolent of the entire jazz era than the work of any other lyric writer. You can feel the twenties in his lyrics as much as in the verse of Dorothy Parker and some of the writing of Scott Fitzgerald. He even gave 'baby' and 'sweetie pie' respectability.

Ira collaborated with George for thirteen years and George was the first to admit that Ira's continually original concept of what a musical could be, his catchy titles and provocative colloquialisms were a constant source of inspiration. For example, the line 'Do do do what you done done done before, baby' was one of those phrases Ira handed to George that sparked his musical invention.

In that year of 1925, George and Ira wrote *Tip-Toes* which was a hit; how could it not have been when it included such songs as 'Sweet and Low-Down' and 'That Certain Feeling'? One of the secondary roles, incidentally, was played by Jeanette MacDonald.

Again in the same year of 1925, George's 'Concerto in F' for piano and orchestra had its premiere at Carnegie Hall. Unlike the 'Rhapsody', it was written for a full symphonic orchestra.

One of the most unfortunate critical diseases is an inability not to compare an artiste's work with his previous efforts. And so even those critics who had

ABOVE: Fred and Adele Astaire: *Lady Be Good*
BELOW: Gertrude Lawrence and O. Shaw in *Oh, Kay!*

quibbled about 'Rhapsody in Blue' could not resist comparing the 'Concerto' unfavourably with it. They were, of course, quite wrong. It was an entirely different work and the second movement is regarded by many as one of the most beautiful pieces produced by American music. Noel Coward once pointed out that the tragedy of paying attention to reviews is that if you believe the good ones, then you have to believe the bad ones. There must be an alternative but so far I have not found it.

It is hard to believe that in that one year of 1925, in which Gershwin wrote *Tell Me More, Tip-Toes* and completed and presented the 'Concerto in F', he had time to contribute to one more show before the year was out. The show was called *The Song of the Flame*, and it was one of those rare occasions when those who were writing operetta and those who were writing musical comedy assembled on the same side of the street and contributed to the same show. The music was by Herbert Stothart, primarily an operetta composer, and George. The book and lyrics were by Harbach and Hammerstein, both, as I have said, operetta lyricists. A further curiosity, Stothart and Gershwin did not contribute separately, but actually collaborated on most of the songs. Despite this mixed bag of diverse talents the play did quite well and enjoyed a healthy run.

In 1926 came one of the most popular and brilliant of all the Gershwin shows of the twenties. It was called *Oh, Kay!* P. G. Wodehouse and Guy Bolton reunited to write the book and Ira wrote the lyrics with two assists from Howard Dietz when he went down with appendicitis. The show starred that most magnetic of ladies, Gertrude Lawrence, and the score featured 'Do, Do, Do', 'Clap Yo' Hands' and 'Someone to Watch Over Me'. The middle strain, or the 'release' as it is known in the trade, was pure Ira at his best:

> Although he may not be a man some
> Girls think of as handsome ...

In 1927 George and Ira collaborated for the first time with George S. Kaufman, one of America's most versatile and prolific playwrights of the twenties and thirties. He was not only a playwright but a brilliant sketch writer for revue, and he and Noel Coward are probably the most frequently quoted wits of our time. He was also, by the way, the author of the most brilliant pun of the twentieth century. At lunch one day, somebody used the word 'horticulture'. George Kaufman looked up and said: 'You can lead a horticulture but you can't make her think.' The musical they wrote, called *Strike Up the Band*, was a noble experiment in musical comedy. Instead of the usual boy meets girl, comedian tells jokes and chorus girls dance, it was a legitimate satire on war. At long last 'The Man I Love' was included in the score, but this time instead of the song being taken out, the whole show was taken off. But not for ever. Three years later it was rewritten with Morrie Ryskind assisting on the book and it came to New York to be greeted with

ecstatic reviews. The score included such Gershwin standards as the title song, 'Soon' (one of George's most haunting ballads), and one of my own personal favourites, 'I've Got a Crush on You', with Ira's wonderful last two lines:

> The world will pardon my mush
> 'Cause I've got a crush, my baby, on you.

The satire, both in the lyrics and music, was a forerunner to their classic satire in 1931, *Of Thee I Sing*. Kaufman once said: 'Satire is a show that closes on Saturday.' He was proven wrong twice, the first being *Strike Up the Band*.

In between the two versions of *Strike Up the Band*, George and Ira crossed the street again to the lush dens of operetta and contributed songs with Sigmund Romberg to the show *Rosalie*. It was one of the rare instances when Ira collaborated on some of the lyrics with none other than our old friend 'Plum'. The score contained another George and Ira classic, 'How Long Has This Been Going On?' It was later interpolated into the film version of *Funny Face* starring Fred Astaire and Audrey Hepburn, and sung by Audrey herself (as opposed to the film version of *My Fair Lady* where most of Eliza Doolittle's singing was dubbed).

The following year Ira journeyed to London alone and provided most of the lyrics to a show for the inimitable Jack Buchanan, called *That's a Good Girl*. Big success. In the same year he was back in America, working with George and writing a show for Gertrude Lawrence called *Treasure Girl*. It was not a success, but I would have liked it because 'I've Got a Crush on You' was in it. The show closed early enough for them to have no compunction about using it again in *Strike Up the Band*. After all, very few people had heard it.

George began working on *An American in Paris* before *Treasure Girl*, continued working on it during the writing of the show, and ten days after it opened he completed the orchestration. He thought of it, as he said himself, as a 'rhapsodic ballet', which indeed it was and was one of the reasons it lent itself so admirably to choreography in the film *An American in Paris*. It had its premiere in 1928 at Carnegie Hall. Outside of one critic who described it as 'nauseous claptrap' – there has to be one of those apples in the critical barrel – the reviews varied from very good to superlative. Even the one critic who did not appreciate the 'Rhapsody in Blue' and the 'Concerto in F' had learned his trade and wrote that the work had 'the tang of a new and urgent world, engaging, ardent, unpredictable'.

George and Ira's last show in the twenties was Florenz Ziegfeld's production of *Show Girl*, which opened in New York in July 1929. Some of the lyrics were written in conjunction with Gus Kahn, essentially a popular-song lyric writer of the time. ('My Blue Heaven' was his.) It was a good score in which by far the most enduring song was 'Liza'. Although, as I mentioned before, the following year they presented the second version of *Strike Up the Band*, the year 1929 saw the Jazz Age come to a grinding halt with the Wall Street Crash

of October of that year. The musical theatre does not function in a vacuum detached from life, and the effect of the beginning of the Great Depression was theatrically dramatic. Because the musical theatre is fundamentally a popular theatre and a spontaneous expression of its time – I am not one who believes there is such a thing as an avant garde musical – it was entirely logical that it would react more quickly than any other theatrical form.

The reaction came with the death of operetta. There were one or two exceptions which I have already mentioned, *The Cat and the Fiddle* and *Music in the Air*, but the theatre-going public was no longer in the mood to see the world through the rose-coloured spectacles of operetta, especially with an administration in Washington that seemed oblivious to the disaster that had befallen the country and the civilized world.

It is hard to believe that the following quote comes from a speech made at that time by the Secretary of the Treasury, Andrew Mellon, who also happened to be one of the richest men in the country:

> I see nothing in the present situation that warrants pessimism. During the winter months there may be some slackness or unemployment, but hardly more than at this season every year. I have every confidence there will be a revival of activity in the spring and that during the coming year the country will make steady progress.

The myopia of politicians seems to be chronic. Even today, with millions unemployed on both sides of the Atlantic and human misery rampant, our leaders fairly bubble with pride at how well we are doing.

So operetta died and musical comedy, brash, satiric and unsentimental, became the language of the theatre. Those affected were, of course, Harbach, Hammerstein, Romberg and Friml. Those unaffected were the Gershwins, Cole Porter, Rodgers and Hart, Arthur Schwartz and Howard Dietz. (More about them later.) Jerome Kern, without a permanent collaborator who suited the times, moved to Hollywood where he wrote some of the best motion picture music of the thirties. His lyricist on five pictures was Dorothy Fields, who had begun her career in the twenties contributing 'I Can't Give You Anything But Love' and 'On the Sunny Side of the Street', among others, to two revues.

11 Rodgers and Hart

Once upon a time, shortly after the First Word War, a bunch of teenage boys who used to play together in the park decided to form a club called, for some reason, the Akron Club. They would play basketball in the winter, baseball in the summer and football in the autumn. One day one of them had a Mickey Rooney–Judy Garland–MGM musical idea. 'Let's put on a show.' Another boy was the son of a rather prominent physician in town and everybody agreed he wrote the best music in the club. His name was Dick Rodgers. The problem was finding a lyric writer talented enough to live up to the music. Another member had a friend called Oscar Hammerstein, who had just graduated from Columbia, and he helped out by writing two lyrics to Rodgers' music. But he could not hang around as his uncle had given him a job as an assistant stage manager in the real-life professional theatre. Suddenly one of them remembered a former class mate, seven years older than the average age of the Akron Club, who he recalled was determined to make a career as a lyricist.

So on a spring day in 1919, the ambitious lyricist, Lorenz Hart by name, came to Dick Rodgers' house where they met for the first time and the collaboration of Rodgers and Hart was born.

Previous to their meeting, Hart, who although born in New York City in 1895 had a fluent knowledge of German, had been making a meagre living by translating some of the successful German operettas for the Shuberts. Among them was a more up-to-date version of Offenbach's *La Belle Hélène*. He also worked for a man named Benjamin Glazer, also fluent in German, who translated some of the German plays that came to Broadway. When Glazer found Larry Hart he saw an easier way to make a living than working, so he paid Larry to do the translating for him – without credit, of course. Ironically, one of the plays Larry translated was Ferenc Molnar's *Liliom*. Some twenty-odd years later, Rodgers and Hammerstein used *Liliom* as the basis for *Carousel*. So although nobody knew it, Larry was a silent collaborator.

Unlike Dick, he did not come from an affluent family and his entire life was blighted by his physical deformity. He was well under five feet tall, and in a way that is difficult to explain, his diminutive body did not seem put together proportionately. When I say his life was blighted by his physical appearance, it

Richard Rodgers and Lorenz Hart at the piano

is a gross understatement. I came to know him well during the last four years of his life. In fact it was Larry who first encouraged me and gave me hope that I might make a career as a lyric writer. There is no doubt that his appearance was the cause of his frequent forays into the bottle, the untidiness of his life and his devastating loneliness. He once attended the wedding of a friend at which he was the best man, and no one, other than the bride and groom, seemed more joyous. Someone suggested to him: 'Larry, why don't you get married?' With a sudden surge of his hidden pain, he answered: 'Yes, I could get a stepladder and get married.' About a year before he died we were at the bar of the Lambs' Club in New York, an actors' and writers' club of the day, and Larry was, in simple language, drunk. He turned to me and said: 'I've got a lot of talent, kid. I probably could have been a genius. But I just don't care.' I do not think that is quite true. Somewhere along the line there obviously did come a time when the joy of his professional success became drowned in the lost misery of his handicapped life. Certainly in the beginning he was a

determined young man. 'Bad luck sticks to me like a disease,' he told a friend. 'They won't let a new man in. But I'll show the bastards I can write lyrics!'

His opportunity came on that spring day in the Rodgers' house. He and Dick discovered they both worshipped Jerome Kern and that they both considered the Princess Theatre shows were models of what good musicals should be. Dick Rodgers remembers that other than the Princess Theatre shows, Larry felt strongly that lyric writers wrote down to the audience as if they thought their own intelligence was superior. He believed that all of his life. I remember him saying to me on many occasions: 'Trust the audience, kid. They're just as smart as you are.'

Dick, up to this point, had written a couple of amateur musicals, for one of which he had also written the lyrics. When he and Larry began working together they continued writing for the Akron Club, invariably for charity, and for the Columbia University Players Varsity Show. In fact they wrote amateur productions even after their first song and their first complete score reached Broadway.

None of these amateur shows was wasted. The more they collaborated, the closer they came to producing that one voice that was theirs and theirs alone.

Their first professional opportunity came through the good offices of Lew Fields who, as part of the team of Webber and Fields, formed one of the great comedy acts of their time. Lew Fields had four children, one of whom was Herbert, who, as time went on, wrote the books for many of the Rodgers and Hart shows in the twenties. The youngest in the family was Dorothy, who started her career as an actress before turning to lyrics. She, I might add, was among that first ten elected into the Songwriters' Hall of Fame on that misguided night when I followed Duke Ellington to the fight.

Lew Fields, besides being a great comedian, also produced, and in 1919 he was starring in his own production of a musical called *A Lonely Romeo*. Dick and Larry had written a song called 'Any Old Place with You' and through a mutual friend were given an introduction to him. Fields not only liked the song but liked it enough to find a place for it immediately in *A Lonely Romeo*. So on 16 August 1919, at a Wednesday matinee, the first Rodgers and Hart song was heard on Broadway.

The following year, Lew Field again called on them for some songs for his production of a musical/revue called *Poor Little Ritz Girl*. An odd combination of people wrote the score for that show. The 'serious' songs were by Sigmund Romberg and a lyric writer who passed in the night named Alex Gerber. The 'lighter' songs were by Rodgers and Hart – except for one song, for which the lyric was written by Herbert Fields. The reviews were good, with the lighter songs faring better in the press than the serious ones. Dear old Alan Dale liked it enormously, but objected to the profanity, by which he meant the use of the word 'hell'. It is worth noting that Richard Rodgers was eighteen years old at the time.

A Connecticut Yankee

In 1924, under the aegis of Lew Fields again, they wrote the entire score for a musical called *The Melody Man*. The score was attractive but the play was defeated by the book. George Jean Nathan, probably the most illustrious and influential critic of the day, wrote: 'The plot is not only enough to ruin the play; it is enough – and I feel I may say it without fear of contradiction – to ruin even Hamlet.' The only aspect of the show worth mentioning was the performance of the leading man, a handsome young actor named Frederick Bickel. The producers persuaded him before the show to change it to Frederic March.

Mr Nathan was not only a brilliant critic of profound theatrical insight, but, along with Dorothy Parker and Robert Benchley, the founder of the American school of critical wit, which in recent times along Broadway has all too often degenerated into 'wise guy' cruelty. It was Nathan who first shone the spotlight on the talents of the unknown Eugene O'Neill. The theatrical organization that produced O'Neill and became the major producing influence in the growing American theatre – as well as presenting the great European luminaries such as Bernard Shaw, Molnar, Strindberg and Ibsen – was the Theatre Guild. Theater, as it is spelt in America, with the Theatre Guild was theatre, as it is spelt in Britain, probably because one of its founders, Lawrence Langner, was Welsh.

The Theatre Guild had developed a roster of young actors and actresses who became something like a stock company. They operated in a small theatre called the Garrick, which, by 1925, had become too small for the flourishing

"Grandpa tickles my tummy
Then my thumb he bites
And glee.
Aand all the great big
older folks
Seem dam childish to
me."
JESSIE MATTHEWS AS
BABY IN HER SONG:
"ONE DAM THING
AFTER ANOTHER."

One Dam Thing After Another:
Jessie Matthews as the Baby for the title song

Guild. In order to help finance the building of a new theatre, their young actors
and actresses suggested that they produce a revue. One of the frequent backers
of the Guild productions suggested Dick Rodgers as composer. Dick Rodgers
suggested Larry Hart as his lyric writer.

The Garrick Gaieties, as it was called, opened at the Garrick Theatre in the
spring of 1925. It was produced on a small budget but what it lacked in
opulence was compensated for by Rodgers and Hart. Mr Nathan, unfortunately, did not like it, but all the other critics in varying degrees did. Robert
Benchley wrote: '... by miles the cleverest and most civilized show in town.
Messrs. Rodgers and Hart's music and lyrics together with the burlesque
sketches and the playing by half a dozen hitherto unknown youngsters should
be a standing taunt and source of chagrin to those revue managers who keep
putting on the same old thing each year.'

It was originally intended that *The Garrick Gaieties* would run for six to
seven performances, which it did. But it reopened within a month and played
for an entire season – a highly successful run in those days. The music was

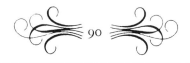

lilting, delightful, melodic and possessed of that one special quality that distinguished Richard Rodgers' work throughout his life: good taste. The lyrics? Well, there was one song that began:

> We'll have Manhattan
> The Bronx and Staten
> Island, too.
> It's lovely going through
> The zoo . . .

It was, of course, 'Manhattan', and all of Larry's wit, warmth and originality, both in thought and rhyme, were in it. The show featured 'Mountain Greenery' too. And Rodgers and Hart were in.

In that same year of 1925 they had another great success with *Dearest Enemy*. The book was by Herbert Fields and one critic accorded them the ultimate accolade of referring to Fields, Rodgers and Hart as the successors to Kern, Bolton and Wodehouse.

The story of *Dearest Enemy* was set during the American Revolution when men wore breeches and white stockings. That it was a success was a tribute to Rodgers and Hart. Let me explain. One time, many many years later, the famous director Elia Kazan was making a film in Hollywood. He wandered on to the set of the filming of a musical called *Knickerbocker Holiday*, which took place in pre-Revolutionary days, but in which the clothes were similar. He ran into a friend who was standing there in his breeches and stockings and asked him how it was going. The actor looked at him sadly, clutched his breeches and said: 'Mr Kazan, you never have a hit in these pants.' Strangely enough he was right. There have only been two other musicals that I can remember that overcame the sartorial handicap.

In 1926 Rodgers and Hart made their first journey to London and wrote a musical called *Lido Lady*, also a success, and in the same year returned to Broadway with still another hit, *Peggy-Ann*. One of the best songs in the show was called 'Where's That Rainbow?' and the second verse could only have been written by Larry Hart. It went:

> Fortune never smiles, but in my case,
> It just laughs right in my face.
> If I looked for a horseshoe, I s'pose,
> It would bop me right in the nose.
> My luck will vary surely,
> That's purely a curse.
> My luck has changed – it's gotten
> From rotten to worse!

In that same year of 1926 they contributed to the score of another show called *Betsy*, which failed (the one hit in it being by Irving Berlin, 'Blue Skies').

They also wrote the immensely popular *The Girl Friend*, where Dick tried his hand at the current craze, the charleston, and did it very nicely, thank you.

Back to London they went in 1927 to supply the music and lyrics for one of the famous Charles Cochran revues that starred that most luminous, adorable and talented lady of the English theatre, Jessie Matthews. The revue was called *One Dam Thing After Another* and it was one dam big hit. The score included 'My Heart Stood Still' which they used again on Broadway the following year in *A Connecticut Yankee*. There were also one or two interpolated songs in the score, one being imported from a recent George White 'Scandals' called 'The Birth of the Blues', and one called 'Play Us a Tune' by a little known composer named Cole Porter. 'My Heart Stood Still' was singled out for praise by almost every critic.

In 1927 came *A Connecticut Yankee* based on Mark Twain's famous novel *A Connecticut Yankee in King Arthur's Court*. The book was again by Herbert Fields and the show was the biggest hit they had had to date. Besides the aforementioned 'My Heart Stood Still', the score included one of Larry's most delicious, cleverest and endearing lyrics, 'Thou Swell'.

In 1928 they added two more shows to the shelf. *She's My Baby* which, starring Beatrice Lillie and Clifton Webb, and with Irene Dunne playing one of the smaller parts, one would have thought would have a predictable result. But there are no guarantees in the theatre and the play had a very short run. The second was *Present Arms* which although successful was hardly the unqualified smash hit that *A Connecticut Yankee* was. That same year Herbert Fields adapted for the stage a novel called *The Son of the Grand Eunoch*. It was called *Chee-Chee* – but not for long. Thirty-three performances and whatever the Chinese word is for goodbye. Brooks Atkinson of the *New York Times*, the most beloved and knowledgeable critic, certainly in my lifetime – in fact the only American critic ever to have had a theatre named after him – wrote: 'The triumvirate of Fields, Rodgers and Hart seems not to have preserved the animation and originality of their *Dearest Enemy* and other musicals.' Critical but respectful.

In 1929 the prominent American playwright Owen Davis adapted one of his earlier plays, *Shotgun Wedding*, and Dick and Larry supplied the score. Brooks Atkinson's review sums it up: '... impudent and endlessly amusing ... a book more solid than the usual conventional plot of musical comedy ... Rodgers' music seems very good indeed ... "With a Song in My Heart" is a lovely moonlight serenade.' Besides 'With a Song in My Heart', certainly one of Dick Rodgers' most glorious love songs – almost operetta – 'Yours Sincerely' and 'Why Can't I?' were also singled out for praise.

Seven months later Wall Street crashed.

12 Cole

In 1911, six years before P. G. Wodehouse's deft lyrics started a new trend in the musical theatre, a young undergraduate at Yale University wrote a fraternity show which included the following lyric:

> On my houseboat on the Thames,
> On my houseboat on the Thames,
> It's a jolly ripping vessel to relax on,
> For it's deuced dull and deadly Anglo-Saxon.
> We have Punch on board, I think,
> One to read, and one to drink.
> And when we're bored and feeling undone,
> We can wander up to London
> On my houseboat on the Thames.

His name was Cole Porter and he came from Peru, Indiana. But where his lyrical style came from is as mysterious as the pyramids. Certainly nothing like it was being written on Broadway.

He was born in 1891 with a platinum spoon encrusted with diamonds in his mouth, and he grew up enjoying all the privileges of the rich that Scott Fitzgerald envied so. When he was of age, he attended an exclusive prep school (public school in Britain) in New England and then went on to Yale, where besides writing two Yale football songs, 'Bingo Eli Yale' and the still-played 'Bull Dog', he also wrote the music and lyrics for eight undergraduate shows. Upon completing his four years at Yale, at his grandfather's insistence – and it was potent insistence indeed because he had all the money – Cole was dispatched to Harvard to study law. Unlike Oscar Hammerstein he did not stay the course and after a year, in 1914, transferred to the Harvard School of Music. He and his mother, to whom he was devotedly attached throughout his life, kept the transfer a secret from Grandfather in order to preserve the steady flow of monthly allowance.

Cole passed his summers on the Hampton 'Gold Coast', East, South and West Hampton, located at the end of Long Island, which was the summer resort of the New York social set. There he met that famous lady agent-producer, Elizabeth 'Bessie' Marbury, who was immediately taken by his songs and introduced him to several of the well-known producers and authors of Broadway. It was because of her that Cole's first song, 'Esmerelda', was interpolated into a Romberg musical called *Hands Up*. The lyric is worth quoting:

> Esmerelda,
> Then Griselda,
> And the third was Rosalie.
> Lovely Lakme
> Tried to track me,
> But I fell for fair Marie.
> Eleanora
> Followed Dora,
> Then came Eve with eyes of blue.
> But I swear I ne'er loved any girl
> As I love you.

Even then, in 1915, it was pure Cole Porter. It was sly, amusing, well-rhymed, and although I have never heard the music I can almost hum it. It was immature Cole Porter, but it was most definitely the signature of a man who once he hit his stride went from the twenties to the fifties and, unlike Kern and Rodgers, never changed the signature that was uniquely his.

Still at Harvard, he found a book writer and they wrote a musical called *See America First* which Bessie Marbury produced. Although it only ran fifteen performances, the first Porter score was on Broadway.

When America entered the war in 1917, Porter became attached to the American Aviation Headquarters in Paris. But four months later he extricated himself and joined the Foreign Legion. Before doing so, he left two songs in London, one of which was interpolated into the score of the English production of *Very Good Eddie*, and the second appeared in a musical called *Telling the Tale*.

When the war was over Porter returned to America. Among the ship's passengers was a producer-comedian named Raymond Hitchcock who was preparing a revue for Broadway called *Hitchy-Koo of 1919*. Porter cornered him on the boat, played him some of his songs, and Hitchcock accepted them. *Hitchy-Koo* opened in October of that year and ran forty-five performances longer than *See America First*. Despite the failure of the show, one of Cole's songs, 'In an Old-Fashioned Garden', caught the public's fancy and became his first big hit. It was not in the usual sophisticated Porter style, in fact it almost seemed as if he were trying to write a hit. And he did.

One other major event occurred as a result of *Hitchy-Koo*. Hitchcock introduced Cole to Max Dreyfus. In typical fashion, Max recognized his ability immediately and from that moment on Cole became one of Max's writers. Although Cole was still receiving his monthly cheque from Grandpa,

it hardly covered his penchant for the lavish life. 'In an Old-Fashioned Garden' helped to fill in the slack, but until he came into half of his trust fund a few years later, Max's advances on future songs were of invaluable assistance.

Of even greater financial assistance, however, was his marriage. In that year of 1919, he married a most gracious, beautiful, elegant and affluent lady called Linda Lee Thomas whom he had met in Paris during the war. Although Linda could trace her ancestry back to one of the signatories of the Declaration of Independence, the source of her wealth was the settlement made upon her by her former husband, the heir to a prominent publishing family. Eight years older than Cole, she loved him deeply, deeply enough to live with the knowledge that Cole was a homosexual who had never seen the closet. Yet his affection for her was genuine, and for his part he managed to keep that affection untarnished by guilt. The life they lived made the complication of their relationship simpler. They were rich, charming and gregarious and were charter members of the international elite – habitués of the Ritz Bar in Paris and well-known hosts to the equally well-endowed in rented palazzos on the Grand Canal. Although they remained married until Linda's death in 1954, as time went on the moments multiplied when the problem became more difficult.

Moss Hart, one of America's great men of the theatre, both as author and director (he directed two shows of mine, *My Fair Lady* and *Camelot*, so I can vouch personally for the word 'great'), once told me a story of an evening he had spent in one of the Porter palazzos. Cole, who by this time was well established in the theatre, was playing a song to a group who had gathered around the piano. Tears suddenly appeared in Linda's eyes and she walked out on to the terrace. Moss followed her. Alone on the terrace she turned to him and said: 'The one thing I always had was that I was the first to hear his new songs. I never heard that one.' But despite the difficulties, no one was prouder of Cole than Linda. Her tombstone reads: 'Linda Lee, wife of Cole Porter.'

Richard Rodgers met Cole in 1926 when Cole had rented the famous Palazzo Rezzonico on the Grand Canal where Robert Browning had died. Invited to dinner there, served by numerous footmen in technicoloured livery, Dick was persuaded later in the evening to play some of his songs. Noel Coward was there, too, and he did the same. Then Cole sat down and to Dick's astonishment played 'Let's Do It' and two or three other numbers. Dick wrote in his autobiography how dumbfounded he was to discover that his host was far from a playboy, but a composer-lyricist of unique ability. Not only did he not know that Cole had studied harmony and orchestration at the Schola Cantorum in Paris and had written a ballet that had been presented in that same city, but when he asked him why he did not try Broadway, he was embarrassed when Cole told him he had written and/or contributed to four shows, and that so little had come of them that he had decided to amuse himself in Europe and merely write songs for his friends. Amusing himself was

Cole Porter with Moss Hart working on *Jubilee*

a necessity to Cole. Boredom was his prime enemy. He once said: 'I have spent my life escaping boredom, not because I am bored, but because I don't want to be.' But at that meeting with Dick, he did admit that he nurtured an abiding longing to be in the theatre and whispered that he had, at long last, found the secret to writing hit songs. 'I'll write Jewish tunes,' he said. And he was serious. Later on he did exactly that; the most obvious examples being 'My Heart Belongs to Daddy', 'You'd Be so Nice to Come Home to' and 'I Love Paris'.

It seems strange that someone as close to the Broadway scene as Richard Rodgers had not heard of Cole Porter, especially when one recalls that Cole had interpolated a song into Rodgers and Hart's *One Dam Thing After Another* in London. Perhaps it was because there was such a vast number of people writing musicals during the twenties, and so many who interpolated a song here or there fell by the wayside. Unsuccessful songs and musicals have a way of disappearing into oblivion. Few even remember the failures of the talented.

In 1927 Cole went back to New York to have another try at Broadway. He caught the attention of one of Broadway's most prominent agents, Louis Shurr, known in the trade as Doc. (I played for Doc, too, when I got out of college, but he saw no budding Cole Porter in me.) Doc was not only famous as an agent but for a mink coat that he kept in his closet. Every time he took a showgirl out for the evening she had to wear that coat.

After a few fruitless attempts to interest some of the producing clique in New York in Cole's music, Shurr finally arranged a meeting for him with a colourful member of the fraternity named E. Ray Goetz. It seems odd that Cole did not go to Goetz in the very beginning, because he had met him in

Venice and it was Goetz's enthusiasm for his songs that had encouraged him to battle Broadway again.

Goetz's wife was a French chanteuse named Irene Bordoni who had begun making a name for herself in one of the Gershwin shows. Goetz was determined that she become a star and had had a book prepared for her called *Paris*. He had tried to get Rodgers and Hart to write the score for it, but they were busy doing *A Connecticut Yankee*, so he decided to believe in his Venetian first impression and Cole was given the assignment.

After months of refining on the road (in the provinces in England), *Paris* opened on 8 October 1928 in New York. I need only quote two critics to indicate some idea of the result. Said Richard Watts of the *Herald Tribune*: 'Cole Porter is the flaming star of the premiere of *Paris*.' Said Charles Brackett of the *New Yorker*: 'No one else now writing words and music knows so exactly the delicate balance between sense, rhyme and tune.' In the score was a song that contained these lines:

> The dragon flies, in the reeds do it,
> Sentimental centipedes do it,
> Let's do it, let's fall in love.
> Mosquitos, heaven forbid, do it,
> So does ev'ry katydid, do it,
> Let's do it, let's fall in love.
> The most refined ladybugs do it,
> When a gentleman calls,
> Moths in your rugs, do it,
> What's the use of moth balls?

It was part of but one chorus of the numerous refrains of 'Let's Do It', when the audience kept demanding more and more.

With *Paris*, Cole at last established himself as the other great American lyricist-composer. Up until then there had been only one great American songwriter who was a team unto himself, writing both music and lyrics, and that was Irving Berlin. Cole Porter became the second.

Many years later, Cole told me that after those ecstatic reviews of *Paris*, every other score he wrote was considered by the critics not as good as his last. I think he exaggerated.

The following year he returned to his beloved Europe to write a score for Charles Cochran in London. It was called *Wake Up and Dream*, it was a resounding success, and one of the songs, 'What Is This Thing Called Love?', achieved the same popularity as 'Let's Do It'.

'What Is This Thing Called Love?' was typical of Porter's special melodic gift, a gift which became more and more apparent as time went on. First of all he wrote the most passionate music of any of the great songwriters, including Gershwin (but not counting *Porgy and Bess*). Secondly, all his songs were built

on his opening melodic statement, which kept growing and growing without leaving the melodic path. When most composers came to the release, there would invariably be a change in the melody line. With Cole the release was simply a more dramatic continuation.

Wake Up and Dream opened on 27 March 1929, and naturally Lady Cunard gave the opening night party.

Later that year Cole joined forces with Herbert Fields, who wrote so many of the Rodgers and Hart books, and *Fifty Million Frenchmen* was the result on Broadway. The score was not as rapturously received as *Paris*, but 'You Do Something to Me' and 'You've Got That Thing' moved the show into the hit class. There were also two songs about Paris, 'You Don't Know Paree' and 'Paree, What You Do to Me?' Other than the Parisians themselves, I do not believe anyone has written so many songs about Paris as Cole Porter.

Fifty Million Frenchmen opened a month after Wall Street crashed and ran well into the spring.

LEFT: Marjorie Robertson (Anna Neagle) in
Wake Up and Dream
RIGHT: Tilly Losch, principal dancer, in *Wake Up and Dream*

13 I Want to be Happy

Vincent Youmans, born on 27 September 1898, the day after the birth of George Gershwin, was the only composer besides Cole Porter who came into the world cushioned and cradled in the lap of luxury. But as the days of the calendar of his life flipped forward, seldom was there a man so beneficently endowed and with so much success who found happiness so elusive. He was as handsome and charming as any member of that feverish group, of which he was considered a part, which was more romantically than factually known as the Lost Generation. He was not only successful but achieved it when still in his early twenties. It almost seems as if occasionally there are those in life whose character cannot withstand the weight of their own gifts. In time, whisky became his crutch and the fear of emotional exposure, with its normal disappointments, was too terrifying for him to find the love that he both needed and sought. His lifespan was short – only forty-seven years. His creative lifespan less than twenty.

As a boy, with his mother's encouragement, he studied the piano, and although he played very well he never once evinced any interest in music as a career. When he went to the theatre for the first time, no bolt of lightning struck him as it had both Oscar Hammerstein and Dick Rodgers. Actually, his first ambition was to be an engineer, but a few weeks of college made him realize that no Henry Ford he. Returning to New York, his piano playing ability attracted the attention of a man who made piano rolls. In those pre-radio days, player-pianos were a popular source of home entertainment. When America entered the war to end all wars in 1917, Youmans enlisted in the Navy. The conductor of the US Navy band was John Philip Sousa, the famous march king. When one of Sousa's associates heard Youmans playing the piano, he suggested to him that he try to write a march for the Navy band. Youmans did, and the band master was so enthusiastic about it he had Youmans play it for Sousa. Sousa was equally impressed, had it orchestrated and included it in the band's repertoire. When Youmans heard his own music orchestrated for the first time, *that* was the moment lightning struck. From then on his goal was clear. He liked the song so much that he placed it in the proverbial 'trunk' and used it in a show ten years later. The song was 'Hallelujah' and it was to become one of the biggest hits he ever wrote, a standard to this day. And he was nineteen when he wrote it.

After the war he got his taste of Broadway by becoming a rehearsal pianist for two Victor Herbert shows, and following the ways of the times, had a song interpolated in one show and several in another. He also, as had Gershwin and Kern, became a song-plugger for a publishing firm. Dissatisfied with his progress, one day he packed up his music and took it to – is there any doubt? – Max Dreyfus. Max listened, put him under contract and gave him the same instruction as he had given Gershwin: 'Go home and write.' The following year a show called *Two Little Girls in Blue* opened on Broadway at the George M. Cohan Theatre. Most of the music was by Vincent Youmans and the lyric writer was 'Arthur Frances'. In his early days, 'Arthur Frances' was the *nom de plume* of none other than Ira Gershwin who took the name from his brother and sister, Arthur and Frances. The reviews were far from ecstatic but those who wrote favourably of the score singled out three songs in particular, all of which were by Youmans.

Although Youmans, Gershwin and Rodgers were all inspired by Jerome Kern and worshipped at his shrine, Kern's influence is only apparent in the music of Dick Rodgers. Kern may have been the innovator, but both Gershwin and Youmans, each in his own way, travelled a road of his own. Dissimilar as they may have been, they shared a melodic power that no one else has ever equalled. It was markedly evident in Youmans' first song, 'Hallelujah', in its strength and simplicity and the feeling that if one did not hold tightly to the reins, the melody would run away. There lay deep in it a controlled passion that was not at all like the sweeping melodic passion of Cole Porter. There was an inner life to many of Youmans' slow tunes that was unique to him.

The year that established him as a major composer was 1923. To a book written by Harbach and Hammerstein called *Wildflower*, he shared the composing credit with Herbert Stothart, and one of his songs, 'Bambalina', not only filled the opening night audience with glee but proceeded to do likewise to the country. *Wildflower* was an alchemy of both operetta and musical comedy which left most of the critics bemused. But all of them hailed 'Bambalina' and despite the mixed bag of reviews, it became one of the longest running musicals of the twenties. A second company, equally successful, carried Youmans' name from coast to coast. (Second and sometimes third companies were as much a part of the theatre then as they are today. The story goes that Sigmund Romberg's *Blossom Time* had so many companies playing throughout the country that the Shuberts, who produced it, lost one. They knew it was out there somewhere, but somehow they just could not find it.)

No one seemed to enjoy the accoutrements of success as much as Youmans. After *Wildflower* he bought himself a yacht and the first of a stream of expensive automobiles. During the twenties it was not uncommon to find a Packard, a Rolls Royce and a Mercedes in front of his door. He was also never completely at home with the members of his profession, and except when he was preparing a show, he lived very much away from the theatre among those

who had enjoyed the same benefits of birth as he. The exceptions were the ladies of the theatre. In fact in one show he married two girls from the same ensemble – though not at the same time.

In that same year of 1923, Youmans crossed paths with a successful Broadway producer named Harry Frazee. In 1919, Frazee had produced a straight play entitled *My Lady Friends* and he was now determined to convert it into a musical. Youmans wanted desperately to write the songs but Frazee had his heart set on more glittery names in the composing arena. Youmans might have lost the show had it not been for his mother, who offered to finance it. The cost of production was $10,000. Otto Harbach was engaged as the lyricist but he and Youmans had artistic differences about the choice of songs to be used. Harbach, being the gentleman he was, suggested another writer be called in. The one selected was Irving Caesar whose most famous song had been Gershwin's 'Swanee'. One of the songs that Youmans played for him Caesar found monotonous – not only monotonous, but because of the repetitive melodic pattern a lyrical back-breaker. To facilitate the writing he made up, as is common practice in the trade, what is called a dummy lyric, meaning just words which fit the music and create a model for the lyric writer to follow. Dummy lyrics, by their very nature, are not supposed to make sense. This was Irving Caesar's dummy lyric:

> Picture you
> Upon my knee
> Just tea for two
> And two for tea
> Me for you
> And you for me alone
> Nobody near us
> To see us or hear us
> No friends or relations
> On weekend vacations
> We won't have it known, dear
> That we own a telephone, dear
> Day will break
> And you'll awake
> And start to bake
> A sugar cake
> For me to take
> For all the boys to see
> We will raise a family
> A boy for you a girl for me
> Can't you see
> How happy we will be.

To Caesar's mixture of horror and surprise, Youmans thought it was perfect. It is not recorded who decided to call it 'Tea for Two' but 'Tea for Two' it became, and although it made little sense it sang well. And one of the greatest popular songs ever written came into being. To this day it is one of the best known, most played standard songs in the world.

Youmans' melody was a stroke of pure genius. No one before had ever written dotted quarter-eighth note, dotted quarter-eighth note, dotted quarter-eighth note from beginning to end. Even the development, which begins with 'Nobody near us to see us or hear us', holds fast to the pattern and was made fresh by merely a key change. When I say no one had written one before, I might add that no one has written one since, although I know of several composers who have tried. There is no question that it was an extraordinary melodic invention. It not only became the classic soft-shoe rhythm, but it can be played in every orchestral interpretation without losing the strength and stature of its melody.

The show was *No! No! Nanette!* and as if 'Tea for Two' were not enough for one score, during the try-outs on the road Youmans added rather prophetically a song of his own title: 'I Want to Be Happy'.

A further addendum to the legend of *No! No! Nanette!* is the way in which it came to New York City. It opened in Detroit in April 1923, but because of its success due to the immediate fame of 'Tea for Two' and 'I Want to Be Happy', it was sold out in every city in which it played. Frazee, not one to turn his back

Vincent Youmans

on an ever growing mountain of money, kept the show on the road for two years. By the time it opened in New York there was already a London production, and nine days before, Youmans had another show, *A Night Out*, opening in Philadelphia. (When the Prince of Wales saw *No! No! Nanette!* in London he requested that the orchestra remain after the curtain came down and play 'Tea for Two' for him repeatedly. Needless to say, this attracted much attention in the press.) Not unexpectedly, there was a slight resentment on the part of the New York critics to have had the ultimate judgement taken from their hands. Said one paper: 'Boston saw it, Philadelphia saw it, Chicago saw it, London saw it, and Guatemala, Medicine Bend and the Canary Islands have probably seen it as well.' Said Alan Dale: 'Why, bless your heart, New York didn't care. No! Nay! We weren't peeved for we really have a lovely nature when you come to know us. If *No! No! Nanette!* wanted to keep away from us until it had been everywhere else – why, let it. Of course, we have such gorgeous shows here, don't you know, that we can afford to be generous.' Later on in his review he said: 'There we were at the Globe Theatre listening to "Tea for Two" after it has become a menace, and to "I Want to Be Happy" after every phonograph and barrel organ and summer hotel orchestra has done it to death.' The *Daily News* said that 'last night we heard "Tea for Two" and "I Want to Be Happy" for the 1,876,934th time'.

Probably because most of the theatre-going public in America had seen the show, it did not enjoy one of those endless runs on Broadway. Nevertheless, when the final accounting was made it was far and away the most successful musical of the 1920s. The producer's earnings were well over $2 million and Youmans' in the vicinity of half a million. The discrepancy irritated Youmans deeply. He was quoted as saying: 'No one is going to make any money off my music but me.' And he meant it. It caused Otto Harbach to say one day: 'He was a nice kid but wanted to be everything. He wanted to be producer. He wanted to be dressmaker. He wanted to raise the money. He wanted to hire the theatre. If he had just stayed a composer he would have been the greatest of them all.' For a moment he had forgotten Gershwin.

A Night Out was a failure, as was his next musical, *Oh, Please!* But buried in the score of *A Night Out* was a song that he was to use later called 'Sometimes I'm Happy', and in *Oh, Please!* was another song of 'Hallelujah' vibrancy, 'I Know that You Know'.

In 1927 Youmans did indeed become a producer. His partner was Lew Fields. The show they embarked upon was *Hit the Deck*, but before it opened on Broadway Youmans bought out Lew Fields and became the sole producer. The most prestigious theatre on Broadway was the Belasco Theatre, a legitimate theatre whose capacity was too small for a musical. But with his dreams of grandeur, Youmans was determined to play the Belasco. The normal ticket price on Broadway in those days was $5. Youmans doubled the price and *Hit the Deck* opened at the Belasco. The score included 'Hallelujah' and 'Some-

Hit the Deck

times I'm Happy', and despite the outrageous price being charged it enjoyed the longest run of any of his shows to date. In short order a second company was dispatched to the hinterlands and the following year it opened in London, starring my dear old friend, Stanley Holloway.

As a rule, after a show opened Youmans would take himself to Europe. His restlessness prevented him from staying in one place too long – except the bar of wherever he was. After *Hit the Deck* opened and before he left for Europe he saw *Show Boat* and made up his mind 'he wanted one of those'. I was told that he always harboured a hidden envy of Gershwin's career in the world of serious music. The same applied to *Show Boat.* Youmans became determined to reach for the larger theme, both in book and in music.

His opportunity came the following year when a producer offered him a new musical called *Rainbow*, for which Hammerstein had co-authored the book and would write the lyrics. The setting, instead of the Mississippi River, was early America in the Far West. Unfortunately, Hammerstein became ill, was unable to work on the score, and a young lyric writer named Edward Eliscu inherited the assignment. It opened on Broadway in November 1928 and Brooks Atkinson best summed up Youmans' effort: 'If Mr Youmans has

not realized his opportunity completely, he has written in an harmonious key and occasionally with genuine distinction.' *Rainbow* was not a success and closed after thirty performances. But Youmans' determination to reach the land where *Show Boat* lived remained undaunted.

By this time he was not only a producer and composer, he had formed his own publishing company. But even that was not enough. In Columbus Circle in New York there was a theatre notorious for failure called the Cosmopolitan. (This strange phenomenon occurs frequently on Broadway. The Mark Hellinger Theatre, for example, which opened in 1930, never had a success until *My Fair Lady* in 1956.) Determined to own a theatre and defying the odds, Youmans acquired the lease on the Cosmopolitan and on 17 October 1929 opened his production of *Great Day*. Moving closer to the locale of *Show Boat*, the plot of *Great Day* took place along the shores of the Mississippi River rather than on a boat. The road to Broadway had been a minefield, with numerous book writers being called in to try and save an ailing play, but there was no cure. In the theatre you cannot make a bad play good, but you can make a good play better. One of the great deceptions when one is out of town is that when a bad play is improved, one thinks it has become good, when all it really is is less bad. Youmans' score, however, was nothing short of magnificent and included three of his most memorable and powerful songs: 'Without a Song', 'Great Day' and 'More than You Know'. *Great Day* lasted thirty-seven performances. It has been said, and rightly so, that no failure in the history of Broadway ever produced so many great songs.

In that same month *Variety*, the showbiz weekly bible, ran its famous headline: 'Wall Street Lays an Egg'.

14 Dietz and Schwartz

W rote Howard Dietz in his autobiography *Dancing in the Dark*: 'I saw newspapermen at work so I became a correspondent. I saw advertising men at work so I became an advertising man: publicity people at work, I went in for publicity. I saw painters at work, so I bought some canvases and covered them with oil. I saw musical shows I liked and I became a lyric writer.' It may seem glib but it was not far from the truth. Dietz became a painter by avocation rather than vocation and painted charmingly throughout his life, that is, as long as he was able to. The last part of his life was spent suffering the agonies of Parkinson's Disease. He also became a publicist and was vice president in charge of public relations for Metro-Goldwyn-Mayer until retirement. It was he who invented the famous lion that identifies all MGM films. But of more importance to us he wrote some of the most felicitous lyrics ever to grace the stage. Not only felicitous, but charming, literate, warm and witty. All of these adjectives could be applied to the man himself. I knew him well and my knowledge is first-hand. He once said: 'I don't like composers who think. It gets in the way of their plagiarism.' Lyric writers also plagiarize, at least this one will because, if I may be forgiven, I would like to quote a passage I wrote for the introduction to Howard's autobiography. 'Howard is the Fred Astaire, the Chevalier, the Molnar, the Lubitsch of lyric writers ... to those of us who have long loved and admired him, this book is not only filled with his memories, but the best of ours.' Underneath the introduction, Howard printed his reply:

Dear Alan,
When I received your introduction to my book I was in the hospital.
When I finished reading the introduction I went home.

As ever,
Howard

In the early twenties there was a famous newspaper column in New York called The Conning Tower. Its editor and regular contributor was a man with a passion for light verse and humorous pieces who signed himself F.P.A. It stood for Franklin P. Adams. From time to time some verse appeared signed 'Freckles'. 'Freckles' was Howard Dietz and it was an apt nickname. He also

LEFT: Howard Dietz   RIGHT: Arthur Schwartz

tried his hand at lyrics and in 1923 contributed a song called 'Alibi Baby' to an ill-fated show called *Poppy*. A little less than two years later he received a phone call from a man who identified himself as Jerome Kern. Dietz could not believe it, but it was indeed Kern. He had read some of 'Freckles" work in The Conning Tower, had heard that he also wrote lyrics, and invited him to his house to discuss doing a show together. The show they did was called *Dear Sir*. It was not one of Kern's major efforts, but the score was appreciated and Dietz received good notices for his lyrics. One of them was typically Howard:

> On our houseboat on the Harlem
> Where the pleasure-seekers flock
> Though it's stuck there
> In the muck there
> It's the best boat on our block
> The breezes sweep along the shore
> And tell us what they cook next door
> On our houseboat on the Harlem
> Off the coal and lumber dock.

The following year Howard received a letter on stationery, at the top of which was stamped 'Arthur Schwartz Attorney at Law'. Schwartz wrote that although he was a lawyer by practice, he was a composer by talent, and invited Howard to collaborate with him. (When one recalls how many lawyers left the

profession for the theatre – W. S. Gilbert, Oscar Hammerstein, Cole Porter and now Arthur Schwartz – one cannot help but speculate what a more pleasant and civilized world this would be if the rest of the legal profession followed suit.) At the time, Schwartz was about to contribute some songs to a revue. Howard answered his letter politely by saying that he did not think the collaboration was a good idea, that he had already written a show in collaboration with a well-established composer, and suggested that Schwartz do the same with a well-established lyric writer. 'In that way we will both benefit by the reputation of our collaborators, then when we both get famous we can collaborate with each other.'

It was a good idea but it did not happen exactly that way. As I have previously mentioned, Howard assisted Ira Gershwin when Ira had appendicitis during the writing of *Oh, Kay!* He also contributed to a not very successful musical in 1927 called *Merry-Go-Round*. But the collaboration of Schwartz and Dietz did not happen until that fateful year of 1929 when neither of them was famous.

A producer of considerable wealth named Dwight Deere Wiman, who was to figure prominently in the 1930s, joined forces with another budding producer named Tom Weatherly to present a small revue called *The Little Show*. What they had in mind was a chic and elegant version of *The Garrick Gaieties*. Howard wrote that Wiman was 'so solvent that he had a wicker-work Rolls Royce built for him. It was the most expensive looking car ever to appear in traffic. It was equipped with a bar and this, to Dwight, was its most important equipment.' Wiman and Weatherly were discussing their prospective venture in a speakeasy in the West Forties one day, and Howard was at the bar and overheard their conversation. On his way out he stopped at their table and said that if they were planning a show, his advice was not to do it. Invited to join them, by the time drinks were over Howard had agreed to write the lyrics. Wiman and Weatherly suggested Arthur Schwartz as composer.

They were introduced and their collaboration began. They did most of their work in hotel rooms from which they were invariably asked to leave because of the noise. (Howard, working at MGM all day, could only work at night.) One night, walking down the street after their third or fourth eviction, Arthur said: 'They don't like what I'm playing.' 'That must be it,' said Howard. 'They never complain about the lyrics.' They finished the score and in the spring of 1929 *The Little Show* opened at the Music Box Theatre on Broadway. There were two interpolations, but the rest of the score was by Dietz and Schwartz and they left their calling card with 'I Guess I'll Have to Change My Plan'. The show ran two years.

With *The Little Show* opening as it did just a few months before the Crash, Dietz and Schwartz had come in just under the wire to join the masters who founded the American musical theatre in the 1920s.

15 'Destiny's Tot'

In 1890 there lived in Teddington, Middlesex, on the edge of London, a Mr and Mrs Arthur Coward, a couple with proper, English middle-class credentials. They produced three sons. The first, Russell, died as a child of meningitis, and the youngest, Erik, was struck down at the age of twenty-eight by cancer. The middle son was born on 16 December 1899. In the twenties he was referred to by Alexander Woollcott as 'Destiny's Tot'; later, by John Osborne, as 'his own invention and contribution to this century'; and, more recently, as the 'impresario of himself' and 'England's solid-gold jazz-baby' by John Lahr, who is one of the two finest theatre critics America has produced in the last four decades, the other being Walter Kerr. Being born so close to Christmas, the boy was named Noel, Noel Peirce to be exact.

The accumulation of his talents was staggering. In the twenties he became a celebrated actor, playwright, director, composer and lyricist – a one-man band, a theatre unto himself, a world unto himself. No one of this or any age has ever been crowned with adulation and acclaim as was Noel Coward. He was Celebrity and Star, Chic and Elegance nonpareil: a geyser of quoted wit both on stage and off. He was also, I might add, a most kind and generous man, both of which I gratefully remember from my early days when I was hungry for hope.

The significance of Noel to this volume is, of course, his music and lyrics. He was a self-taught musician, and although he played the piano rather well, better than some trained composers I have known, he could not write down one note and relied upon an assistant to commit his music to paper. At times, when a melody came to him on the street or in a taxi, as in the case of 'I'll See You Again', his most famous song, it meant dashing home to the piano as quickly as possible before he forgot it, as opposed to having a bit of paper on him upon which he could draw the musical staff and jot it down.

In the case of Porter and Berlin, one cannot say which of their dual talents was superior. But until he became musically more ambitious in 1929 with *Bitter Sweet*, Coward's lyrics far outshone his music. There was, of course, the

LEFT: Noel Coward

occasional melodic flash of brilliance, such as 'Poor Little Rich Girl', the verse of which he accidentally borrowed from César Franck's 'D Minor Symphony', and the equally delightful melody of 'A Room with a View'. But it was his lyrics that were special and irresistible. His ballads were literate, graceful, and glistened with the polish of Coward's readily identifiable language. His comedy lyrics were the funniest of anyone to come down the lyrical pike, be they witty, silly in the best sense, outrageous or glibly cynical. I offer in evidence two songs from the thirties, 'Mad Dogs and Englishmen' and 'Don't Put Your Daughter on the Stage, Mrs Worthington', which, to my mind, is the most hilarious lyric ever written.

His first published song was an attempt to be apple-pie American. It was called 'The Baseball Rag' and, like Berlin in the beginning, Coward provided only the lyrics. By 1922 his playwriting and acting skills were already on public view, and ideas for sketches and songs began to tumble through his head and on to the page. They were brought to the attention of André Charlot, one of London's most active producers, and the result was the 1923 hit revue *London Calling*. The hit song was 'Parisian Pierrot' and the lady who sang it was Gertrude Lawrence – to wit:

> Parisian Pierrot
> Society's hero
> The Lord of the day
> The Rue de la Paix
> Is under your sway,
> The world may flatter
> But what does it matter,
> They'll never shatter
> Your gloom profound . . .

And there was the Coward style. The world-weary, glossy romanticism, the multiple rhyming, and the inverted adjective and noun of 'gloom profound'. All that was missing was his perennial use of the anti-penult rhyme that usually ended with a clipped 'it', as in 'mad for it', 'sad for it'; 'know of it', 'glow of it', etc., etc.

In 1925 he joined forces for the first time with the illustrious Charles B. Cochran, in a way the English Ziegfeld. But where Ziegfeld's scarcely-clad lovelies were called the Ziegfeld Girls, in Cochran's revues they were the beautifully gowned Mr Cochran's Young Ladies. The revue Cochran and Noel did together was *On with the Dance*, and from it came 'Poor Little Rich Girl', which was lyrically laced with the mood of the twenties by someone who was not only a part of it but on the balcony looking down. There was also one of Coward's outrageous numbers, which went:

ABOVE: The entire company, for the Finale: *This Year of Grace*
LEFT: A young Noel Coward in the New York Production of *This Year of Grace*

We're six dirty little choirboys,
With really frightful minds,
We scream and shout and run about
And pinch our friends' behinds.
Nobody could admire boys
With dirty hands and knees,
But the countryside rejoices
At our sweet soprano voices,
So we do what we damn well please.

The star of *On with the Dance* was Noel himself. His understudy was John Gielgud.

Three years and three plays later, Noel returned to the musical scene with another sparkling revue, *This Year of Grace*, starring Jessie Matthews and Sonnie Hale, and with a score that starred 'Dance Little Lady', 'A Room with a View' and 'World Weary'.

I have always envied the exotic places where Noel found inspiration. With me it is invariably a small room with a boring wall a few feet away. But Noel? The idea for 'Parisian Pierrot' came to him on his way home after a fascinating evening in a Berlin café; 'A Room with a View', walking on a beach in Hawaïi; and the first draft of *Bitter Sweet* on a luxurious ocean liner on his way back to London.

ABOVE LEFT: Gertrude Lawrence as the
'Parisian Pierette' in *London Calling*, 1923
ABOVE RIGHT: 'Cosmopolitan Lady'
Alice Delysia, from *On With the Dance*

Bitter Sweet was his first book musical. It opened in London in May 1929 and the reception was thunderous. At the final curtain, the audience not only rose from their seats en masse to applaud and cheer, but reports have it that some actually stood on their seats, which seems to me rather precarious. For Noel, the score was a departure. It was pure operetta, French operetta at that. But it contained his most memorable and touching song, 'I'll See You Again', and another, 'If Love Were All', the lyrics of which took on an added significance during the closing years of Noel's life. The last four lines of the lyric are:

> But I believe that since my life began
> The most I've had is just
> A talent to amuse.
> Heigh-o, if love were all.

Although written when he was still a young man, it later seemed to be a clairvoyant and moving summing-up of his own life.

I remember one of the last parties given for him in London in the early seventies to celebrate the successful revival of *Private Lives*. The full roster of the giants of the British theatre were on hand, as well as a few fortunate foreigners such as myself. Noel was not well, but upon inducement falteringly made his way to the piano, and with an uncertain touch and with a slight tremble in his voice sang two of his songs, and ended with 'If Love Were All'. When he came to those last four lines, people who as a rule never wept unless the script called for it suddenly joined those like myself who cry at ushers, and the room was filled with tears of affection, nostalgia, grief and gratitude.

It was one of those moments that could only occur in the theatre. Never at British Petroleum, never at General Motors, never at IBM. Only in the theatre. It is one of the reasons I have always regarded myself as among the blessed to have been able to spend my life in it.

Of Noel, the pure and simple fact is he was the most original composer/lyricist to emerge in England during the post-war years; the only one to rise to the international level of the Gershwins, Kern and Hammerstein, Youmans, Rodgers and Hart, and Cole Porter. Ivor Novello did not come into his own until the thirties, and even then he remained a product for home consumption. This was also true of composer Vivian Ellis and librettist A. P. Herbert, two of Britain's most accomplished and prolific writers of the period, whose most famous musical, *Mr Cinders*, captivated the British audiences in 1929. But like the above-mentioned Yanks, whose musicals were as popular in Britain as they were in America, only the songs and musicals of Noel Coward safely crossed the Atlantic to reappear on Broadway with equal success.

FAR LEFT: Evelyn Laye in *Bitter Sweet*, 1929
LEFT: 'I Went to a Marvellous Party'
from *Set to Music*, 1939: Beatrice Lillie

16 Postscript to the Twenties

With all the fresh, innovative and remarkable music that emerged from the musical comedies of the 1920s, there was one tragedy. The books that accompanied those great scores were so unsubstantial – with the exception of *Show Boat* – that they are almost impossible to revive. One of the reasons was that it was the age of the musical, dancing and comedic star, something which this impoverished theatre world of the post-sixties not only knows little about but makes no effort to develop. Authors, composers and lyric writers wrote shows for Fred and Adele Astaire, Marilyn Miller, Beatrice Lillie, Bert Lahr, Harry Richman, Joe Cook, the Marx Brothers, Jack Buchanan, Jessie Matthews, Gertrude Lawrence, etc. The love story was invariably of little consequence and developed 'in one', which means before the front cloth to cover a change of scenery. Occasionally, as in the recent case of *No! No! Nanette!* and a 1920 operetta called *Irene* – which featured the famous 'Alice Blue Gown' – the books were rewritten and updated (hopefully), but fundamentally it has always been only the melodies that survive. Fortunately, those melodies are so infectious, so vital, so timeless, and of such musicianship that they always will linger on. With radio, television, motion pictures and the recording industry, Gershwin, for example, is played more today, fifty and sixty years after creation, than ever before.

The same handicap does not apply to operetta. The books may have been spun candy, but unlike musical comedy, operetta was written for baritones, sopranos, tenors and coloraturas, and although we may not be saturated with good ones, there are enough pear-shaped tones around to continue to delight audiences with *The New Moon, Rose-Marie, The Desert Song* and so on. Not necessarily on Broadway or in the West End, but certainly in the regional theatres.

But let us be grateful for all we were given. In a world not distinguished for either happiness or melody, thank God for those moments of joy when we chance to hear the music of Jerome Kern, George Gershwin, Richard Rodgers, Arthur Schwartz, Vincent Youmans, Cole Porter, Irving Berlin and Noel Coward. And thank God again that most of them continued into the thirties and forties, and a few thereafter.

17　The Depression

In the United States by the end of 1930, 4.5 million people wandered the streets in search of employment and filled makeshift soup kitchens across the country for nourishment to keep alive. By the end of that same year, 1,300 banks had failed, culminating with the collapse of the Bank of the United States with its 60 branches and 400,000 depositors. By 1932, unemployment had reached 11 million and at its peak in the thirties was over 14 million. Yet in the midst of all this human misery, the rich continued their ways and habits, seemingly impervious to the sea of misery that surrounded them. Being one of the fortunate few, I remember the car and chauffeur picking me up from boarding school, and at the age of sixteen walking down the street in white tie and tails on my way to debutante parties, unaware of the unintentional cruelty of my presence as I passed men on street corners selling apples. The ocean liners were still crowded, evening dress was obligatory in the ship's dining room for dinner, and the jewels that festooned the stately necks outshone the chandeliers. Every cabana on the Lido in Venice was taken for the summer (my mother insisted upon the same one every year), and there was not an empty mansion in Palm Beach. (In one, all the bathrooms had solid gold fixtures.) The cost of debutante parties ran into thousands of dollars and they vied for splendour. And when President Franklin Roosevelt raised income taxes, by not very much by today's standards, in order to accelerate the redistribution of the nation's wealth and pay for projects that would put men back to work, an almighty cry of outrage went up against him and he was branded a socialist by some and a communist by others. Never in current history has there been a public figure so hated by everyone but the people as was Franklin Roosevelt, who was guilty of nothing more than saving the capitalist system in America. Even after leading America victoriously through the war, when he died in 1945 one of New York's country clubs gave a ball to celebrate his death. Franklin Roosevelt who, with Abraham Lincoln, saved the Republic.

Yet in that first year of the Depression, thirty-two musicals opened, only five less than the year before. It was not until the year-end that the full effect of the prevailing and growing economic catastrophe struck Broadway. In 1929 the

profits of the Shuberts ran well over one million dollars. In 1930 they produced nine musicals and showed a loss.

But the humour and subject matter of the best of the musical comedies immediately reflected the new and tragic circumstances of life. Gone for ever were the silly, skittish plots of the Flapper Age. Without losing any of its humour, comedy became deftly edged with satire, poking good-natured fun at politicians, government, the rich, business and the human plight.

The rewritten *Strike Up the Band* by George and Ira Gershwin opened right after the New Year and heralded the comedic style of the thirties. The plot concerned America imposing a high tariff on Swiss chocolate and then declaring war on Switzerland when it discovers the Swiss are retaliating by using Grade B milk instead of Grade A in their chocolate production. In the course of the evening, bumbling politicians and shady businessmen served as dartboards for humour and no one was bothered when a communist was a 'good guy'. Gershwin's music contained a spirited mockery of patriotic songs and the lyrics were barbed and satiric.

Rodgers and Hart wrote a musical, *Simple Simon*, for Ziegfeld, which starred one of America's great funny men, Ed Wynn. At one point in the show, said the straight man to Ed Wynn: 'Business is looking up.' Replied Wynn: 'It has to. It's flat on its back.' Big laugh. The score was overshadowed by the antics of Ed Wynn, but not when Ruth Etting sang 'Ten Cents a Dance', which contained one of Larry's most ingenious rhymes:

> Sometimes I think
> I've found my hero,
> But it's a queer ro-
> Mance.

'Dancing on the Ceiling' was also in the score, but was taken out on the road to reappear the following year in London in *Ever Green*, which Dick and Larry wrote for Jessie Matthews.

Cole Porter had two entries on Broadway in late 1929 which carried over into 1930. One was *Fifty Million Frenchmen*; the other was *Wake Up and Dream*, imported from London bringing Jessie Matthews with it. Her understudy was a young English girl named Marjorie Robertson, who later became Anna Neagle. It was the last musical of the twenties. At the end of 1930 Cole wrote *The New Yorkers* which was advertised as a 'sociological musical satire' about New York City. Brooks Atkinson of the *New York Times* said the show 'managed to pack most of the madness, ribaldry, bounce and comic loose-ends of giddy Manhattan into a lively musical'. One of the best songs Cole ever wrote was in *The New Yorkers*. It was called 'Love for Sale' and it became a minor *cause célèbre*. The audience took it in its stride, but one or two of the critics felt it was in extremely bad taste and it was barred from the radio. The producer, however, became uneasy and changed the street-walker from a

white singer to a black singer – street-walking being considered less offensive in Harlem. God bless hypocrisy!

The biggest hit of 1930, in performances if not quality, was *Flying High* by De Sylva, Brown and Henderson, a musical starring the Cowardly Lion, Bert Lahr, and in which he was never funnier. The plot took full comedic advantage of the public's sudden interest in flying, because of Lindbergh and Amelia Earhart.

In June, the Theatre Guild had a go at another *Garrick Gaieties*. One dozen lyric writers and ten composers were responsible for the score. Among the lyric writers were the well-established Ira Gershwin, one relative new-comer, E. Y. (Yip) Harburg, and one genuine newcomer, Johnny Mercer. Among the budding composers was Vernon Duke who wrote serious music under his real name, Vladimir Dukelsky. Duke proved to be more successful than Dukelsky. There was one other composer/lyricist who contributed and that was Marc Blitzstein who in later years, under the influence of Kurt Weill, turned his talent to more serious works for the theatre. This second edition of *The Garrick Gaieties*, while modestly successful, did not compare to the first in originality and freshness.

The nights of 14 and 15 October proved to be two of the most illustrious of that or any other musical year. On the 14th, *Girl Crazy* opened with a trunkful of creative and performing talent. The score was by the Gershwins and included such timeless wonders as 'Bidin' My Time', 'Embraceable You', 'But Not for Me' and 'I Got Rhythm'. One night, Ira and I were comparing lyrical agonies – the lines that we could not get, that almost drove us to cyanide – and Ira told me of the struggle he had had over one line in 'Embraceable You'. As I recall, he said that he had to hide out in a hotel for a couple of days to escape from the pressure of everyone screaming for that missing line. When he finally got it, the line was: 'Come to Poppa, Come to Poppa, Do.' It was sung by an *ingénue* making her Broadway debut, Ginger Rogers. The comedian was one of Broadway's most hilarious Jewish comics, Willie Howard. Among the musicians in the pit were Benny Goodman, Glenn Miller, Gene Krupa, Jimmy Dorsey, Red Nichols and Jack Teagarden. But with all that, the unquestion-able star of the evening was another girl, also making her debut, who became from that night on one of the greatest stars ever to light the musical stage – Ethel Merman. Her first song was 'Sam and Delilah', which took the audience from their seats, but when she came to 'I Got Rhythm' there was pande-monium, the like of which has rarely been equalled in the whole panoply of the musical theatre. If there ever was a voice that put chandeliers in danger – and I mean chandeliers in another theatre – it was Ethel Merman's. Irving Berlin said to me once: 'If you ever write lyrics for Ethel Merman they had better be good, because *everybody* is going to hear them.' It was a night that left the critics thumbing through *Roget's Thesaurus* in search of fresh superlatives.

BROADWAY
1930–1

Bert Lahr in *Flying High*

Fred and Adele Astaire in
The Bandwagon

The following night, 15 October, was also an occasion for rejoicing. Although by its very nature and cast it was not as explosive an evening as *Girl Crazy*, nevertheless, Dietz and Schwartz's new revue, *Three's a Crowd*, was embraced to the collective theatrical bosom. By this time Howard Dietz had become the master craftsman of the revue form, and the show he assembled was witty, elegant and melodic. It starred another of the leading comedians of the day, Fred Allen, and one of his monologues reflected the times. It was a satire on the exploits of Admiral Richard E. Byrd, a national hero who had recently returned from exploring the Antarctic. Said Allen: 'After a year and a half's hard work in the Antarctic region, we discovered and claimed for the United States not fifty, not one hundred, but five hundred thousand square miles of brand new snow ... the United States now has enough snow to meet any emergency for the next two hundred years. Enough snow to settle the unemployment problem in every city in the country. Four million men are now out of work. It will take seventeen million men thirty-one and a half years to remove all the snow and they won't even make a dent in it.' During this lecture, the pictures he showed of his aeroplane, his living quarters, Eskimos and the South Pole itself were all blank – because of the snow. The score, besides Dietz's usual medley of humour, featured one of their loveliest songs, 'Something to Remember You By', and an interpolated song by a talented young composer named Johnny Green called 'Body and Soul'. 'Body and Soul' was not just another song. It was almost blues, of rare melodic invention, and for many years it was the most recorded song in America. Its composer, had he remained in the theatre, would undoubtedly have been a major creative force, but he was a brilliant pianist, arranger and conductor, and the urge to perform superseded all else. He did, from time to time, write some sterling popular songs such as 'Out of Nowhere', but eventually he settled in Hollywood where for many, many years he was the head of the music department at Metro-Goldwyn-Mayer.

A few operettas came and went in 1930, but Noel Coward's *Bitter Sweet*, which opened in November, was a success although it never achieved the glittering popular acceptance it had received in London.

Vincent Youmans was also represented in 1930 with a show called *Smiles*. It was produced by Ziegfeld and not only starred Marilyn Miller, but Fred and Adele Astaire. Featured in a smaller role was Larry Adler, and Bob Hope was in the chorus. The score included one of Youmans' most enduring songs, 'Time on My Hands'. Despite this extraordinary assortment of talent, *Smiles* was one of those musicals that just did not work and ran less than three months. There were three lyric writers. Among them was Ring Lardner, one of America's most brilliant short story writers and celebrated wits who did not venture into the lyrical field often. I mentioned earlier George Gershwin's irrepressible habit at parties of sitting at the piano from the moment he arrived and never leaving it until the party was over. On one of those occasions Ring

Lardner was listening as Gershwin ecstatically played one of his latest songs. Gershwin looked up at Lardner and said: 'God! What a strain!' Lardner replied: 'Then why do you do it?' (Oscar Levant was once asked if he thought Gershwin's music would live for ever, and he answered: 'If Gershwin's around it will.')

The first musical of 1931 was a show called *You Said It* and it occupies a special shrine in the temple of my memory. Members of the business community were understandably under severe strain in those days, and many turned to the bottle more than usual for respite. One of them was my father, who returned home late one evening and the following morning discovered that somewhere during the night he had met the producer of *You Said It* and had signed a contract to finance a good part of the show. Although I was only twelve years old at the time, my passion for the musical theatre was already sharp and clear and I was overjoyed at the prospect of being able to go backstage – which I later did repeatedly. But personal interest aside, the musical importance of *You Said It* was that it was the first complete Broadway score of Harold Arlen, who came to be one of America's most individual, respected and talented composers. The previous year he had contributed to an unsuccessful revue a song called 'Get Happy' – later immortalized by Judy Garland – which Gershwin thought so well of he sought out Arlen to tell him. In the same year he composed some of the songs for Earl Carroll's *Vanities* and finally, in 1931, wrote *You Said It*. Arlen was (and is) the master of the blues – 'Stormy Weather' and 'Blues in the Night' being among his most famous – and became a frequent contributor to the revues at the Cotton Club in Harlem. Legend has it that he was the only white composer the black musical fraternity regarded as one of their own.

A few weeks after the opening of *You Said It*, Herbert Fields rejoined Rodgers and Hart and the result was *America's Sweetheart*. Beginning with Moss Hart and George Kaufman's celebrated *Once in a Lifetime*, there was a medley of shows devoted to the comedic problems of the conversion in motion pictures from silent to talkies. *America's Sweetheart* was one of them. With the exception of Brooks Atkinson, who nevertheless found words of praise for the score, the show was on the whole extremely well received and a very good run was had by all. In one of the papers was a line which, unfortunately, you will never read in a review of a musical today. The critic wrote: 'For all the ingratiating music and ingenious rhythms, it lacks a star ...'

Dwight Deere Wiman and Tom Weatherly produced another *Little Show*, *The Third Little Show* starring Beatrice Lillie – but this time without Dietz and Schwartz. As in the case of the second *Garrick Gaieties*, the score was written by a veritable parade of lyric writers and composers including Noel Coward, whose 'Mad Dogs and Englishmen' was imported from an earlier London revue and sung to a fare-thee-well by Beatrice Lillie.

Dietz and Schwartz were otherwise engaged in writing what was undoubtedly the most elegant, wittiest and most melodic revue of the decade. It opened two nights after *The Third Little Show*, starred Fred and Adele Astaire and was called *The Band Wagon*. The score included 'New Sun in the Sky', 'I Love Louisa' and one of the great show songs of that or any other year, 'Dancing in the Dark'. The show was produced on revolving stages which blended one scene into the next, and for the first time footlights were abandoned and all the lighting came from the balcony rails, a practice that has invariably been followed ever since. The show consisted of a variety of settings from New York to Paris to Bavaria, all of which were magnificently mounted. Among the musical numbers was a story told in dance by Fred Astaire and Tilly Losch, a most famous ballerina, which was one of the first glimpses of ballet to appear on the Broadway stage. All in all it was a band wagon that audiences and critics alike got on, and for those fortunate enough to have seen it, it remains an unforgettable evening in the theatre. The equally unforgettable Brooks Atkinson wrote: 'Mr Schwartz's lively melodies, the gay dancing of the Astaires, and the colorful merriment of the background and staging begin a new era in the artistry of the American revue. When revue writers discover light humors of that sort in the phantasmagoria of American life, the stock market will start to rise spontaneously, the racketeers will all be retired or dead, and the perfect state will be here.'

The only sad note was that it was the last show in which Fred Astaire danced with his sister Adele. After *The Band Wagon* she married Lord Cavendish and retired from the theatre. Brother and sister had been dancing together since they were children in 1908.

Ethel Merman made her second appearance on Broadway that year in the eleventh edition of 'George White's Scandals', and when she sang 'Life Is A Bowl of Cherries', for one moment in those depressing times everybody thought so. The score was by Brown and Henderson, formerly De Sylva, Brown and Henderson, the most frequent contributors to the 'Scandals', and Rudy Vallee made his debut on Broadway. He sang a song called 'My Song' surrounded by a half-dozen, long-stemmed beauties, one of whom was Alice Faye. It also starred Merman's former associate from *Girl Crazy*, Willie Howard, and his straight-man brother, Eugene. The eleventh edition was a great success.

So was the ninth edition of 'Earl Carroll's Vanities' for which the score was mostly written by a young up-and-coming team named Harold Adamson and Burton Lane. The biggest hit in the score, however, was an English import that replaced 'Three O'Clock in the Morning' as the classic last song of every ball, party and nightclub for years to come: 'Good Night Sweetheart'.

The Shuberts also produced a modestly successful musical called *Everybody's Welcome*. There was one interpolated song in it that passed unnoticed

BROADWAY
1932–2

for almost ten years, when it reappeared in that immortal, romantic film *Casablanca*. It was, of course, 'As Time Goes By'. The words and music were by Herman Hupfeld who usually wrote silly songs like 'Sing Something Simple', which was in *The Second Little Show*, and 'When Yuba Plays the Rumba on the Tuba', which appeared in *The Third Little Show*. Little did he know in 1931 that he had written what was to become one of the great standard songs of all time.

At the beginning of the summer Ziegfeld produced another 'Follies', written by nineteen collaborators and starring a host of Broadway favourites. One song, 'Half-Caste Woman', was by Noel Coward and borrowed from a Cochran revue in London. But the best and most enduring was 'You Made Me Love You' sung by Harry Richman which, as in the case of 'Get Happy', reached its peak of fame years later when Judy Garland sang it to a photograph of Clark Gable.

Max Gordon, who had produced *The Band Wagon*, struck gold again in mid-October when he presented *The Cat and the Fiddle* by Jerome Kern and Otto Harbach. It was a noble and, on the whole, successful attempt to make operetta a contemporary form. It was truly a story told in music and lyrics which bravely did without what would have been an unnecessary chorus. Kern's score was hailed by the critics, one even declaring that it was the finest score Broadway had ever heard (debatable), and it was readily and enthusiastically received by audiences for one of the longest runs in Kern's career.

The inimitable Ed Wynn followed *Simple Simon* with another success called *The Laugh Parade*, but it was the day after Christmas that Broadway was treated to the first musical ever to win the coveted Pulitzer Prize for the best play of the year – and over such competition as Eugene O'Neill's *Mourning Becomes Electra*. George Kaufman and Morrie Ryskind had written a brilliant, political satire to which George and Ira Gershwin added an equally brilliant score. When the curtain rose on a parade of John P. Wintergreen for President supporters singing 'Wintergreen for President!/He's the man the people choose/Loves the Irish and the Jews ...' *Of Thee I Sing* was off and running. Hardly an institution of government from the Presidential office to Congress to the Vice President to the Supreme Court was not hilariously and exuberantly lampooned in the book and in George and Ira's Gilbert and Sullivanesque score. Victor Moore, one of America's favourite bumbling comedians, played the Vice President, Alexander P. Throttlebottom, whose only way of seeing the White House was to join a conducted tour, and gave undoubtedly one of the great comic performances of a lifetime.

Brooks Atkinson wrote that it 'substituted for the doddering musical comedy plot a taut and lethal satire of national politics ... it is funnier than the government and not nearly so dangerous'.

The title came from a patriotic song which is sung to the music of 'God Save the Queen'. The first three lines are:

My country 'tis of thee
Sweet land of liberty
Of thee I sing.

For the title song Ira added 'baby' so that it became 'Of thee I sing, baby' – and not only a love song but the campaign song of John P. Wintergreen who was running on the platform of 'Love'.

Of Thee I Sing was the longest running of any of the Gershwin shows. After playing over four hundred performances on Broadway, it went out on tour and then returned to New York two years later for a limited revival.

On the debit side of the year, Oscar Hammerstein collaborated on three failures, Al Jolson appeared in a book show which only lasted two months, and a revue called *Shoot the Works* which included a sketch by Dorothy Parker, some music and lyrics by Irving Berlin, some lyrics by Dorothy Fields, Yip Harburg and Ira Gershwin, and some music by Vernon Duke, suffered the same fate as Al Jolson and lasted two months. The shortest run of the year was a show called *The Singing Rabbi* which opened on Thursday and never saw Monday. (I do not know if they gave a performance on Saturday.)

Vincent Youmans spent most of the year being deserted by lyricists who found his drinking and midnight work habits too difficult for them, and Cole Porter went to Venice by way of Hollywood and China.

After *America's Sweetheart*, Rodgers and Hart were lured by the gold fields of Sunset Boulevard and left the Broadway scene until 1935. In 1932 they were responsible for Hollywood taking a giant leap forward when they wrote *Love Me Tonight* for Maurice Chevalier and Jeanette MacDonald. It was directed by Rouben Mamoulian who was later to figure prominently not only with George Gershwin but with Rodgers and Hammerstein. The music was imaginatively presented both cinematically and in the way it was embedded in the story, and the score included 'Mimi', 'Isn't It Romantic?' and 'Lover'.

On Broadway 1931 had begun with *Through the Years*, produced and composed by Vincent Youmans. Still determined to create something on a grander level than musical comedy, the result belonged more to the operetta of the twenties and closed after three weeks. But as in all of Youmans' shows, including the failures, there was something in the score of genuine melodic stature. In this case it was the title song and 'Drums in My Heart'. It was to be his last complete score on Broadway. Not only was his drinking beginning to show its wear and tear, but his failures and lavish lifestyle had depleted him financially. To add to his economic woes, his parents had lost everything in the Crash and it had fallen upon Youmans to support them. To producers, his wayward ways caused him to be regarded as a risk and offers diminished rapidly. I know of no more tragic waste in contemporary Broadway history.

Moss Hart, who had successfully collaborated with George Kaufman on

the hilarious comedy *Once in a Lifetime*, now turned his hand to musicals and he and Irving Berlin collaborated on a satire on the rich called *Face the Music*, directed by none other than George Kaufman. Although Moss's sharply-edged libretto was not a perfect companion to Irving Berlin's effervescent optimism, the show enjoyed a respectable run.

BROADWAY
1932–3

By 1932, the Depression was beginning to takes its toll on Broadway with the special victims being musicals, which although costing but a fraction of what they do today obviously were more expensive to produce. Including *Through the Years* and *Face the Music*, the curtain went up on only twenty-two musicals and only four could be classified as genuine hits. By far the most successful was *Music in the Air* by Jerome Kern and Oscar Hammerstein, which opened the night Franklin Roosevelt overwhelmingly replaced Herbert Hoover as President of the United States. Despite the fact that it was fundamentally an operetta and reminiscent of the twenties, it was so skilfully crafted and the score possessed of such soaring enchantment that even Herbert Hoover would have enjoyed it. The reviews were unanimous and audiences flocked to it over 340 times, and the following year its success was duplicated in London at His Majesty's Theatre. The leading lady was a beautiful girl named Katherine Carrington. When she auditioned for the role, Kern was astonished to discover that her accompanist was the celebrated composer of *The Band Wagon*, Arthur Schwartz. Why he? Shortly after *Music in the Air* opened, he and Katherine Carrington were married.

Howard Dietz and Arthur Schwartz contributed another delightful revue called *Flying Colors*. In the score were 'A Shine on Your Shoes', 'Louisiana Hayride' and 'Alone Together'. There was also in the show a song called 'Smokin' Reefers' – which was about smoking reefers. Very few people were doing it then, so nobody objected. Most of the vocal arrangements, incidentally, were by André Kostelanetz and the original choreographer was Agnes de Mille, but she was replaced before the show came to Broadway. *Flying Colors* was the second of the four musicals to 'make it' that year.

The third was *Take a Chance* starring Broadway's now blazing star, Ethel Merman. The lyrics were by Buddy De Sylva and the music by Richard A. Whiting, one of the best popular songwriters of the era who seldom ventured into the theatre, and Nacio Herb Brown. There were also three interpolated songs by Vincent Youmans, one of which, 'Rise 'n' Shine', was an Ethel Merman special.

Take a Chance was the last time Vincent Youmans was to be represented on Broadway. Because of his financial difficulties he turned to Hollywood, and the following year composed the score for *Flying Down to Rio*, one of the best film scores ever written and which introduced the dancing team of Fred Astaire and Ginger Rogers. In the score was an absolutely brilliant piece of music called 'The Carioca', which swept the country and started a whole wave

of 'doing the' songs. Soon the country was doing 'The Continental' and then doing 'The Piccolino'. The following year even Youmans' motion picture career came to a grinding halt when he became ill with tuberculosis and was forced to retire to Colorado. He tried frequently to leave Colorado but in the end his failing health brought him back there. Years later, in 1944, he tried his hand at a revue which proved a dismal failure and closed without ever reaching New York. Two years after, he journeyed west to see Louis B. Mayer, the head of production at MGM, in an effort to interest him in a film biography based on his life. Mayer rejected the idea on the grounds that no one remembered Youmans' name. He even called in his secretary and asked her if she had ever heard of Vincent Youmans, and the secretary shook her head. A few months later he lapsed into a coma and died the following day.

Louis B. Mayer's comment may seem cruel, but only because it was said in Youmans' presence. It happened to be the truth. To the theatre-going public Youmans' name disappeared quickly. Perhaps if he had been part of a permanent collaboration, such as Rodgers and Hart, it might have been different. The tragic fact is he died in virtual anonymity, and despite his enduring legacy and even the recently successful revival of *No! No! Nanette!*, few outside the profession remember the name of Vincent Youmans, one of the most talented and blighted composers the musical theatre ever produced.

The fourth long-runner of the year was Cole Porter's *Gay Divorce* which starred Fred Astaire in his first outing without his sister, and his last appearance on Broadway. The critical reaction to the book was tepid, but in the score was 'Night and Day' and its immediate popularity soon overcame the lack of critical enthusiasm.

Beatrice Lillie had an 'almost' that year in a revue called *Walk a Little Faster*, with a score by Vernon Duke and Yip Harburg that featured 'April in Paris'.

It was Yip Harburg's second show of the year, the first being *Ballyhoo of 1932* which did not fare well. He also contributed to a revue called *New Americana* which also had lyrics by Johnny Mercer. One of the songs by Harburg and composer Jay Gorney became the theme song of the Depression: 'Brother, Can You Spare a Dime?'

There was a run-of-the-mill musical starring Bert Lahr called *Hot-Cha!* which was the last Ziegfeld musical comedy. Two months after it opened he revived *Show Boat*, but he was too ill to attend the opening night. Shortly after, Florenz Ziegfeld, Broadway's greatest show man, died at the age of sixty-four. The cast of *Hot-Cha!* included a young dancer named Eleanor Powell, and in the chorus was a tall brunette whose name was listed as Rose Louise. In the coming years she became better known as Gypsy Rose Lee.

Seven musicals ran less than a month and one with the inspired title of *Yeah Man* only four performances. But in the debris could be found some very good songs indeed. In the score of the tenth edition of 'Earl Carroll Vanities'

was 'I Gotta Right to Sing the Blues', with music by Harold Arlen and lyrics by Ted Koehler. In 'George White's Music Hall Varieties' was another Arlen and Koehler hit, 'I Love a Parade', and in the same score, that writer of silly songs, Herman Hupfeld, faced the Depression with a song called 'Let's Turn Out the Lights and Go to Sleep', which became immensely popular.

The years 1933 and 1934 were dark for the musical theatre on Broadway. There were only fourteen entries in 1933 and twenty in 1934, and of those only four could be classified as genuine hits. All four were written by composers and lyricists of note. There were no newcomers who entered the divine circle, nor would there be for another decade and a new generation – with one exception, Harold Rome, who made his debut in 1937.

By far the most original musical of 1933 and the one rewarded with the longest run was a brilliant revue called *As Thousands Cheer*, with sketches by Moss Hart and a score by Irving Berlin. The sketches were all satires of real people and events of the day, such as the inauguration of President Roosevelt, the ninety-fourth birthday of John D. Rockefeller, the divorce of Joan Crawford and Douglas Fairbanks Jr, Noel Coward, Gandhi and so on. The score was Berlin at his best, with one song in particular becoming one of his and the world's most treasured standards. Having difficulty in finding a finale to Act One, Berlin suddenly remembered a song he had written in 1917 called 'Smile and Show Your Dimple'. He rewrote the lyric and it became 'Easter Parade'. The stars were Marilyn Miller, Clifton Webb, a great comedienne of the day named Helen Broderick (mother of Broderick Crawford), and one of the most gifted black singers of her time, Ethel Waters. Berlin took full advantage of her remarkable voice with 'Heat Wave' and 'Supper Time'. Ethel Waters eventually left the theatre and devoted the rest of her life to working for Billy Graham.

The other success was *Roberta* by Jerome Kern and Otto Harbach, which I discussed earlier.

The Gershwins, amazing as it may seem, had two failures in 1933. *Pardon My English* suffered from terminal book trouble, but although the score was not a masterpiece, it was still Gershwin. The second was *Let 'Em Eat Cake*, an ill-fated attempt to write a sequel to *Of Thee I Sing*. The curtain rose again on 'Wintergreen for President', which set the audience on edge with excitement, but from then on it became proof of the old theatrical adage that sequels rarely work. But in the score was a beautiful and inventive song called 'Mine', which was a love song that had a contrapuntal melody sung against the main theme, and the first of its kind.

Cole Porter was in London that year, where he wrote a show for Cochran starring Gertrude Lawrence called *Nymph Errant*. Cole regarded it as his best score to date and the critics received it ecstatically. It included 'How Can We Be Wrong?', 'It's Bad for Me', 'Experiment', and that anatomical song of

Ethel Merman and William Caxton
singing 'You're the Top'
from *Anything Goes*, 1934

Anything Goes

staggering lyrical ingenuity, 'The Physician', the second chorus of which began:

> He said my cerebellum was brilliant,
> And my cerebrum far from N.G.,
> I know he thought a lotta
> My medulla oblongata,
> But he never said he loved me.

The choreography, also praised, was the first breakthrough of Agnes de Mille. Unfortunately the book, which concerned itself with the sexual adventures of a young girl with a voracious appetite, proved a little too head-spinning (or, perhaps, a little too near the mark?) for the British theatre-going public, and *Nymph Errant* had only a modest run.

The following year, 1934, began with an almost-hit, *Ziegfeld Follies*, presented by Ziegfeld's widow Billie Burke, a famous actress in her own right, and the Shuberts. The best of the score were two songs by Vernon Duke and Yip Harburg, 'I Like the Likes of You' and 'What Is There to Say?', but the most popular was a Western number called 'The Last Roundup'.

There was a delightful revue called *Life Begins at 8:40* which starred Bert Lahr and Ray Bolger, with a score by Harold Arlen and lyrics by Yip Harburg and Ira Gershwin, and it was one of the popular hits of the year. But by far the most successful show of 1934 was Cole Porter's *Anything Goes*, starring the magical Ethel Merman. The title song, 'I Get a Kick out of You', and 'You're the Top' are both part of history.

In typical Porter fashion, when the show was trying out, his butler was sent ahead with paintings to hang on the walls of his hotel suites, and during rehearsals he would frequently arrive at the theatre in black tie with a group of friends. They would stay for 'an hour's entertainment' and then move on to the next port of call in the evening's frolic. Although his mode of living may have seemed that of a dilettante, when he was at work he suffered the labour pains familiar to all professionals. I met him many years later, when I was still green in the theatre, and inanely asked him how it felt to hear his songs wherever he went. He looked at me and said: 'My dear boy, I'm stuck on a lyric.' I also remember him being kind and encouraging.

BROADWAY 1934–5

In the autumn of 1934 two shows came to Broadway from London, where operetta still reigned: *The Great Waltz* and Noel Coward's *Conversation Piece*. Both had been highly successful in the West End, especially *The Great Waltz* which ran over six hundred performances. Alas, neither caught the fancy of Broadway, although *The Great Waltz*, for which Moss Hart had rewritten the book, attracted customers for almost a year because of the sheer magnitude of its production: 42 principals, 100 members of the singing ensemble, 40 dancers, and 53 musicians in the pit. The critics were dismissive,

if you can dismiss anything of that size, but the show nevertheless ended up in the black.

The year's most adventuresome entry was an opera, with a text by Gertrude Stein of all people, and music by one of America's most celebrated composers and music critics, Virgil Thomson. The music was highly praised, but Gertrude Stein's words left everyone in a state of confusion, starting with the title *4 Saints in 3 Acts* when it had four acts. But failure though it may have been, it was more than a mere footnote in the history of the musical theatre. It was a serious work and, although no one realized it at the time, a straw in a slowly changing wind.

For the first time in their illustrious career, Howard Dietz and Arthur Schwartz left the revue form and attempted a book musical. The score was an

Lotte Lenja in *The Threepenny Opera* (*Die Dreigroschenoper*)

absolute gem, including such truly beautiful songs as 'If There Is Someone Lovelier than You' and 'You and the Night and the Music'. There was also a number typical of Howard's wisdom wrapped in charm that began:

> You're never lonely when you love only one.
> You're only lonely having two or none.

Unfortunately, Howard was not at home in dramatic story-telling, and *Revenge with Music* never achieved the success of their revues. I do not know how many musicals have had a song called 'Maria' before Leonard Bernstein finally led the lady to glory in *West Side Story*, but there was one in *Revenge with Music* and a month later there was one by Rudolf Friml in an operetta inappropriately called *Music Hath Charms*.

Also among the 'almosts' was *Thumbs Up!*, a revue by the usual rash of composers and lyric writers. In it was another song that years later achieved a measure of fame through the good offices of Judy Garland, 'Zing! Went the Strings of My Heart!', and Vernon Duke wrote a melodic sequel to his *April in Paris*, *Autumn in New York*, for which he also supplied the lyrics. And surprisingly good lyrics they were. Another 'almost' was *New Faces*, among whom was Henry Fonda.

Finally, the ubiquitous gypsies made a brief appearance in a show called *Gypsy Blonde*, and the Kurt Weill–Bertholt Brecht musical, *The Threepenny Opera*, which had swept Europe in the twenties, made its way to Broadway and passed unappreciated. Then in 1935 came *Porgy and Bess*.

18 Porgy and Bess

The first appearance of *Porgy* was between the covers of a novel written by DuBose Heyward who, not long after its publication in the mid-twenties, converted it into a play which was produced by the Theatre Guild. This passionate southern story of a black community on Catfish Row was received respectfully but not, by Broadway's financial terms, successfully. Nevertheless, it attracted the attention of both George Gershwin and Jerome Kern.

In 1932, just before he left for Europe on a brief holiday, Gershwin wrote to Heyward and told him that *Porgy* had been on his mind for several years, and that upon his return he would love to meet with Heyward and discuss the setting of it to music. What Gershwin had in mind was a folk opera. Heyward replied immediately, saying that the rights were available. Upon Gershwin's return, he discovered to his surprise that the Theatre Guild also nurtured the same idea of musicalizing *Porgy*, and had not only spoken to Kern and Hammerstein, but Al Jolson, famous for singing in black-face, to play the lead. Realizing that Heyward was in financial straits and that a musical by the authors of *Show Boat* with a star of the magnitude of Jolson seemed like a guaranteed hit, Gershwin generously bowed out. But Heyward's artistic ambition for his work overcame the lure of lucre, and Gershwin's proposed opera seemed more appropriate to him than a simpler musical version, no matter how distinguished, starring Al Jolson. So, in 1932, DuBose Heyward began his libretto and two years later George Gershwin began devoting all his time to composing *Porgy and Bess*. Heyward was intelligent enough to realize that he needed a more experienced hand than his to collaborate on the lyrics. The experienced lyricist on hand was Ira.

Rouben Mamoulian, who had staged the original play, returned from Hollywood to direct – he agreed to do so without hearing one note of the music – and Alexander Smallens, who had conducted *4 Saints in 3 Acts* and whose work had made a deep impression on Gershwin, was offered and accepted a similar role.

Porgy and Bess opened in Boston, but before it left New York it was presented for one performance in concert form at Carnegie Hall. It ran over four hours, but for years to come there were many who considered it the finest

'It Takes A Long Pull To Get There' from the 1935 production of *Porgy and Bess*

rendition of the opera they had heard. But four hours would not do in the theatre, and during the week before the Boston opening, two songs were dropped, and there was general trimming wherever possible.

On 30 September 1935, *Porgy and Bess* gave its first performance. Boston, a reserved and conservative city by nature, was not so that night. The curtain descended to a stunning ovation. Koussevitzky, the world famous conductor of the Boston Symphony, was quoted as saying that it was 'a great advance in American opera'. The reviews were unanimously superb, with one critic referring to it as: 'Gershwin's most important contribution to music.'

Ten days later it opened in New York. The reaction on opening night was a duplicate of Boston. Even the authors were called to the stage to receive their share of appreciation. But little of the opening night enthusiasm was reflected the following day in the press, which ranged from good – with reservations – to decidedly bad. Only in one paper was it hailed for the achievement it was.

Said the usually reliable Brooks Atkinson of the *New York Times*: 'To the ears of a theatre critic ... Mr Gershwin is still easiest in mind when he is writing songs with choruses ... promoting *Porgy* to opera involves considerable incidental drudgery for theatre-goers who agree with Mark Twain that "classical music is not as bad as it sounds".' And the *Evening Journal* wrote: 'Mr Gershwin has written quite a lot of music, some very happy and pleasant, some self-consciously operatic, and some that went in one ear and out the other. If a critic can be shot for one paragraph, let it be this: I found two-thirds of it mighty dull.' Even the one excellent notice failed to recognize the beauty of 'My Man's Gone Now', 'I Loves You, Porgy' and 'Summertime'. On the whole, one must pity the critics more than Gershwin. They had missed a memorable event.

What Gershwin had done was take the song form and give it a depth, a height and an emotional expansion that on the normal operatic stage would be achieved by aria. He called it a folk opera and that is precisely what it is. There was recitative, but there was also dialogue, which by strict definition was *opéra-bouffe*. But intellectual definitions in the case of *Porgy and Bess* seem irrelevant. It was the first of its kind and remains to this day the greatest triumph of the modern musical theatre.

In time all the critics saw the error of their ways, and when it was revived a few years later it was greeted with universal rejoicing. Recently it became part of the repertoire of the Metropolitan Opera and, seen in a classic setting, some of the critics again returned to carping, primarily finding it musically awkward in places. But nothing too serious, and certainly nothing to impair the stature of Gershwin's remarkable work.

Once, while walking out of a theatre on opening night, I ran into a famous Hollywood agent. I asked him how he liked the show. He replied: 'I don't know. I haven't read the reviews.' Unfortunately, this has become more and more a Broadway disease. It certainly was for *Porgy*, for despite the opening night acclaim the reviews proved to be too damaging. It had only a limited run. But unlike Bizet, who died of grief because of the critical reception to *Carmen*, Gershwin never lost faith in *Porgy*. He even began thinking of a new opera which was to be based on the ancient Yiddish fable 'The Dybbuk'. But it remained only in his mind and never reached manuscript.

The following summer at the Lewisohn Stadium, a New York outdoor concert hall now no longer in existence, Alexander Smallens conducted an all-Gershwin evening. Gershwin played his 'Rhapsody in Blue' and 'Concerto in F', and the programme included a medley of songs from *Porgy and Bess*. As wretched, senseless fate would have it, *Porgy* was his last composition for the theatre, and that night at the Lewisohn Stadium was the last time New York was ever to hear George Gershwin playing his own music.

Shortly after, he journeyed west to Hollywood where, in 1937, he and Ira wrote the scores for two films starring Fred Astaire and Ginger Rogers. The

John A. Bubbles, Todd Duncan (Porgy) and
Anne Brown (Bess) in the original production.

first was *Shall We Dance*. In it, besides 'Beginners' Luck', 'Let's Call the Whole
Thing Off', and 'They All Laughed', was one of George and Ira's most
haunting numbers, 'They Can't Take That Away from Me'.

The other film was *A Damsel in Distress* in which the sun came out when
Fred Astaire sang 'A Foggy Day in London Town'. They were also commissioned by Sam Goldwyn to write the *Goldwyn Follies*. One of the songs in it
was 'Love Is Here to Stay', which years later Gene Kelly and Leslie Caron
danced to in *An American in Paris*. Another was 'Love Walked In', and it was
the last song George Gershwin ever wrote. On 11 July 1938, at the age of
thirty-eight, he died of a brain tumour.

Praise is superfluous. Euologies are inadequate. There are times when
there is nothing to say.

All we can do is listen.

The finale, 1935

19 A Muesli of Musicals

Economically, 1935 was a bleak year in the theatre. Besides *Porgy and Bess*, there were only nine other musicals, and despite the fact that three of them, one by Moss Hart and Cole Porter, one by Dietz and Schwartz, and one which brought Rodgers and Hart back to Broadway, received what would normally have been critical invitations to success, not one of the ten shows retrieved the cost of its production.

In these days, when both the governments of Britain and the United States consider it economic wisdom to reduce the national grants to the arts, the hallmark of any civilization (conservative governments are invariably disinterested in culture), it is hard to believe that once upon a time in the United States there was a president with enough appreciation of the performing arts to try, in the midst of far greater unemployment than exists now, to reach out a helping hand. But in 1935, President Franklin Roosevelt created the Federal Theatre Project which put actors to work in plays that could be presented at reduced prices, and preserved the flow of dramatic creativity.

Rodgers and Hart returned with a circus musical called *Jumbo*, produced by the diminutive impresario Billy Rose. When anyone ever asked George Kaufman what Billy Rose was up to, his immediate reply was always: 'Your waist.' A superb cast was headed by Jimmy Durante and the score included 'My Romance', 'Little Girl Blue' and 'The Most Beautiful Girl in the World' ('Isn't Garbo, Isn't Dietrich, It's my sweet trick ...'). It had all the paraphernalia of a circus from trapeze artistes to elephants. It even had a healthy run. But it was not enough.

Moss Hart and Mr and Mrs Cole Porter took sumptuous suites on the Cunard liner *Franconia* and sailed around the world writing a new musical. Is there any other way? They called it *Jubilee* and the critics felt it was aptly titled. Brooks Atkinson gave it the accolade of 'the aristocrat of American festivals and music'. The play was about a king and queen of an untitled country, and the young prince was played by a handsome boy named Montgomery Clift. In the score were 'Begin the Beguine' and 'Just One of Those Things', neither of which became an immediate hit. Gilbert Gabriel, the critic of the now defunct *New York American*, wrote: 'You hear a song of his [Cole's] for the first time and say "Oh, yes!" or something as ungrateful as

Kurt Weill at Brook House, circa 1948

that, but by the fourth or fifth time you hear it you realize, as everybody else from Manitoba to Mississippi has already realized by then – that it's a honey. "Begin the Beguine" is probably that kind of honey . . .' 'Begin the Beguine' did not become a part of American folk lore for three years, when it was recorded not as a beguine by Artie Shaw, the famous clarinettist.

The third success that was not a success was 'At Home Abroad' by Dietz and Schwartz, which starred Beatrice Lillie and Ethel Waters.

GEORGE
BALANCHINE
AND
KURT
WEILL

The next year, 1936, saw the first appearance on Broadway of two men who were to have a profound influence on the musical theatre. Both had left the land of their birth by necessity, one because of Stalin and the other because of Hitler. They were George Balanchine and Kurt Weill. Both had come to America in 1934.

Balanchine had fled Russia in the early twenties and joined Diaghilev's ballet company, where for five years during the twenties he became Diaghilev's greatest choreographer since Nijinsky. In 1933, Balanchine organized his own troupe in London, where he met an American patron of the arts, Lincoln Kirstein, who persuaded him to go to America and create a ballet company in New York. The result was the School of American Ballet and eventually the New York City Ballet, which became and still is one of the outstanding ballet companies in the world.

Kurt Weill barely escaped from Nazi Germany. Late one afternoon, a music-loving Nazi came to his house and warned him that the order was out for him to be picked up in the morning. His wife, Lotte Lenya, was in Switzerland. They were separated at the time. Throwing the minimal necessities into a suitcase, and leaving behind everything else he owned, Weill took the first train to Paris, where Lotte rejoined him. After a short sojourn in the French capital, and later in London, he went to New York by invitation of Cheryl Crawford, one of the founders and directors of The Group Theatre, the most prominent and influential theatre of protest in America and a spin-off of the Theatre Guild. Among the playwrights produced by The Group were Irwin Shaw and Clifford Odets. Elia Kazan, most certainly one of America's greatest directors for both stage and film, began his career as an actor with The Group, as did Lee Strasberg, who in the late forties became the guru of that celebrated organization of overblown value, the Actors Studio.

Weill's music was the quintessence of despairing German romanticism, and when in the twenties he sought collaboration to compose for the theatre, he turned not to the popular practitioners but to two of Germany's leading dramatists, first Georg Kaiser and then Bertholt Brecht. In 1928, he and Brecht produced one of the great works of the modern musical theatre, *The Threepenny Opera*. There was a state theatre, as they were called, in every reasonably sized hamlet and town in Germany, and at one time there were fifty-six companies of *The Threepenny Opera* playing simultaneously. In the score was a song that became famous many years later in the English-speaking countries as 'Mack the Knife', when in 1955 *The Threepenny Opera* finally received the popular recognition it deserved in America.

In America, Weill followed the same collaborative path as he had done in Germany and his first musical, *Johnny Johnson*, produced by The Group Theatre, was composed to a text by Paul Green, a major American playwright. It was an imaginative, often hilarious, imperfect but provocative anti-war play. It was directed by Lee Strasberg and in the cast were Robert Lewis (who later directed *Brigadoon*, among other shows), Sanford Meisner, who became one of the theatre's most famous acting coaches, John Garfield, Elia Kazan, and Lee J. Cobb who later created the role of Willie Loman in *Death of a Salesman*. Although far from the towering achievement of *Porgy and Bess*, *Johnny Johnson* was a serious musical play which caused it to suffer in the popular marketplace, as had *Porgy*. But it did bring literate, legitimate drama to the musical theatre, which slowly began to widen the theatrical horizon.

Balanchine had contributed a balletic production to a Cochran revue in London in 1930, and now on Broadway did the same in a new edition of *Ziegfeld Follies*. The score was by Ira Gershwin and Balanchine's old friend from his schooldays in Moscow, Vladimir Dukelsky (Vernon Duke). In the cast were Fanny Brice, Josephine Baker and Bob Hope, who sang the score's best song, 'I Can't Get Started with You'. Into a choreographic world that was a melange of decorative movement, legs and taps, Balanchine opened the door and ballet leapt on to the popular musical stage, directed by a supreme artist.

That ballet could be more than a graceful, isolated scene in a revue, that it could be woven into the dramatic fabric of a story, dawned first on Richard Rodgers, who, in the thirties and forties, did more to change the course of the musical theatre than any single man. Inspired by, or envious of, George Gershwin's serious work, he and Larry Hart conceived a show which would conclude with a ballet that required a genuinely dramatic piece of music. The show was to be called *On Your Toes*. It was to depict the struggle between ballet and tap and the finale was to be a ballet called 'Slaughter on Tenth Avenue'.

The year before, in 1935, Balanchine's ballet company had given a recital in New York which both Dick and Larry attended. They left the theatre convinced that what they had in mind could best be realized by George Balanchine.

Thus is was that on 11 April 1936, Dwight Deere Wiman presented *On Your Toes* at the Imperial Theatre in New York City. In the score were 'It's Got to Be Love', 'Too Good for the Average Man', 'There's a Small Hotel', 'Glad to Be Unhappy' (Larry was invariably applauded for his wit, but to me he was at his best when he was at his most touching, as in this song) – and Richard Rodgers' 'Slaughter on Tenth Avenue', choreographed by George Balanchine and starring Tamara Geva and Ray Bolger, who became famous to the world as the Scarecrow in *The Wizard of Oz*. The reviews were on the whole favourable, but only one critic seemed fully to understand what was not only attempted but achieved, and wrote: 'A definite milestone in the musical theatre', which indeed it was.

Between 1937 and 1942 Rodgers and Hart wrote seven musicals, all but one of which, *Higher and Higher* in 1940, were not only critically and publicly successful but represented the absolute bloom of their collaboration. George Balanchine choreographed three of them, *Babes in Arms* in 1937, *I Married an Angel* in 1938 in which ballet was so integrated into the story that the leading lady was played by a ballerina, Zorina, and in that same year of 1938 *The Boys from Syracuse*.

Babes in Arms may well have been their greatest score and it is impossible not to quote some of the lyrics, which have never lost their youth:

Verse
I've wined and dined on Mulligan stew
And never wished for turkey.
As I hitched and hiked and drifted, too,
From Maine to Albuquerque.
Alas, I missed the Beaux Arts Ball,

And what is twice as sad,
I was never at a party
Where they honored Noel Ca'ad.
But social circles spin too fast for me.
My Hobohemia is the place to be.

1st Refrain
I get too hungry for dinner at eight.
I like the theatre, but never come late.
I never bother with people I hate.
That's why the lady is a tramp.
I don't like crap games
With barons and earls.
Won't go to Harlem
In ermine and pearls.
Won't dish the dirt
With the rest of the girls.
That's why the lady is a tramp.

I like the free, fresh wind in my hair,
Life without care.
I'm broke – it's oke.
Hate California – it's cold and it's damp.
That's why the lady is a tramp.

And –

My funny Valentine,
Sweet comic Valentine,
You make me smile with my heart.
Your looks are laughable,
Unphotographable,
Yet you're my fav'rite work of art.
Is your figure less than Greek?
Is your mouth a little weak?
When you open it to speak
Are you smart?
But don't change a hair for me,
Not if you care for me,
Stay, little Valentine, stay!
Each day is Valentine's Day.

And –

It seems we stood and talked like this before,
We looked at each other in the same way then,

But I can't remember where or when.
The clothes you're wearing are the clothes you wore.
The smile you are smiling you were smiling then,
But I can't remember where or when.
Some things that happen for the first time
Seem to be happening again.
And so it seems that we have met before,
And laughed before, and loved before,
But who knows where or when!

And –

The sleepless nights,
The daily fights,
The quick toboggan when you reach the heights –
I miss the kisses and I miss the bites.
I wish I were in love again!
The broken dates,
The endless waits,
The lovely loving and the hateful hates,
The conversation with the flying plates –
I wish I were in love again!
No more pain,
No more strain,
Now I'm sane, but ...
I would rather be gaga!
The pulled-out fur of cat and cur,
The fine mismating of a him and her –
I've learned my lesson, but I wish I were
In love again.

Larry Hart was a distant descendant of Heinrich Heine and there are times when the bitter-sweet flavour of Heine's poetry seems to cast a shadow over some of Larry's most moving lyrics. I think of it in particular when I hear one of the songs from *I Married an Angel*, which ends:

Spring is here!
Why doesn't the breeze delight me?
Stars appear!
Why doesn't the night invite me?
Maybe it's because
Nobody loves me.
Spring is here, I hear!

And I think of it again in this lyric from *The Boys from Syracuse*, which was probably the saddest and most personal statement Larry ever wrote:

Falling in love with love is falling for make-believe.
Falling in love with love is playing the fool.
Caring too much is such a juvenile fancy.
Learning to trust is just for children in school.
I fell in love with love one night
When the moon was full.
I was unwise, with eyes
Unable to see.
I fell in love with love,
With love everlasting.
But love fell out with me.

For the music of 'Falling in Love with Love', Dick Rodgers composed a kind of fast waltz which he later developed in his collaboration with Oscar Hammerstein. To those of us who wrote (and write) musicals, it became known as the Rodgers Waltz, and although many tried to copy it, the results were simply that: copies.

Dick and Larry's most significant effort came in 1940 when, to a book by the immensely respected and popular novelist and short story writer, John O'Hara, they wrote the nearest thing to a genuine musical play yet produced, but which still retained the musical and lyrical genre of the thirties. It was called *Pal Joey*, starred a young dancer named Gene Kelly (his understudy was Van Johnson), and featured a ballet created by one of Broadway's most talented choreographers, Robert Alton.

The evolution in the musical theatre that produced *Pal Joey* included in its genealogy *The Cradle Will Rock*, with book, music and lyrics by Marc Blitzstein and a plot that concerned the struggle of union versus industry. Produced by the Federal Theatre Project, it was directed by its mentor, Orson Welles. The score departed from the musical idiom of the day and was much more indebted to the influence of Kurt Weill. In fact, on the opening night Marc Blitzstein was standing in the wings with Kurt Weill when cries for 'Author!' were heard. Blitzstein turned to Kurt and said: 'You should take the bow.'

In 1938 Weill again joined forces with one of America's most famous playwrights, Maxwell Anderson, and the result, although imperfect, was a musical of unfamiliar dramatic literacy called *Knickerbocker Holiday*. It will be best remembered for one song, 'The September Song', the lyric for which Maxwell Anderson wrote in less than an hour. I mention it because lyrical speed is a rarity in my profession. The three who took the longest, to my knowledge, were Ira Gershwin, Oscar Hammerstein and me. Oscar would frequently disappear for as long as three weeks, and over the years I find I average between a week to ten days, sometimes considerably longer. Both

BROADWAY
1936–8

Irving Berlin and Cole Porter always had more trouble and took more time with the lyrics than the music, although Irving invariably began with a lyrical idea. The most damnably facile were Larry Hart and Howard Dietz. Larry could stand in a cocktail party and while the pianist was playing something else, sequester himself in a corner and write a lyric. Howard Dietz was equally amazing. One time, he and Arthur Schwartz were strolling down the street and Arthur asked him exactly how quickly he thought he could dash one off. Howard replied: 'Give me a melody.' Arthur hummed the first few bars of the well-known tango, 'Jealousy'. Within ten seconds Howard sang:

> Cyd Charisse!
> Up there on my mantlepiece!
> You're quite a shock there.
> We need a clock there.

Between 1936 and *Pal Joey*, Broadway was populated with the usual mixed bag of doomed operettas, revues and musical comedies. During this last half of the decade there were actually eight operettas that stormed the barricades, and all but one, *The White Horse Inn*, were critically vanquished. *The White Horse Inn* was also mauled, but, as in the case of *The Great Waltz*, it was another 'King Kong' in size and won on sheer weight.

Kay Street and Gene Kelly in *Pal Joey*

There were four successful revues, two of which ran for years. Both were unexpected. The first was in 1937 and opened at a theatre called the Labor Stage, which was formerly the Princess Theatre. It was a show about labour and sponsored by the International Ladies Garment Workers Union. It was called *Pins and Needles* and, unlike *The Cradle Will Rock*, it poked fun at the problems of labour versus management with immense good humour. It introduced Harold Rome, who wrote both music and lyrics, to Broadway and the score was witty, topical and so engaging that even Republicans were forced to enjoy it. The other oddity was a brash, outrageous, corny, fast-moving grab-bag vaudeville called *Hellzapoppin*, which opened in 1938 and closed four years later.

In 1937 Arthur Schwartz and Howard Dietz again tried their hand at a book show, *Between the Devil*, and again found the form elusive. But the score, as usual, contained some Dietz-Schwartz jewels including 'I See Your Face Before Me', sung by Evelyn Laye making her first appearance on Broadway since *Bitter Sweet*; 'By Myself', sung by the one and only Jack Buchanan; and a very funny song, 'Triplets', which was about triplets and began:

> We do everything alike
> We look alike, we dress alike
> We walk alike, we talk alike
> And what is more
> We hate each other very much.
> We hate our folks. We're sick of jokes
> On what an art it is to tell us apart.
> If one of us gets the measles
> Another one gets the measles
> Then all of us gets the measles
> And mumps and croup.
> How I wish I had a gun – a little gun
> It would be fun to shoot the other two
> And be only one.

Years later in the film *The Band Wagon*, which was a composite of all the great Dietz and Schwartz songs and starred Fred Astaire, Cyd Charisse (down off the mantlepiece), Jack Buchanan and Nanette Fabray, Astaire sang 'By Myself', not Jack Buchanan, and Fred, Buchanan and Fabray, dressed up as babies and all in a pram, brought universal laughter with the above lyric.

One of the most unusual events of the period was by Noel Coward who, in 1936, took *Tonight at 8.30* to Broadway, which consisted of nine one-act plays that covered the entire spectrum of the musical and dramatic theatre. He not only wrote the plays, he composed the music and wrote the lyrics, and directed and starred in them with Gertrude Lawrence. Three plays were presented each night, two dramatic and one musical, and it gave the critics

three nights of steady employment. Although the plays were appreciated, in truth they did not receive their due. But fortunately time corrected the error. To this day they are constantly being performed, more in Britain than in the United States where, largely due to the pretentious influence of the Actors Studio, for a while the country suffered from an acute shortage of actors with style, panache, and a nodding acquaintance with the English language. (So sacrosanct was this thespian gymnasium that once, about a dozen years ago, when I was asked by the drama editor of the *New York Times* to write a piece on a subject of my choosing for the Sunday drama section and I did an article on the damaging effect of the Actors Studio on the contemporary theatre, it was rejected on the grounds that it was too controversial.)

COLE
PORTER
While Rodgers and Hart, Kurt Weill and George Balanchine were slowly changing the direction of the musical theatre, one of the constants, and in this case a constant joy, was Cole Porter. After the short run of *Jubilee*, he took up residence in Hollywood for a while, wrote a film *Born to Dance*, in which appeared two of the best songs he ever wrote, 'I've Got You Under My Skin' and 'Easy to Love' (the latter sung by James Stewart), and then returned to Broadway in 1936 with a new musical. It was called *Red Hot and Blue!* and starred Ethel Merman, his favourite singer, Jimmy Durante and Bob Hope. The show suffered from book trouble and it would be inaccurate to call it a hit, but when Ethel Merman sang 'Ridin' High', and when she and Bob Hope sang three choruses of 'It's DeLovely', it certainly seemed like one. There was also

FAR LEFT: *Red Hot and Blue*

CENTRE LEFT: Mary Martin singing 'My Heart Belongs to Daddy' in *Leave it to Me*

LEFT: Ethel Merman in *Something for the Boys*

another song called 'Down in the Depths', which was Cole writing at the peak of that world that was uniquely his. The imagery and sheer artistry of it are breathtaking. It went like this:

> With a million neon rainbows burning below me
> And a million blazing taxis raising a roar
> Here I sit, above the town
> In my pet pailletted gown
> Down in the depths on the ninetieth floor.
> While the crowds at El Morocco punish the parquet
> And at '21' the couples clamour for more,
> I'm deserted and depressed
> In my regal eagle nest
> Down in the depths on the ninetieth floor.
> When the only one you wanted wants another
> What's the use of swank and cash in the bank galore?
> Why, even the janitor's wife
> Has a perfectly good love life
> And here am I
> Facing tomorrow
> Alone with my sorrow
> Down in the depths on the ninetieth floor.

Following *Red Hot and Blue!* Cole went back to Hollywood to do another film, *Rosalie*, and then to his house in Paris, 13 rue Monsieur. (I visited that house years later when it was up for sale and I will never forget the way Linda

had arranged Cole's studio. It overlooked the courtyard and the facing wall was a solid sheet of frosted glass. In the centre of the courtyard was a Japanese tree of a variety unknown to me, of which Cole was especially fond. In the centre of the frosted glass was plain glass that outlined the shape of that tree in the courtyard, so it was always visible to him.) After a reasonable respite in Paris, Cole returned to New York, to begin work on a new musical to star his good friend Clifton Webb.

Cole was never known to be a snob with his professional associates, although his social life was peopled with counts and countesses, lords and ladies, and qualified members of the Social Register. One weekend he was at Oyster Bay, Long Island, an exclusive area of the North Shore, and in the morning decided to go horseback riding. As he was cantering blithely along the bridle path, his horse suddenly reared. Unable to extricate himself from the stirrups quickly enough, the horse fell upon one of his legs and crushed it. In trying to rise, the horse fell again, shattering Cole's other leg. It was an accident from which he was never to recover. One leg healed, the other should have been amputated, but for Cole the idea of spending the rest of his life with only one leg became a disproportionate handicap he was incapable of accepting. To preserve that other leg he endured thirty-six operations and was never again in his life without pain. Even had he been able to save the leg the agony would not have been worthwhile, but twenty years later the degeneration made it a matter of life or limb, and the leg was amputated from the hip.

I visited him in the hospital two or three times after the amputation and Cole was still Cole. I was notified by his secretary of the precise time in the afternoon when I might see him. When I arrived at the floor, his butler was waiting for me at the elevator. Cole had converted the room next to his into a pantry, where his butler prepared cocktails and hot hors d'oeuvres. During the hour I would spend with him in the visiting room, I was served by the butler as if I were in Cole's house.

Cole bore his cross with astounding courage and during those moments when the pain subsided returned to work. He finished the musical for Clifton Webb, called *You Never Know*, and although it was not successful it included, as always, a Cole Porter 'honey', 'At Long Last Love'. That same year he wrote *Leave It to Me* which was a hit and one scene of which became a legend on Broadway. It appeared at the end of the show. An unknown girl named Mary Martin, dressed adorably in a fur coat that ended above the knee, sang 'My Heart Belongs to Daddy' and raised the roof of the Imperial Theatre several feet. The chorus boy to whom she sang it was Gene Kelly. Until her retirement years later after *The Sound of Music*, Mary Martin was the unqualified leading lady supreme in the musical theatre.

The following year, in 1939, Cole wrote one of the biggest hits of his career, *Dubarry Was a Lady*, starring Ethel Merman and Bert Lahr. A young lady who had not been doing too well in Hollywood returned to play one of

the minor parts, and although there was no danger of her stealing the show from Ethel Merman, she set the style for legs for the next twenty years and became the pin-up girl of the United States Army in the Second World War. Betty Grable.

In late 1940, he wrote still another show for Ethel Merman called *Panama Hattie*, and the combination continued its merry way. After a film for Fred Astaire, Cole came back to Broadway in 1941 with yet another hit, *Let's Face It*. It starred Danny Kaye, who had made a huge success earlier in the year in *Lady in the Dark*. Two years after, he wrote again for Ethel Merman, *Something for the Boys*, which although an addition to his string of hits, was not Cole at his best. In fact both *Panama Hattie* and *Let's Face It*, while always Cole Porter, were indications of the depression that was slowly but surely overcoming him as he fought hopelessly to try and save his leg. Nevertheless, somehow he pressed on through 1944, writing two shows and producing a hit song in each. One was 'I Love You' from *Mexican Hayride*, and the other was one of his most enduring ballads, 'Ev'ry Time We Say Goodbye', from *Seven Lively Arts*, a revue produced by Billy Rose, whose ego was not only far larger than he was but considerably greater than his talent. (I knew Mr Rose better than I wanted to. He was the original producer of *Brigadoon* and even before the contract was signed, my partner Fritz Loewe and I decided that even a production was not worth it – and we walked away.)

Between *Pal Joey* in 1940 and 1943, the latter being the dramatic turning point in the history of the musical theatre, the usual muesli of musicals, some good and some bad, dropped in on Broadway, the most significant being *Lady in the Dark*. In 1941 Kurt Weill, continuing his drive for legitimate books, went to Moss Hart and suggested to him a musical on the hitherto untouched subject of psychoanalysis. Fired by the idea, Moss successfully persuaded Ira Gershwin to write his first book show since George's death, and the result was a highly imaginative musical. It starred Gertrude Lawrence and featured the newcomer I mentioned above, Danny Kaye. The lady lay on the couch and recounted her dreams to her doctor, all set pieces of music and lyrics.

BROADWAY
1940–3

There was a famous story about the opening night of *Lady in the Dark* in Boston which, I suppose, can be classified as the definition of a star. There was a song to be sung by Gertrude Lawrence called 'The Saga of Jenny'. She did not like it and so refused to rehearse it. Kurt and Ira promised her a new song after the out-of-town opening. The number preceding 'The Saga of Jenny' was a bit of Ira Gershwin virtuosity, which was a song that consisted of nothing but a list of Russian composers and writers sung at breakneck speed. It was performed by Danny Kaye to a show-stopping ovation. That was too much for Miss Lawrence. She arose, took over the stage, and using every trick and invention from the vast repertoire of her experience, she bumped and grinded and everything-elsed her way through 'The Saga of Jenny' – to an even greater

Ray Bolger and Nanette Fabray starring in *By Jupiter*

ovation than Mr Kaye's. Needless to say 'The Saga of Jenny' remained in the show. As so frequently happens with all works of enterprise, the critics quibbled but not the audience, and the show became a triumphant hit.

In 1942, the two most prominent efforts were a successful musical by Rodgers and Hart, *By Jupiter*, starring the old Scarecrow, Ray Bolger, which, in fact, was one of their longest running shows, and Irving Berlin's stunning army show, *This Is the Army*, with an all-military cast except one: the great man himself.

LONDON The theatre in London during the thirties and early forties changed remarkably little. There were the medley of revues, the occasional American import; and operetta, to which the theatre-goers of the West End remained dedicatedly loyal. There were at least six instances when operettas that enjoyed enormous success in London came to America with disappointing results. Ivor Novello, who had been writing songs since before the First World War – 'Keep the Home Fires Burning' being his most famous – starting in 1934 wrote a series of operettas, most of which took place in imaginary kingdoms, to which the British public flocked. Novello wrote the book, music and starred in his own shows, and among his operettas were *Glamorous Nights*, which contained songs with such titles as 'Fold Your Wings of Love around Me' and 'Shine through My Dreams'; *Careless Rapture*; *Crest of the Wave*; *The Dancing Years* – his greatest success; *Arc de Triomphe*; and *Perchance to Dream*.

Noel Coward's operettas were the aforementioned *Bitter Sweet* and *Conversation Piece*. In 1932 he also wrote another tremendously successful revue, *Words and Music*, in which 'Mad Dogs and Englishmen' first appeared. The score also included 'The Party's Over' and one of my favourite Coward songs,

'Mad About the Boy'. Four lines of the lyric are the essence of Cowardiana:

> Will it ever cloy?
> This odd diversity of misery and joy –
> I'm feeling quite insane and young again
> And all because I'm mad about the boy.

There was a show in 1936 by Eric Maschwitz called *Balalaika*, with a charming score by George Posford, which ran for 570 performances, and in 1937 came Noel Gay's *Me and My Girl* which featured 'The Lambeth Walk'. *Me and My Girl* was revived in the West End with even greater success in 1985.

If London did not enjoy the creative boom that did New York between the wars, it certainly had a heaven full of stars. Jack Buchanan, Mary Ellis, Bobby Howes, Evelyn Laye, Jessie Matthews, Gertrude Lawrence, Leslie Henson, Jack Hulbert, Cicely Courtneidge and Anna Neagle come readily to mind. But with the exception of Coward, it would be many years before London would find a musical voice of its own that would cross the dateline.

This is the Army. Irving Berlin is sixth from the right in the line-up

20 Oklahoma!

The story of *Oklahoma!*, written by Richard Rodgers and Oscar Hammerstein II, must necessarily begin with the heartbreaking end of Rodgers and Hart.

In the theatre, failure can bring grief to the happy but success cannot bring happiness to the unhappy. At its best it is a palliative. For the lonely, deprived of the consuming ambition to achieve it, success can shine down with a merciless glare and illuminate the emptiness. So it was that the more successful Larry Hart became during those last five years of the thirties, the more unbearable did his life become. To escape he turned to alcoholic insensibility, and despite the brilliance of his work – when he could be found, which was not always simple – the strain on his collaboration grew more and more taut. On more than one occasion Dick Rodgers persuaded him to check in to the Doctors' Hospital in New York to dry out. When they were writing the score of *Too Many Girls*, Dick moved a piano into an adjacent room at the hospital and that was how the score was finally written. But after *By Jupiter*, Dick,

Margaret Auld Nelson dancing as Aggie 'Pigtails'

whose constitution absolutely demanded that he compose (he once told me that if he went too long without writing he actually felt constipated), slowly and painfully began to consider the possibility that the day might come when he would be forced to work with someone else.

The day came in 1942. The Theatre Guild suggested to Dick a play they had produced a dozen years before called *Green Grow the Lilacs*. It was a lyrical play set at the turn of the century in the Southwest that fundamentally concerned itself with the struggle between farmers and ranchers, with, of course, an appropriate love story. It was unlike anything Rodgers had done before and he was eager to work on it. He approached Larry, but Larry was determined to take a vacation. Dick said that if he did, it would leave him with no alternative but to turn to someone else. Larry understood. In fact he said that he could not see how Dick had put up with him all these years. But he also said, without rancour, that he did not think *Green Grow the Lilacs* would make a very good musical. They were in Max Dreyfus's office at the time. Larry said goodbye and closed the door. And the partnership of Rodgers and Hart, after twenty-three years of endowing the theatre and the world with some of the best music and lyrics ever known, was over.

Dick turned to Oscar Hammerstein, whom he had known since the Akron Club. They began work on *Green Grow the Lilacs*, and when the curtain rose, the musical theatre would never be the same again.

Through the 20/20 vision of hindsight, one can look back over the fourteen years between the Depression and *Oklahoma!* and perceive the influences and social changes that created it. The lyrical satire and, in the case of George Gershwin, the musical as well, that invaded the theatre starting with *Strike Up the Band* and *Of Thee I Sing*, had the automatic effect of adding weight. This was also true of book shows and, to a lesser degree, revues. Satire was a maturing force. The effect of the several serious attempts to raise the level of the libretto, while not always successful until *Pal Joey* and *Lady in the Dark*, proved that it was possible for a musical to be something more than an evening of light-hearted entertainment, and the introduction of ballet offered promise of unlimited horizons for the use of movement as an integral part of the play.

All that was needed was the atmosphere in which the proper lyrical and romantic subject matter required to bring all these elements together could bloom. The atmosphere was provided by the war. Political and social satire, which by their very nature are critical, no longer suited the mood of a country that was rallying together to preserve a way of life that suddenly was seen clearly and deeply as precious as existence itself. If anything, people wanted to be reminded of who they were and the roots from which they had sprung; not what was wrong but what was right. Looking back to earlier times may be an escape, but it can also be a reaffirmation.

In theatrical terms, writing of the past is intrinsically lyrical. And so consciously or unconsciously, Rodgers and Hammerstein fell into step with

LEFT: Henry Clarke as 'Jud Fry' and Howard Keel as 'Curly' and ABOVE: 'Jud Fry' and 'Curly' (centre) with (right) Mary as 'Aunt Eller' and Betty Jane Watson as 'Laurey'

their time and found exactly the right subject in which all the theatrical arts could merge into what became known as lyric theatre.

Searching for a choreographer, Theresa Helburn, one of the directors of the Theatre Guild, had seen a ballet in the repertoire of the Ballet Russe de Monte Carlo called *Rodeo*. The choreographer was that often replaced lady Agnes de Mille. Theresa Helburn recommended that Dick and Oscar see the ballet, which they did. They loved it. They thought Agnes was ideal. They approached her. She accepted. The Guild, remembering Rouben Mamoulian's contribution to *Porgy and Bess*, suggested him as director and there was no hesitancy. Alfred Drake, the young leading man who had sung so beautifully in *Babes in Arms*, was selected to play Curly, and Joan Roberts, who had sung the lead in Oscar's 1941 ill-fated operetta *Sunny River*, was chosen for Laurey.

Raising the money was not simple. The show was to cost $75,000. MGM, who owned the rights to *Green Grow the Lilacs*, were asked to invest and turned it down. (MGM, I might add, also turned down Fritz and me when we asked them to finance *My Fair Lady*. I would estimate offhand that those two astute decisions deprived MGM of well over $100,000,000.) But Max Gordon, the redoubtable producer of many of the Kaufman–Hart shows, made a considerable investment and lived happily ever after.

Away We Go!, as it was initially called, opened in New Haven on 11

March 1943. The reception was rapturous. A week later when it opened in Boston the result was the same. It was in Boston that Dick and Oscar added the song 'Oklahoma' in the second act and it became the title of the show. For some reason which nobody can remember, the song did not have an exclamation point but the title did. It opened in New York at the St James Theatre on 31 March, where it remained for the next five years and nine weeks. The critical reaction was delirious and Howard Barnes of the *Herald Tribune* put his finger on it when he wrote: 'Songs, dances and story have been triumphantly blended. The Rodgers' score is one of his best, which is saying plenty. Hammerstein has written a dramatically original libretto and a string of catchy lyrics; Agnes de Mille has worked small miracles . . . a striking piece of theatrical Americana.'

Oklahoma! was the most totally realized amalgamation of all the theatrical arts. The book was legitimate play writing, every song flowed from the dramatic action, and Agnes de Mille's ballet at the end of Act One, in which Curly and Laurey were skilfully replaced by two dancers as the plot continued, was one of the most imaginative uses of choreography yet set in the theatre. Whereas Hammerstein was never the wit that Larry Hart was, he was far superior as a dramatic lyricist, and certainly no one ever wrote a lyric that sang better. Lyrically, *Oklahoma!* was a masterful work, lighter than Hammerstein had been before and with none of the 'poetic' excesses that to me frequently marred some of his future writing. Dick's music adjusted itself to the new collaboration, and together they produced a new voice and a style that was distinctly their own.

One of the reasons for the change in the style of each may well have been the change in manner of creation. There are fundamentally three ways a song can be written. A composer composes the music to which the lyric writer lyricizes, or it may be the reverse. The lyrics are written and the composer sets them. Or it is something in between. I, for example, prefer giving the composer the title and he composes to that title, and then I add the lyric. When Dick and Larry were collaborating, Dick invariably wrote the music first and then Larry added the lyrics. When Dick and Oscar, however, were writing *Oklahoma!*, Oscar began more and more to write the lyrics first, and as time went on it almost became the rule.

America's most coveted award for journalism, fiction, history, poetry, music, political cartoon and drama is the Pulitzer Prize. As I mentioned earlier, it had only been given to one musical before, *Of Thee I Sing*. The requirements for candidacy in the field of drama are that the play be on an American theme and not be an adaptation of a former play. Nevertheless, the committee recognized the unique achievement of *Oklahoma!*, and for the first and only time gave a special award.

With *Oklahoma!* the musical theatre began its *belle époque* which lasted for a quarter of a century.

21 From Lyricism to Reality: the Forties

Dick Rodgers and Oscar Hammerstein were obviously determined to continue their collaboration, but the plight of Larry weighed heavily on Dick's mind. He met with Herbert Fields and they decided to try and do a revival of *A Connecticut Yankee* with additional new lyrics, if Larry was able. Larry leapt at the opportunity and over the summer collaborated with Dick on six new numbers including a charmer, 'You Always Love the Same Girl', and another, 'To Keep My Love Alive', which was as witty and original as anything he had ever written. This was the first refrain:

BROADWAY
1943–4

I married many men,
A ton of them,
And yet I was untrue to none of them
Because I bumped off ev'ry one of them
To keep my love alive.
Sir Paul was frail;
He looked a wreck to me.
At night he was a horse's neck to me.
So I performed an appendectomy
To keep my love alive.
Sir Thomas had insomnia;
He couldn't sleep at night.
I bought a little arsenic.
He's sleeping now all right.
Sir Philip played the harp;
I cussed the thing.
I crowned him with his harp
To bust the thing.
And now he plays where harps are
Just the thing,
To keep my love alive,
To keep my love alive.

While they were working together, Larry was always punctual and always sober. Fritz and I saw a good deal of him in those days and if sobriety was the rule of the day, it was not of the night. But somehow he always pulled himself together before he met Dick.

The show opened in November, seven months after *Oklahoma!* The reviews ranged from fair to wonderful, but one of the critics wrote: 'Mr Rodgers' new music offers no top-flight tunes but one light number, "To Keep My Love Alive", gives Lorenz Hart a chance to go to town with his wittiest and funniest lyric in years.' But the strain of that opening night was the beginning of the end of Larry Hart. He had started drinking when the show was out of town in Philadelphia, and on the opening night he had to be removed from the theatre.

The following evening, a cousin of Larry's rang Fritz and me to ask us to help find him. I took the bars on Sixth Avenue and Fritz covered Eighth Avenue. Fritz found him, literally sitting on a kerb in the pouring rain in a state of drunken paralysis. Fritz put him in a cab and took him to the hotel where he was staying. He made Larry promise he would go right to bed. The following day he was taken to the Doctors' Hospital suffering from pneumonia. Because of the war, there were regular blackouts in New York City. At 9 p.m. on 22 November 1943, a siren sounded and there was a brief blackout. By the time the lights went on, Larry was dead. He was forty-eight years old.

I believe in reincarnation, and I pray the next time he returns he is six feet tall and that he will be repaid in kind for the joy he gave and never shared.

Carmen Jones

Over the summer, while Dick Rodgers was engaged with *A Connecticut Yankee*, Oscar Hammerstein busied himself with a project that had long been on his mind, a modernized black version of Bizet's *Carmen*. Robert Russell Bennett, Broadway's premier orchestrator, 'rhythmized' the score, Carmen worked in a parachute factory, and the entire play took place in a Southern town. It was called *Carmen Jones*, and Hassard Short, famous for his lavish and tasteful productions of revues, staged each scene with a uniform palate: one scene was all blue, one all red, etc. Spoken passages that were in the original production of *Carmen* and that were later eliminated after Bizet's death were also left on the floor by Hammerstein, and he received unanimous and justifiable kudos for his splendid adaptation. *Carmen Jones*, presented by the waist-high producer, proceeded to run over five hundred performances.

That same year, Kurt Weill composed the closest score he had written to date to pure musical comedy. America's famous writer of light verse and the most inventive rhymer the country ever produced, Ogden Nash, did the lyrics. Called *One Touch of Venus*, it was based on *The Tinted Venus* by that impish, English fantasist of the early 1900s, F. Anstey. In a song called 'How Much I Love You' there was a lovely line:

As a dachshund abhors
Revolving doors,
That's how much I love you.

And in a delicious trio, 'The Trouble with Women', the last line was 'The trouble with women is men'. There was also a haunting pseudo-beguine called 'Speak Low', which is still heard today. What is most significant, however, is that *One Touch of Venus* was Agnes de Mille's first assignment after *Oklahoma!*, and in two brilliant ballets she left no doubt that she was indeed Broadway's most creative choreographer.

Cheryl Crawford of the old Group Theatre, who had just done an enormously successful revival of *Porgy and Bess*, was the producer. They had great difficulty finding a leading lady to play Venus, who comes to life. The famous ballerina Zorina turned it down. It was then offered to Marlene Dietrich, and the story goes, perhaps apocryphal, that when some of the angels went to her hotel suite, she greeted them with all, and I mean all, of her luscious skin on display. But in the end she refused the role. Finally they turned to Mary Martin, who had gone to Hollywood after 'My Heart Belongs to Daddy', where her vast talents were left fallow. She was originally feared by the creative staff to be too 'Amurrican' for the part, but with the aid of some magnificent costumes by the great American couturier, Main Boucher, or Mainbocher as he later called himself, and with her own extraordinary charm and ability, she became Venus personified and a full-fledged star on Broadway.

In November of 1943, a musical called *What's Up?* made a brief visit to town with music by Frederick Loewe, choreography by George Balanchine,

Hirschfeld cartoon of *One Touch of Venus*

and co-authored and with lyrics by your embarrassed scribe. Fritz and I had begun working together the year before in Detroit, Michigan, where we had been hired to add some music and lyrics to a successful play of the twenties, *The Patsy*. I had been writing radio programmes, sometimes as many as nine a week, and working on plays in the later hours when we met at the Lambs Club, an actors' and writers' club in New York. Fritz had been offered the Detroit assignment and having been told that I wrote lyrics at Harvard, invited me to join him. *What's Up?* was not even promising.

In 1944 there were two unsuccessful musicals by Howard Dietz and Vernon Duke, *Jackpot*, and a musical version of Somerset Maugham's famous

Bloomer Girl

novella *Rain*; a highly successful operetta, *Song of Norway*, based on the music of Edvard Grieg for which George Balanchine contributed some appropriate classical ballet; a hit musical comedy of the old school, *Follow the Girls*; and Cole's two shows, *Mexican Hayride* and *Seven Lively Arts*.

Seven Lively Arts, which attempted to touch base with all of the performing arts, starred Beatrice Lillie, Bert Lahr, Benny Goodman, Anton Dolin and Alicia Markova. For the latter two, producer Rose had commissioned Stravinsky to compose a fifteen-minute ballet. After the opening in Philadelphia, Rose, with characteristic sensitivity, sent Stravinsky a telegram which read:

YOUR MUSIC GREAT SUCCESS STOP COULD BE SENSATIONAL SUCCESS IF YOU WOULD AUTHORIZE ROBERT RUSSELL BENNETT RETOUCH ORCHESTRATION STOP BENNETT ORCHESTRATES EVEN THE WORKS OF COLE PORTER STOP

Stravinsky wired back:

SATISFIED WITH GREAT SUCCESS

But of major importance to the developing musical theatre was *Bloomer Girl*, a story of the Civil War with a score by Harold Arlen and Yip Harburg and another stunning ballet by Agnes de Mille. A great success, it was influenced by *Oklahoma!*, which was all to its credit, but it was not as fully realized a work. Harold Arlen, certainly one of the great songwriters of our time, never quite mastered the dramatic form.

At the beginning of 1944 the ballet world was jolted into jubilation by the new work of a new choreographer, Jerome Robbins. Called *Fancy Free*, the music was composed by 25-year-old Leonard Bernstein, who had dramatically come to the public's attention the previous year by substituting for the famous conductor, Bruno Walter, at a concert of the New York Philharmonic. In December 1944, with book and lyrics provided by Betty Comden and Adolph Green, also fresh names to the trade, *Fancy Free* became *On the Town*, a full-scale musical and a full-scale hit. The choreography lost none of its originality and verve. The score, although not studded with hits, was dynamic and melodic, and the lyrics of Comden and Green showed neither the influence of Hammerstein nor the tightly-rhymed and witty style of the thirties. Comden and Green had been cabaret performers and appeared in the show themselves. As a total work, *On the Town* cut a path of its own which was appreciated by press and public alike. At the end of the forties it repeated its success as a film starring Gene Kelly and Frank Sinatra.

In the same year there was another version of Offenbach's *La Belle Hélène*, this time called *Helen Goes to Troy*. The music, as always, received the notices it was due, but the time was not right and the run was not long. There was an unfortunate and lavish musical called *Allah Be Praised*, produced by Alfred Bloomingdale of the famous department store family. When the show was out

of town, a 'play doctor' was called in, hopefully to aid the ailing patient. His advice to Mr Bloomingdale was: 'Close the play and keep the store open nights.'

Broadway has a calendar of its own which does not begin on 1 January and end on 31 December. The Broadway season begins in September and ends in June. The reason was that plays usually did not open during the summer and many would close then to reopen again in the autumn. Despite the fact that during the war years there was such a continual influx into the city that the hot summer months made little dent in theatrical attendance, and plays no longer took the summers off, the Broadway season continued to be known as beginning in September and ending in June. On Broadway the Antoinette Perry (better known as the Tony) and the Drama Critics' Awards are given at the end of the season in late spring, unlike in Britain, where theatrical awards are presented in December.

In the 1944–5 season, there was a musically and lyrically ambitious show by Kurt Weill and Ira Gershwin, *The Firebrand of Florence*, in which Kurt Weill's famous wife Lotte Lenya made her debut on the American stage. It was she who sang the lead in the original *Threepenny Opera* in Berlin. Unfortunately, it was a work that did not work and must be recorded as a failure. Sigmund Romberg's musical, *Up in Central Park*, with lyrics by Dorothy Fields, opened mid-season and, as mentioned earlier, it was the great man's last hit.

But it was on 19 April 1945 that one of the major musicals of the *belle époque* opened at the Majestic Theatre on Broadway. It was Rodgers and Hammerstein's first effort since *Oklahoma!* and the Theatre Guild not only assembled the same creative group, which included Rouben Mamoulian and Agnes de Mille, but again suggested the subject matter. In 1921 they had produced one of Ferenc Molnar's most touching plays, *Liliom*, a fantasy of imaginative invention. Dick and Oscar moved the setting from Budapest to New England, pre-dated it to 1873 and changed the title to *Carousel*. In the score were such glowing songs as 'If I Loved You', 'You'll Never Walk Alone', 'June Is Bustin' Out All Over', and the famous 'Soliloquy' at the end of Act One. The score as a whole reached higher and deeper than that of *Oklahoma!* without any loss of popularity, and, if it were possible, Agnes de Mille's choreography surpassed anything she had done. In the future when Dick Rodgers was ever asked which was his favourite musical, his reply was always *Carousel*.

The reviews were unanimous, the *Herald Tribune* pointing out that 'Music and real drama can be combined outside the opera with very good entertainment results'. John Chapman of the *Daily News* summed it up by saying: '. . . one of the finest musical plays I have ever seen and I shall remember it always. It was everything the professional theatre can give it and something else

besides; heart, integrity and an inner glow. The score and lyrics are by Rodgers and Hammerstein and the musical theatre does not have two finer creative artists.'

In style, both *Oklahoma!* and *Carousel* could musically be classified as modern operetta. But the legitimacy of the books, the dramatic use of lyrics and the wedding of choreographic movement to the story produced a new form of musical theatre, which very properly was called musical play. The total emotional impact of *Carousel* could not have better suited the times and for all time. There is no doubt that Rodgers and Hammerstein deserved the acclaim they received. Part of that acclaim was the Award for Best Musical of 1944–5, given by the newly-formed New York Drama Critics' Circle.

After two black musicals that failed, despite one of them starring that greatest of tap dancers, Bill 'Bojangles' Robinson, George Kaufman brought the season to an end by trying his hand at lyrics in a version of *HMS Pinafore* called *Hollywood Pinafore*. It was a wild and witty satire on the Hollywood scene, and Kaufman showed that besides being an expert writer of drama, comedy, musicals and direction, he also had a hitherto unrevealed ability as a lyricist. Significantly, it also brought the celebrated English choreographer, Anthony Tudor, to the theatre for the first time. But this was indeed the period when 'satires closed on Saturday', and *Hollywood Pinafore* suffocated in the summer heat.

BROADWAY 1945–6

The season of 1945–6 had two hits of major proportion, three efforts to tread the path of the musical play, a follow-up to *On the Town* by Comden, Green and Jerome Robbins, and the usual group of misfortunes.

The Comden, Green, Robbins' effort, *Billion Dollar Baby*, was the first satire on the twenties. The music was by another conductor/composer, Morton Gould, the choreography was brilliant, and the book and lyrics filled with

Richard Rodgers and Oscar Hammerstein II in a mid-1950s pose

ABOVE: The cast of *Carousel*, 1945 and BELOW: Ethel Merman in *Annie Get Your Gun*

bright ideas. What was missing was the built-in emotion of *On the Town*, and the omission was costly.

The three efforts began with *Lute Song*, based on an ancient Chinese fable and with ravishing sets by one of America's most illustrious designers, Robert Edmond Jones. It was Mary Martin's first musical since *One Touch of Venus* and although the play failed, her performance enhanced her reputation.

The second was *St Louis Woman*, another slice of period Americana. It was directed by the firm hand of Rouben Mamoulian and the music and lyrics were by Harold Arlen and Johnny Mercer. Brilliant as Arlen and Mercer were, neither of them was at home in the dramatic musical. Their songs were better than the score. Among them was the Arlen-Mercer classic, 'Come Rain or Come Shine'. The songs were so good, in fact, that they almost overcame the faults of the book, but despite some marvellous moments *St Louis Woman* failed to live up to its potential.

To describe the third effort I will, for obvious reasons, quote from Gerald Bordman's comprehensive tome, *American Musical Theatre*. He wrote: '*The Day Before Spring* was an innovative melodic musical that didn't quite work and didn't quite make it. It reunited Alan Jay Lerner and Frederick Loewe and furthered what soon became one of the most fruitful of partnerships . . . the happiest aspect of *The Day Before Spring* was its wide-ranging, infectious collection of songs: the sober considerations of the title song and 'You Haven't Changed at All", the bubbling gaiety of "I Love You This Morning", and the simple joys of "A Loaf of Bread, a Jug of Wine and Thou, Baby".' The trouble, as usual, was the book. Period.

But unlike *What's Up?*, I am not prickling with embarrassment as I write its name. I was determined to write musicals with original stories, that is to say not based on other plays, novels or short stories, and in doing so doubled the pitfalls. Anthony Tudor did the choreography which included a delightful ballet about the pursuit of romance. While the production was in the talking stage, Fritz asked Tudor if he would like to do the ballet first to improvised music, following which Fritz would compose it, or if he would prefer to have the music written first. Tudor preferred the latter. Fritz then asked him what he wanted. Tudor thought for a moment and then said: 'Paris. At five in the morning.' To my astonishment, Fritz was not at all bewildered and said: 'Fine. How long?' To which Tudor replied: 'About twelve minutes.' Fritz proceeded to lock himself up for a week and he then called Tudor to come and hear what he had written. Tudor lay on the floor – why, I do not know – and Fritz played him the ballet. When he had finished there was a long, long silence. Finally, Tudor looked up at Fritz and said: 'It sounds more like six in the morning.' Fritz pondered a while and then said: 'Yes, I see what you mean. Come back next week.' (I thought they had both gone mad.) Tudor returned a few days later and listened again. 'Just right,' said he. And that was that. I never knew why it was six in the morning and I never knew why it was five in the morning. But they did and that was all that mattered. *The Day Before Spring* was what George Kaufman used to call a 'success d'estime', which means a success that runs out of steam. (Lawrence Durrell used to call novels that failed 'suck eggs d'estime'.) But it ran the season, MGM bought the film rights, and Fritz and I became solvent professionals.

One of the two great hits of the season was *Call Me Mister*, a revue by Harold Rome about the problems of soldiers returning to civilian life. It was a wonderfully funny collection of lyrics, including an absolute wow sung by an exhausted canteen hostess called 'South America, Take It Away!'

The other, produced by Rodgers and Hammerstein, was the show Jerome Kern had come East to write, *Annie Get Your Gun*. It starred 'La Merman', and in contrast to the strides they had made as creative authors, *Annie Get Your Gun* was an out and out musical comedy. But the score by Irving Berlin was so magical, the book by Herbert and Dorothy Fields so expert, and the

entire production assembled with such perfection, that it was a work of popular art unto itself.

There are two songs that can be classified as the anthems of show business. One was in *Annie Get Your Gun*, 'There's No Business Like Show Business'. (The other, written many years later by Howard Dietz and Arthur Schwartz, is 'That's Entertainment'.)

Among the handful of operettas that went down the drain was *Polonaise*, based on the music of Chopin and with a plot that revolved around Kosciuszko, a renowned Polish soldier who went to America during the Revolution and fought bravely on the side of freedom. Of course, with those breeches it was a failure, but it starred the famous light opera team of Jan Kiepura and his wife Marta Eggerth. Kiepura, although possessed of a splendid tenor voice, was famous for being the quintessence of ham. When he read one of the reviews, he looked at his wife and said: 'How can they say I stink when I'm better than ever?'

There was also that season an old-fashioned musical comedy called *Are You With It?* that laid the groundwork for *Oh, Calcutta!* and consequently attracted the tired businessman long enough to be classified as a hit; and a brave attempt at a Haitian musical starring the gifted and beautiful choreographer and dancer, Katherine Dunham.

Before flipping the theatrical diary to the next season, I am impelled to give a few words to a musical that had a weak score by Cole Porter, was as far off the beaten track of the lyric theatre as it is possible to be, in fact bore no relation to any hitherto known form of musical, was wholeheartedly scoffed at by the critics and lasted but a few weeks. But was, with all that, an uproarious, mad piece of theatre. Directed by and starring Orson Welles, it was a musical version of Jules Verne's *Around the World in Eighty Days*. It had more scenery than Switzerland, was the first attempt at multi-media, meaning the interpolated use of film during the action, and for a handful, including me, it was a treat. Years later, when the flamboyant showman Mike Todd produced his hugely successful film on the same subject, most of the ideas originated on the stage of the Adelphi Theatre in Orson Welles' outrageous extravaganza.

The first half of the 1946–7 season was hardly distinguished. The first two entries were two old, old-fashioned operettas, *Yours Is My Heart*, an American version of Franz Lehár's last effort, and another of the mystifying gypsies, *Gypsy Lady*, which was a medley of Victor Herbert favourites encapsulated into an unfortunate book. The music of both was, of course, lovely, but in those times and with those books the moving vans were soon waiting by the stage door.

A sad failure of the late autumn was *Park Avenue*, which seemed impervious to the new direction of the musical theatre. It was sad not because it was without merit – how could it have been with a book by George Kaufman and

BROADWAY
1946–7

the celebrated screenwriter Nunnally Johnson, and music by Arthur Schwartz? – but because it was Ira Gershwin's last Broadway musical.

The great Ira was still in evidence, the wonderfully witty lyric, for instance, 'Don't Be a Woman if You Can', but despite the lyrical brilliance of *Lady in the Dark* and some of his contributions to revues, part of Ira's love and enthusiasm for the theatre had been buried for ever with his brother George. He returned to his house in Beverly Hills, and apart from his frequent afternoons at the races he seldom left his favourite chair or the pool table downstairs. From time to time he would write the lyrics for a film, and it was obvious his talent remained unimpaired. For the remake of *A Star Is Born* starring Judy Garland, he and Harold Arlen wrote a superb score which included one song that was Ira at his peak, 'The Man that Got Away'. I happened to be at Ira's house the day he finished it, and that evening he and Harold played it for a few of us. Harold, incidentally, is one of the most maddening demonstrators I have ever known. He plays beautifully and sings probably better than any other composer. But when he performs his own songs, he does what we songwriters complain about in singers: he does not sing the melody. Although Ira was pleased by our reaction to 'The Man that Got Away', I believe he was at his happiest in 1950 during the preparation of *An American in Paris*, because he was once again working with George's music.

One night at the pool table, Arthur Freed, Hollywood's greatest musical producer and one of Ira's closest friends, suggested a film in which the climax would be a ballet danced by Gene Kelly to George's famous orchestral suite. The rest of the score would be culled from the Gershwin catalogue. Ira's response was spontaneously enthusiastic. Arthur asked me to write the story and screenplay and Ira threw himself into the enterprise with long-lost joy. Under Vincente Minnelli's unerring direction, *An American in Paris* reached the mountain top of everyone's hopes, even winning the Academy Award for the best film of the year. To my astonishment, I received an Oscar for the best original screenplay, but I am certain there was no one connected with *An American in Paris* who enjoyed the deep, deep satisfaction of that dear, shy, and lovable man.

In mid-season, what on paper should have been a fascinating musical came to town. Called *Beggar's Holiday*, it was a modern retelling of *The Beggar's Opera* with a score by the incomparable Duke Ellington and lyrics by John LaTouche. The danger of the ambitious musical is that it must almost be perfect to succeed. One cannot interpolate a life-saving, splashy production number or an irrelevant comedy scene now, as one could in the earlier days of featherweight books. *Beggar's Holiday*, despite brilliant moments, was far from perfect and suffered accordingly.

The second half of the season was an improvement of major proportions. Kurt Weill, who had long nurtured a desire to attempt a 'Broadway opera',

finally realized his ambition with a musical adaptation of *Street Scene*, a famous play of the late twenties by one of America's major playwrights, Elmer Rice. It was the story of ill-fated love and infidelity on a shabby street in Manhattan. Although there was the occasional song, Weill, unlike Gershwin, reached his dramatic heights with operatic aria – one of which, 'Somehow I Never Could Believe', was a melody of soaring dramatic beauty. There was recitative as well as dialogue, but the overall style was indisputably operatic. Langston Hughes' lyrics were pure, unadorned and as powerful as the play itself. But the subject matter may have been too uncompromising for popular Broadway taste and *Street Scene*, despite the encouragement of the reviews, proved not to be the stuff that made for long runs. Moss Hart used to say that in the theatre one receives either more or less than one deserves. It is not an infallible generality, but certainly *Street Scene* received less.

Later in the season came another operatic evening which introduced Giancarlo Menotti to New York. Writing not only his own music but text as well, his first opera, *Amelia Goes to the Ball*, had been presented ten years earlier in Philadelphia when he was still a student. He made his debut on Broadway with two intimate one-act operas called *The Telephone* and *The Medium*. He also directed them. They were completely original in concept and not without humour. *The Telephone* was the type of comedic operatic sketch that might well have suited Offenbach's Bouffes-Parisiens. The critics and public alike were enchanted, and Giancarlo Menotti became Broadway's first commercially successful operatic composer.

The coincidence of two operas, Weill's and Menotti's, appearing between January and June 1947 was further compounded by two fantasies, one Gaelic and one Scottish, opening on Broadway within three months of each other. The first was *Finian's Rainbow*, a delightful Irish tale with distinctly social overtones, with a book by Yip Harburg and Fred Saidy, lyrics by Harburg, and an exuberant score by Burton Lane which had one foot in the thirties and one in the forties. The choreography was designed by Michael Kidd, a fresh name in the balletic world of the musical theatre. Influenced by Jerome Robbins, his contribution was vital and joyous, and the entire evening was as magical as the subject. Lyrically, Yip Harburg surpassed himself with such numbers as 'When I'm Not Near the Girl I Love, I Love the Girl I'm Near', 'The Begat' and the instantly popular 'How Are Things in Glocca Morra?'

Finian's Rainbow was a smash.

With *Finian's Rainbow*, Burton Lane finally came into his own and received the appreciation he deserved. The tragedy of Lane, however, was that this amazingly gifted composer was to write so little thereafter. Only two other shows in the next twenty years. Both with me.

In March, the Scottish fantasy *Brigadoon*, written by Fritz Loewe and me, opened in New York. The journey that culminated with that evening had been a long and bumpy one. We had auditioned it for literally almost every musical

producer in New York and it had been unanimously rejected. The Theatre Guild, deeply embedded in Americana with *Oklahoma!* and *Carousel*, said they were interested if we could make one alteration: change the locale from Scotland to America. Somehow we did not know how to do that. We finally played, sang and read it to Billy Rose who registered immediate enthusiasm and agreed to produce it. It was to be staged by Reginald Hammerstein, who had had a singularly less successful career than his brother Oscar, but it meant that Oscar would be silently involved and we all would have the benefit of his guidance. All well and good – so far. But the early meetings with Mr Rose were far from congenial, being studded with such expressions from him as: 'Never argue with a man who has more money than you have.' The contract that he wished us to sign negated Abraham Lincoln's Emancipation Proclamation that freed the slaves. Rose would have the right to call in other authors or composers should he so desire; Fritz, an expert vocal arranger, would not be allowed to do so; Mr Rose would have the final say on casting. Etcetera, etcetera, *ad nauseam*. When we questioned the terms, Mr Rose simply said: 'Sign it or else.' Fritz and I took a long walk and decided that even if it meant no production of *Brigadoon*, the answer would have to be 'or else'. When he was notified, Rose sent us a telegram stating that if the play were produced and any of the ideas he had suggested appeared on the stage, he would take legal action. I wrote him a very polite letter asking him please to send me a list of his ideas and we would certainly avoid infringing on his creative genius. I received no reply.

So all the producers had now heard *Brigadoon* but one, Cheryl Crawford, who was on the road. Our lawyer was her lawyer and when Cheryl returned to New York for a weekend, he arranged for Fritz and me to play it for her. And Cheryl Crawford became the producer of *Brigadoon*.

But our auditioning days were not over. The show was budgeted at $150,000 and Fritz and I gave fifty-eight performances, sometimes three a

David Wayne with the children of Rainbow Val in *Finian's Rainbow*

Brigadoon

day, to raise the money. The last audition was three days after the show was in rehearsal.

To our everlasting good fortune, Agnes de Mille agreed to provide the choreography, and one of Cheryl's former compatriots at The Group Theatre, Robert Lewis, who had directed William Saroyan's *My Heart's in the Highlands* before disappearing to Hollywood, returned to direct the book.

After a break-in half week at New Haven, as was the custom in those days, we opened in Boston to decidedly unfavourable reviews. One critic said that he had never liked James Barrie so why should he like an inferior copy. But Bobby Lewis and Agnes remained firm in their intentions, and during the entire run in Boston I only changed one page. The audience reaction was far more encouraging than the reviews and by the end of the second week, we were selling out. We moved on to Philadelphia for another two weeks and there the reviews were ecstatic. Agnes's work was as original and creative as anything she had done and Bobby directed the play with a rare sensitivity. Being one of the best acting coaches in America, he guided the cast into performances that were all any author could hope for.

And so, finally, on 13 March 1947, we opened. Where? The only theatre available in New York at the time: the Ziegfeld. The owner? Billy Rose. An illustration of George M. Cohan's famous comment about an actor: 'Throw that son of a bitch out of the theatre and I never want to see him again, unless I need him.'

The audience on opening night seemed to me more appreciative than enthusiastic, but perhaps I was too numb to distinguish the difference. I do remember, however, that during the second act there were several departures. It may have been less than half a dozen, but to me it seemed like a thundering

herd. There was an opening night party being given by one of the backers, but I was so fearful of the outcome that I decided not to go, and after a quick drink with one or two friends I returned to my lodgings at the Algonquin Hotel. About one o'clock in the morning I received an urgent call from Cheryl telling me, nay ordering me, to come to the party instantly. When I arrived I was handed the first editions of the morning newspapers. This is what I read:

Brooks Atkinson in the *New York Times*, first paragraph: 'To the growing list of major achievements on the musical stage add one – *Brigadoon*, put on at the Ziegfeld Theatre last evening. For once, the modest label "musical play" has a precise meaning. For it is impossible to say where the music and dancing leave off and the story begins in this beautifully orchestrated, Scottish idyll.' His last paragraph: 'This excursion into an imagined Scottish village is an orchestration of the theatre's myriad arts, like a singing storybook for an idealized country fair long ago.'

John Chapman in the *Daily News*: '*Brigadoon*, with book and lyrics by Alan Jay Lerner and a score by Frederick Loewe, is an enchanting musical about an enchanted village – a work of imagination and beauty.'

Howard Barnes in the *Herald Tribune*: 'A musical fantasy of rare delight and distinction has opened at the Ziegfeld Theatre. *Brigadoon* is a jubilant and brilliantly integrated show.' His last paragraph: 'A scintillating song and dance fantasy that has given theatregoers reason to toss tam-o-shanters in the air.'

The *Daily Mirror*, second paragraph: 'It took courage to produce *Brigadoon*, an unconventional show of marked originality.'

Later in the day when the evening papers appeared, the *Journal American* said: 'Believe me, *Brigadoon* has everything, including my theatre-going love and admiration.'

The headline in the prestigious *Sun* read: '*Brigadoon*, An Enormous Hit at the Ziegfeld, Best Musical Play of the Season.'

And finally, the *New York World Telegram*: '*Brigadoon* is absolute enchantment. The new musical is tender and exciting, fantastic and real, stirring and soothing.'

In recounting this biography of *Brigadoon*, if I seem to have given it inordinate space, it is not merely because it was mine, but because it is an illustration of what I am certain other authors, in their own but related ways, must experience.

Later in the spring, *Brigadoon* won the Drama Critics' Award for the Best Musical of the season, and in the ensuing years joined the ranks of the most frequently performed musicals around the world.

BROADWAY
1947–8

The star of the 1947–8 season was Jerome Robbins. In two shows, one the hit of the year, *High Button Shoes*, and in the other, *Look, Ma, I'm Dancin'*, less successful, his choreography gave the Broadway year its distinction.

Defying the usual practice of not opening during the summer, one show did, called *Louisiana Lady*, and it is only worth mentioning because one of the collaborators on the score was named Monte Carlo. The casino closed after four days. A few months later came an operetta, *Music in My Heart*, based on the music of Tschaikowsky and his romance with a French chanteuse, thus making it the first sexual fantasy of the century. After a brief visit by an English musical starring Cicely Courtneidge, *High Button Shoes* with a merry, melodious score by Jule Styne and lyrics by the talented and irrepressible Sammy Cahn (who can probably write a lyric even faster than Howard Dietz and Larry Hart) opened to a splendid reception. The show was good-natured and funny, but the outstanding moment was a Keystone Cop ballet by Jerome Robbins which left the audience breathless, not only by its pace but by its sheer comic brilliance. *Look, Ma, I'm Dancin'* followed several months later, and the highlight again was Robbins' choreography. Unfortunately, the rest of the show never approached the level of the dancing.

Rodgers and Hammerstein's third effort, *Allegro*, opened in the early part of the season to reviews that ranged from magnificent to disappointing. Departing from his previous custom of adapting former plays, Oscar bravely attempted an original, and Agnes de Mille not only choreographed, but directed. Brooks Atkinson ended his notice by saying: 'If this review sounds ungratefully reluctant it is because Rodgers and Hammerstein have just missed the final splendour of a perfect work of art.' The *Herald Tribune* called it: 'A musical play of rare distinction', but the *Daily News* said: 'Moments of levity may be found in *Allegro* ... but in the show itself, they [the authors] seem to disapprove of levity.' To the *New York Post*, it was: 'A distinguished musical play, beautiful, imaginative, original and honestly moving', but to the *Journal American*, it was: 'As pretentious as artificial jewellery and just about as valuable.' And so it went. Both the score and the choreography were handicapped by expectations and in the final accounting, *Allegro* must be labelled a near miss.

As musical stars kept moving to Hollywood and television variety shows began to multiply, the number of revues began to dwindle. There were only three that season but two of them did surprisingly well. Beatrice Lillie, still loyal to Broadway, starred in one, *Inside USA*, by those masters of the revue, Howard Dietz and Arthur Schwartz, and it ran for over a year. The second was a more modest effort, *Make Mine Manhattan*, which created a star in Sid Caesar and also lived long enough to circle the sun. The third, *Angel in the Wings*, even more modest not only in size but success, had the virtue of bringing Elaine Stritch downstage centre.

Near the end of the season there was also an evening of three one-act musicals called *Ballet Ballads*, with music by Jerome Moross and lyrics by John LaTouche, which, though appreciated by the critics, probably opened too late in the season to attract the kind of theatre-loving public it needed to

succeed. *Ballet Ballads*, to recall Moss Hart's observation, received less than it deserved.

The Broadway season of 1948–9 not only produced two of the greatest musicals of the era but, of equal importance, there began a definite shift away from the lyric aspiration of the five years that followed *Oklahoma!* Ballet began to be a diversion and no longer an essential part of the story-telling process, the accent on the book became stronger, and more laughter began to be heard in the theatrical land. The reason for the growing change was, as usual, more sociological and historical than theatrical. The war was over, taking with it the nostalgic appetite, lyricism shifted to reality, the present was no longer too grim to face, and humour locked arms with sentiment.

Frank Loesser, who had written a few numbers of little importance for a revue in the thirties and had then abandoned Broadway for Hollywood, where he functioned mainly as a lyricist, returned to Broadway with a charming and often hilarious musical version of the famous farce *Charley's Aunt*, now called *Where's Charley?* He not only supplied the lyrics but the music as well, and his debut as composer/lyricist was auspicious. George Balanchine did the choreography, but it was Ray Bolger's taps that danced *Where's Charley?* to success.

Sigmund Romberg said a last and unhappy farewell with *My Romance*; there was an out-and-out musical comedy, redolent of the thirties, *As the Girls Go*; a genuinely funny revue called *Lend an Ear* which introduced Carol Channing to Broadway and Gower Ghampion, formerly a dancer, as a choreographer; Benjamin Britten's opera, *The Rape of Lucretia*, which proved too operatic for Broadway; and a too ambitious musical by Kurt Weill and me called *Love Life*.

Love Life was an attempt to show the effects of the industrial age on marital relations and covered the period from 1800 to the present, the couple never ageing. The story was told in the style of a vaudeville show with sketches that carried the couple through the years, each followed by a vaudeville act that served as a comment. It began with a magician who sawed a lady (the leading lady) in half, raised the leading man three feet off the stage in the time-honoured elevation trick, and then disappeared, leaving the couple to figure out how they had arrived in this awkward position, where the woman was half home-maker and half breadwinner and part-time mother, and the man up in the air. For all its good intentions, *Love Life* was too uneven a work, but the score was well received with Kurt Weill supplying music that was both satiric and melodic and all written in the vaudeville genre. Unfortunately, *Love Life* opened in the middle of a recording strike and no cast album was ever made that preserved the true quality of Kurt's orchestrations, which were very much an integral part of his work. Michael Kidd provided an imaginative Punch and Judy ballet which took place in a divorce court. There were

vaudeville quartets, song and dance acts and even a trapeze artiste who swung out over the theatre, but despite Elia Kazan's expertise as a director, the variety of styles seemed more like breaches of style and *Love Life* barely ran out the season.

Then, on the night of 30 December 1948, at the New Century Theatre in New York, the curtain rose on Cole Porter's *Kiss Me Kate*.

Following the demise of *Around the World in Eighty Days*, Cole went West to his house in Hollywood, with its conservatory – walls, furniture and all – made entirely of glass. By request of Arthur Freed he wrote a score for *The Pirate*, starring Gene Kelly and Judy Garland. 'Be a Clown' was a smashing number, but the score as a whole was not up to Porter-par and *The Pirate* was one of the least successful of Arthur Freed's incredible medley of musical films. During this period, a young production assistant of great ability but still unfulfilled promise named Arnold Saint Subber was backstage one night when Alfred Lunt and Lynn Fontanne were performing *The Taming of the Shrew*. Overhearing them argle-bargling, it gave him the idea to do a musical version of *The Taming of the Shrew* as a play within a play. He was and is a beloved friend, and I remember long evenings spent listening to him thinking his idea out loud. He found a co-producer in Lemuel Ayers, who, with Oliver Smith, was one of the two reigning scenic designers on Broadway. They first went to Burton Lane, who, for reasons unknown to me, was either unable or unwilling to accept the assignment. Searching for book writers, they approached the well-known husband and wife team of many Broadway hits, Bella and Sam Spewack, who instantly saw the possibilities and having agreed to do it, began campaigning for Cole Porter. Because Cole had seemed out of the swim for so long (but times were changing) and his recent work less than inspiring, there was resistance from the producers, but Bella, a powerful contestant in any ring, in the end prevailed and Cole was invited to supply the music and lyrics. He, too, resisted, primarily feeling that it was courting disaster to try and supply lyrics to Shakespeare. But Bella was Bella and her persuasions finally wore him down.

The show was budgeted at $180,000, but with two untried producers at the helm and a composer who had not had a hit in years, the 'Saint', as he was called, and Lem Ayers went through the same agonizing and exhausting experience in securing backing as had *Brigadoon* and *Oklahoma!* The auditions were numberless before the $180,000 was eventually raised. Finally, with Alfred Drake and Patricia Morison from Hollywood playing the leads, choreography by Hanya Holm, a gentle and talented lady from the ballet, and directed by John C. Wilson, who had redirected many of Noel Coward's plays in New York as well as *Bloomer Girl*, *Kiss Me Kate* opened in Philadelphia. The reaction was such that within twenty-four hours the word was all over New York that a hit was on its way to town.

And on that glorious night of 30 December, the hit came in. The reviews

were dazzling, best summed up by Robert Garland in the *Journal American*, who wrote: 'If this isn't the best musical comedy I ever saw, I don't remember what the best musical comedy I ever saw was called.' For Cole, after all those years of suffering, failure and self-doubt, the reviews were like a rebirth. Someone connected with the play said later: 'I never saw anyone enjoy good notices as much as Mr Porter.' And if ever a man deserved them, he did. To paraphrase Robert Garland, if better lyrics ever appeared in a musical, I do not remember what that musical was called. 'Another Op'nin', Another Show', 'I've Come to Wive It Wealthily in Padua', 'Were Thine That Special Face', 'Where Is the Life that Late I Led?', 'So in Love', those and a dozen others were musical and lyrical wonders. The celebrated showbiz weekly, *Variety*, called it: 'The triumphant return of Cole Porter, the prodigal composer, to the ranks of the theatrical great.'

Kiss Me Kate was not only Cole Porter's masterpiece, but a masterpiece of musical theatre. In 1949 the Antoinette Perry Award was given for the first time to a musical. The winner was *Kiss Me Kate*.

The significance of *Kiss Me Kate* was that even though it was pure musical comedy it bore no relation to the musical comedy of the thirties. The advances that had been made in the legitimate construction of the book were maintained, albeit in this case the subject was comedic and not lyric.

It is hard to imagine that only four months later Broadway would behold another musical of equal stature. The show was *South Pacific* with a book by Oscar Hammerstein and Joshua Logan, lyrics by Hammerstein, music by Richard Rodgers, and based on two stories from James Michener's Pulitzer Prize-winning *Tales of the South Pacific*. Oscar had prepared the first draft, but director Joshua Logan's creative contribution to the final script was such that he and Oscar shared credit as co-authors. The word went out that *South Pacific* was a hit when it was still in rehearsal, and when it opened in New Haven the rumour was confirmed. It opened in New York to the biggest advance sale in history.

The two principal roles were brilliantly played and sung by Mary Martin and Ezio Pinza, one of the leading operatic bassos of our time. Pinza's part called for a man in his early fifties, and he not only became a matinee idol but gave all middle-aged men a new lease on life. The play dealt exhilaratingly and romantically with soldiers on an island in the South Pacific during the war, and the love story of a native French planter, a widower with Polynesian children, and an American nurse from Arkansas who was unable to accept the colour of his children. By its very subject matter, *South Pacific* was more a musical play than *Kiss Me Kate*. It was told realistically and without any formal choreography. Dick Rodgers' score was one of the most beautiful he had ever written, and Oscar's lyrics, with the exception of the occasional moment where he became philosophical and polemic, were superb. This time the reviews were unanimous, as well they should have been. Brooks Atkinson: 'A tenderly,

beautiful idyll of genuine people'; the *Herald Tribune*: 'Pearls, pure pearls'; *Variety*: 'It is one of the most enjoyable and satisfying musicals in theatre history.'

South Pacific not only became the second musical to win the Pulitzer Prize for Drama, but also won the Drama Critics' Award for the Best Musical. Because it opened too late in the season to be eligible for the Tony Awards that year, it was considered part of the 1949–50 season and proceeded to win in every category: best musical, best book, best music (an award for lyrics was not added until 1962), best direction and performances.

The first commerical success of 1949–50 did not open until mid-season. It was a musical version of Anita Loos's famous book of the twenties, *Gentlemen Prefer Blondes*, and with it, Carol Channing became a major musical star. It was musical comedy marvellously assembled, with an irresistible musical comedy score by Jule Styne and lyrics by Leo Robin, which were not only skilful but genuinely funny. The proceedings came to an uproarious halt when Miss Channing, with those huge eyes that seemed never to blink, sang 'Diamonds Are a Girl's Best Friend'.

Leo Robin had written lyrics back in the late twenties for Vincent Youman's *Hit the Deck*, but after two or three failures and with the enticement of the growing number of musical films, he went West where he and his

Kiss Me, Kate, 1949, with Lisa Kirk, Alfred Drake,
Harold Lang and Patricia Morrison

Ezio Pinza and Mary Martin, with children, in *South Pacific*

equally gifted collaborator, Ralph Rainger, became composer and lyricist in residence at Paramount Studios. They wrote countless hits, among them 'Thanks for the Memory'. He returned to the theatre with *Gentlemen Prefer Blondes*.

The season had started many months earlier in July with a much-heralded and seemingly guaranteed bonanza, which had a book by Pulitzer Prize-winner Robert Sherwood, a score by Irving Berlin and direction by Moss Hart. But as everyone in the theatre knows, there are no guarantees, and as illustrious as this trio was, their effort, *Miss Liberty*, was far from Sherwood and Berlin at their best. The reception was tepid and it barely made it through to the following spring.

There was an uneven revue called *Touch and Go* which originated at Catholic University in Washington and which is of considerable significance because of the authors it brought to New York. They were Jean Kerr, who later wrote several enormously skilful comedies, and her husband Walter Kerr, who was to inherit the mantle of Brooks Atkinson as America's most knowledgeable and respected critic. He later did indeed take over the post on the *New York Times*. In recent years, he has confined his activities to a Sunday column and has abandoned daily reviewing, much to the theatre's loss.

Three musicals of noble aspiration came to Broadway that season. One was *Regina*, an opera based on Lillian Hellman's famous play *The Little Foxes*. Marc Blitzstein composed the score to his own text. Faithful to its

subject, with an accomplished cast, it was an unremitting musical drama, appreciated by the music critics but apparently out of place in the Broadway milieu. Years later, it was revived by the New York City Opera where it seemed more at home.

The second was *Lost in the Stars*, adapted by Maxwell Anderson from Alan Paton's stunning novel of racial strife in South Africa, *Cry, the Beloved Country*. Its deeply moving score was by Kurt Weill and the title song is as touching and heartbreaking a blend of music and lyrics as I know. The reviews, with the occasional qualification, were appropriately enthusiastic and the morning after it opened it seemed as though *Lost in the Stars* had conquered the resistance to the serious musical. Bur as the year progressed it was not to be so. Opening in November, it closed at the beginning of the summer.

During the winter Kurt had a heart attack. It was not fatal, and after a spell in the hospital he returned home to recuperate. We lived near each other in the Hudson River Valley, and when I saw him in March he seemed in fine spirits and anxious to work. I was writing a film in California at the time, where I had rented a small house. At the end of March, for some reason I suddenly began to worry about him, and I wrote him a letter suggesting that he come and stay with me and stretch out for a bit in the California sun. My letter arrived the day he died. He was fifty years old and one of the warmest, kindest, most intelligent and enchanting men I have ever known. My affection for him was not unique. He was as beloved as much as he was respected, and he left a void in the life of the theatre as well as in the lives of those who were fortunate enough to have been his friend.

The acceptance of the dramatic musical that Kurt had struggled so to achieve was realized a month after he died by Giancarlo Menotti. Called *The Consul*, it was the tale of the heartless insanity inflicted on a woman attempting to get the proper papers for herself and her family to leave an unnamed Iron Curtain country. Defeated by dehumanized red tape, she is finally driven to suicide. Again directed by Menotti himself, it was a shattering story, expertly written, composed and performed, and *The Consul* won the Drama Critics' Award for the Best Musical of the season. Menotti also received the Pulitzer Prize for music.

Bob Fosse came to public attention in an unsuccessful little show, *Dance Me a Song*; there was an equally ill-fated attempt by composer Morton Gould and lyricist Dorothy Fields to adapt a success of former years, *The Pursuit of Happiness*; and still another ambitious musical based on a play by Goldoni, *Il Bugiardo* – 'The Liar' in English – co-authored by and starring Alfred Drake. It lasted but a few weeks.

In London, with the final All Clear about to be heard, Noel Coward, after LONDON

having spent the war entertaining the troops around the world and writing and starring in that most splendid and inspiring film, *In Which We Serve*, returned to the theatre with a happy revue aptly entitled *Sigh No More*. It starred, among others, one of the most talented and endearing artistes ever to grace the English stage, Joyce Grenfell, and the headline of Beverley Nichols' review summed up the general reaction: 'No Sighs In New Coward Show'.

I cannot move on without a brief quote from one of the most sharply satiric songs Coward or anyone else has ever written. It was called 'Don't Let's Be Beastly to the Germans' and part of it went:

> It was just those nasty Nazis who persuaded them to fight
> And their Beethoven and Bach are really far worse than
> their bite.
> Let's be meek to them
> And turn the other cheek to them
> And try to bring out their latent sense of fun.
> Let's give them full air parity
> And treat the rats with charity
> But don't let's be beastly to the Hun.

The song had no greater fan than Winston Churchill for whom, by request, Noel once had to play it repeatedly.

In that same year of 1945 Ivor Novello brought another excursion to Ruritania (in this case it was referred to as Murania) to the London Hippodrome, where it proceeded to rack up over one thousand performances. This great hit was *Perchance to Dream*.

In 1946 Coward reopened the Drury Lane Theatre with a semi-operetta, *Pacific 1860*, which starred Mary Martin. Noel always felt that *Pacific 1860* was his best score, but that the play was too intimate for the size of the Drury Lane. Perhaps it was and perhaps it accounted for the raft of negative reviews and its early demise.

In April the following year, the first of the new American musicals took possession of the Drury Lane, where it remained for almost four years. The Equity rules concerning the interchange of actors between Broadway and the West End were far less rigid then than they are today, and the star of *Oklahoma!* at the Drury Lane was an American, then unknown in his own country, Howard Keel. *Oklahoma!* was received as rapturously and appreciatively as it had been in America. Two months later, Rodgers and Hammerstein brought their production of *Annie Get Your Gun* to the Coliseum, again starring two American actors, Dolores Gray and Bill Johnson. It, too, repeated its Broadway success.

That same year, Britain contributed a smash hit of its own, *Bless the Bride* by Vivian Ellis and A. P. Herbert. It not only became one of London's longest

Camelot: Julie Andrews, Richard Burton and Robert Goulet
in the Throne Room Scene at the end of Act 1

running musicals, but proved that the West End's great producer, Charles Cochran, had not lost hs touch.

Brigadoon arrived at His Majesty's Theatre, undamaged by the crossing, in the spring of 1949 and one more American musical proceeded to fill one more West End theatre. The final import of the decade was *Carousel*, which followed *Oklahoma!* into the Drury Lane and settled in for a long run.

There had been two other highly successful British musicals during the five years between the end of the war and the end of the decade, *Under the Counter* and *Blue for a Boy*, but both were of the old school. Noel Coward once wrote that the principal difference between the English musical theatre and the American is that in America they take light music seriously, and in Britain they do not. Only recently has that changed, but there is no question that the effect of the American lyric theatre and its development did not take root in Britain for many years. And even then it was infrequent. But when it did, it emerged not as an American imitation but as a British interpretation, with a character of its own.

22 One Extended Season: the Fifties

On Broadway, no decade began as splendiferously as did the 1950s. After one or two stumbles, one of which was *Mike Todd's Peep Show* that stumbled into a hit because of a liberal sprinkling of stripteases and locker-room humour, the season officially and respectably began with a new show for Ethel Merman written by Irving Berlin. It was musical comedy at its almost best, which became something better when Ethel Merman and a young performer named Russell Nype sang a duet in which Nype sang thirty-two bars of one melody, Ethel Merman answered him with thirty-two bars of another, and in the third chorus the two themes meshed. It was called 'You're Just in Love' and required four to five encores every night before the play could continue. Encores are the special possession of musical comedy denied to a musical play. *Call Me Madam* kept the seats warm at the Imperial Theatre for over a year and a half.

But it was a month later, the twenty-fourth day of November to be exact, that one of the great triumphs of the musical theatre made its debut on Broadway. Based on stories, characters and, in truth, a language invented by the Broadway chronicler Damon Runyon, with a book by Jo Swerling and Abe Burrows (actually it was almost exclusively Burrows), and above all a musical score of brilliant originality by Frank Loesser, *Guys and Dolls* became legend after one performance. The idea of bringing Runyon's world to the musical theatre was the producers', Ernest Martin and Cy Feuer who was formerly head of the music department at Republic Pictures. Their first joint effort had been *Where's Charley?*, and with *Guys and Dolls* they established themselves as that rarity in the theatre, two genuinely creative producers. Abe Burrows' book was a comedic masterpiece for which Frank Loesser wrote a score that captured every character and every situation without one bar that breached the style. One song, 'A Bushel and a Peck', became an immediate hit, but none of the score, including 'A Bushel and a Peck', passed into the musical literature known as standards. In a way it was a tribute to the meticulousness with which Loesser remained within the confines of the play. *Guys and Dolls*

ranks as one of the great and most beloved achievements of the musical theatre.

The other major event opened in March 1951. It was Rodgers and Hammerstein's musical based on the film version of the book, *Anna and the King of Siam*, which starred Rex Harrison who was turned down for the role on the stage. Retitled *The King and I*, it had been the idea of Gertrude Lawrence who acquired the rights and took them to Dick and Oscar. After much searching they found a king in Yul Brynner, who had appeared several years earlier playing opposite Mary Martin in *Lute Song*. (One of the favourite guessing games in the theatre was Where Did Yul Brynner Come From? Even I, an old friend, never knew. I am certain it was only a secret because it amused Yul for it to be so.)

After the usual try-out in New Haven and Boston, *The King and I* opened in New York to a generally fine press. Brooks Atkinson wrote: 'This time Rodgers and Hammerstein are not breaking any fresh trails. But it is a beautiful and lovable musical play'; the *New York Post*: 'Another triumph for the masters'; and the *Daily News*: 'A distinguished musical play'. There was praise for the one ballet in the show, Jerome Robbins' Siamese version of *Uncle Tom's Cabin*, and huzzahs for Gertrude Lawrence and Yul Brynner. As was her custom, Miss Lawrence brought magic to the theatre. She never had a great voice (Kurt Weill once said to me that she had the greatest range between

The crap game from *Guys and Dolls*

Gwen Verdon in *Can-Can*, 1953

Yul Brynner and Gertrude Lawrence in
The King and I, 1951

C and C Sharp of anyone he ever knew), but when she sang she somehow made music, and you knew that something special was happening on the stage. Yul *was* the King of Siam, and together, when she taught him how to dance in 'Shall We Dance', they miraculously brought tears to your eyes. I have always thought of it as one of the loveliest moments I have ever had in the musical theatre.

Tragically, *The King and I* was Gertrude Lawrence's farewell. A year and a half after the show opened she died of cancer. Although she was only fifty-four years old, she had been in the theatre for forty-two years. Impoverished as the theatre became without her, no one was more affected by her passing than Noel Coward. Besides his deep affection for her, which had begun when they

both started in the theatre, he wrote in his obituary notice for her in *The Times*: 'No one I have ever known, however brilliant and however gifted, has contributed quite what she contributed to my work.'

When *The King and I* became a film, Yul won the Academy Award for Best Actor, and in 1976 he began a revival tour which, with intermittent holidays and a period when he courageously overcame a dangerously serious illness, he played until June 1985. In all, he gave four thousand performances. Four months later the illness, also cancer, returned and dealt him a fatal blow. Tragic, tragic. He was an implosion of life.

With *Guys and Dolls* and *The King and I* as curtain raisers, the 1950s can almost be viewed as one extended season. There were no breakthroughs that influenced the future musical theatre. There were a handful of wonderful musical comedies. The musical play was brought to its ultimate fruition. There were three other major attempts at Broadway opera. There were several enterprising ventures that barely missed the mark. There was a powerful dance musical with an enduring score. There was the use of musical comedy to tell a moving story. And several new faces appeared on the creative scene.

Following the hysterical evil of the McCarthy period, the death knell of which was sounded not by the press or the government as it should have been, but by television, America during the next few years enjoyed the last relatively comfortable and peaceful period it has known to the present day, and probably for the foreseeable future. There was the customary medley of social injustice and rumble of racial and urban strife, but there was no clatter of social rebellion and in the theatre it was a time of *l'art pour l'art*.

COLE PORTER

During the fifties, Cole Porter wrote his last three musicals for Broadway. The first was *Out of This World* in 1950. The score was good but the book was not and it had a limited run. Cut from the play before it opened was 'From This Moment On', which later, when it was interpolated in the film version of *Kiss Me Kate*, became a Porter-permanent. In 1953 came *Can-Can*, and *Silk Stockings* in 1955. Both were produced by Feuer and Martin. Abe Burrows wrote the book for *Can-Can* and doctored *Silk Stockings*. Both were hits. As had happened so often in Cole's career, neither score was critically appreciated – after *Kiss Me Kate* it was inevitable that too much would be expected of him. But both scores made significant contributions to his immense catalogue of standards. In *Can-Can* was another of his memorable paeans to his beloved Paris, 'I Love Paris' with its marvellous octave leap from minor to major in the middle of the chorus, and 'It's All Right with Me'. From *Silk Stockings* came the delicious ballad 'All of You', which began:

> I love the looks of you, the lure of you,
> I'd love to make a tour of you,
> The eyes, the arms, the mouth of you,
> The East, West, North and the South of you.

The world had the opportunity of hearing 'All of You' under ideal circumstances when it was sung and danced in the film by Fred Astaire and Cyd Charisse.

One of the events of *Can-Can* was the introduction to Broadway of Gwen Verdon, who had been a choreographic assistant in Hollywood and who became an overnight star.

In 1954, shortly before the opening of *Silk Stockings*, Linda Porter died. In 1956 Cole underwent an operation to remove a large and painful ulcer, and while recuperating he wrote *Aladdin*, a musical for television which had little of the Porter gift for melody and rhyme. Two years later he lost his long struggle to preserve his leg. And from then until his death in 1964 he never wrote again.

RODGERS
AND
HAMMERSTEIN

Following *The King and I*, Rodgers and Hammerstein's work during the decade was far less adventurous. They wrote four shows, all of which took place in the approximate present. For the first three Oscar also supplied the book, and although one was a hit, he seemed less at ease in a contemporary setting. Their last effort became one of their longest running successes.

In 1953, for the first time since *Allegro*, Oscar again attempted an original story with *Me and Juliet*, a backstage play within a play, with disappointing results. Brooks Atkinson had high praise for Dick's music, but wrote: '*Me and Juliet* had just about everything except an intelligible story.' And Walter Kerr, then critic of the now defunct *Herald Tribune*, wrote: 'A dizzying collection of independently attractive fragments, so eager to embrace everything that half its treasures slipped through its outstretched arms.'

In 1955 they presented *Pipe Dream*. It was based on John Steinbeck's novel *Sweet Thursday*, Steinbeck's affectionate view of the poverty-stricken citizens of a seedy section of Monterey, California, called Cannery Row. The settings were a shabby marine biology laboratory, a flophouse and a rundown café, all of which were beyond the periphery of Oscar's creative habitat. As John Chapman in the *Daily News* wrote: 'Perhaps Hammerstein and Rodgers are too gentlemanly to be dealing with Steinbeck's sleazy and raffish denizens.' The score, inevitably, had its captivating moments, but *Pipe Dream* was too far from the popular preconception of a Rodgers and Hammerstein musical to overcome a less than enthusiastic press.

Flower Drum Song, which opened in 1958, was a definite success. The reviews were restrained but uniformly good. Brooks Atkinson said: 'Everything is done with ease, taste and pride in the theatre ... *Flower Drum Song* is not one of their master-works.' The *Journal American*: 'A big, fat Rodgers and Hammerstein hit ... remarkably good, but not a stupendous musical ... everything is fine, nothing is sensational.' Based on a novel by C. Y. Lee, it was adapted by Oscar and Joseph Fields, the uncle of Herbert and Dorothy who, with his partner Jerome Chodorov, had written several hit comedies. The

setting was San Francisco's Chinatown and Gene Kelly returned from Hollywood to direct. It was far and away the best score they had written since *The King and I* and one song, 'Love Look Away' – which for reasons I cannot understand was overlooked by recording artistes – was one of their most beautiful creations, musically and lyrically.

The following year they were responsible for the season's biggest hit, *The Sound of Music*. The book, taken from Maria Trapp's autobiography *The Trapp Family Singers*, was adapted by two of Broadway's most celebrated playwrights, Russel Crouse and Howard Lindsay, who had written among many others *Life with Father* and won the Pulitzer Prize for *The State of the Union*. The show starred Mary Martin. The score was universally praised, but, according to Brooks Atkinson, 'It is disappointing to see the American musical stage succumbing to the clichés of operetta.' And Walter Kerr in the *Herald Tribune* wrote: 'The show is handsome, it has a substantial plot and it is going to be popular . . . but before the play is halfway through its promising chores, it becomes not only too sweet for words but almost too sweet for music.'

There is a phrase in the theatre, 'it's an audience show', which is usually the optimistic battle-cry of producers to justify continuing when the press has been negative, and it is almost invariably illusory. The reviews of *The Sound of Music* were mixed, but it was one instance where 'it's an audience show' was not wishful thinking. Audiences everywhere, good reviews or not, adored *The Sound of Music*. It ran well over three years on Broadway, over five in London,

Mary Martin as Maria with the children in *The Sound of Music*

ABOVE: Rex Harrison and Julie Andrews (Eliza Doolittle) in *My Fair Lady*
BELOW: The Ascot scene from *My Fair Lady*

and is revived as often as *Oklahoma!* The film, starring Julie Andrews, became the largest grossing film up to that time and won the Academy Award.

During the fifties Dick and Oscar never stopped working, despite the plague of serious illness that afflicted them both. While preparing *Pipe Dream*, Dick endured fierce pain in his lower jaw. It was diagnosed as cancer and he went into hospital where half of his lower jaw was removed. Ten days after the operation, he was back at rehearsal, returning to the hospital each night. Before they began work on *The Sound of Music*, Dick conquered a severe depression by committing himself briefly to an institution for therapy. Then,

at the beginning of rehearsals, Oscar went into hospital for what was thought to be an ulcer. It was discovered to be an incurable malignancy. When the play was trying out in Boston and a song was needed for Captain Von Trapp, Oscar somehow made his way there, where he and Dick wrote 'Edelweiss' – the last lyric Oscar was ever to write. During the summer of 1960, they had lunch one day at the Plaza Hotel where Oscar told Dick that the doctors wanted him to re-enter the hospital to try, by any and all means possible, to arrest his deteriorating condition. Very calmly, sitting there over lunch, he told Dick that he had decided against it. He had had a good life and he wished to leave it peacefully. That afternoon he would return to his beloved farm in Pennsylvania where he would remain until the end came. All of this was said as matter-of-factly as if they were discussing a scene from a play. After lunch they shook hands and said goodbye.

Oscar Hammerstein died on 23 August 1960. That night, for the first and only time in the history of the theatre, all the lights on Broadway and in the West End of London were dimmed for three minutes in tribute.

The two major triumphs of the 1950s were *My Fair Lady* in 1956 and *West Side Story* in 1957.

TWO TRIUMPHS

Fritz and I had previously written *Paint Your Wagon* which opened in November 1951. It was the tale of the life and death of a town during the gold rush. Dear Cheryl produced it and Agnes de Mille opened the second act with a moving ballet – which was so long it was difficult to remember the plot when it reappeared. Brooks Atkinson's review was excellent, and although the rest

Robert Coote as Pickering, Stanley Holloway as Doolittle
and Rex Harrison as Higgins, in *My Fair Lady*

of the critics had fine words to say for the score, there were definite qualifications. *Paint Your Wagon* ran for almost a year, followed by a reasonably successful tour. Then, during the summer of 1952 while I was in Hollywood, I was approached by the producer of the film version of *Pygmalion*, Gabriel Pascal, whose idea it was that Fritz and I convert *Pygmalion* into a musical. We worked on it for six months and then decided it was impossible. (We did not know that Dick and Oscar had had the same experience before us.) In 1954, we picked it up again, and this time we stayed with it to completion. The major factor that influenced us was – whether we were aware of it or not – the changing style of musicals. It now seemed feasible to preserve the text as much as possible without the addition of a secondary love story or choreographic integration. What *was* essential was that every song and every addition to the play not violate the wit and intelligence of Shaw's work. He was an ideal 'collaborator' because there was so much oblique and unstated emotion that could be dramatized in music and lyrics.

Rex Harrison, with fear and trepidation, finally agreed to appear in a musical. Every one of Higgins's songs was written expressly for him so that adjustments could be made to accommodate his non-singing singing.

In his stage directions Shaw states that Eliza is eighteen years old. The original Eliza was Mrs Patrick Campbell who was in her high forties. Both Lynn Fontanne and Gertrude Lawrence, who appeared in revivals of *Pygmalion*, were well into their thirties or more. We decided to believe the stage direction and were fortunate enough to find Julie Andrews, who had bewitched Broadway in the 1954–5 season in an English import, *The Boy Friend*. (To be discussed later.) And for the role of Alfred P. Doolittle, one of England's most famous music hall and musical comedy performers as well as a superb actor, Stanley Holloway, agreed to leave home. Cecil Beaton, who I believe invented the Edwardian era, designed costumes that are still discussed; Oliver Smith designed magnificent and fluid scenery; Hanya Holm's choreography was exactly what was needed when it was needed; and the entire production was shaped into a unified whole by director Moss Hart. Produced by Herman Levin, *My Fair Lady* was a glittering success from its first performance in New Haven to its opening in New York on 15 March 1956.

Brooks Atkinson called it: 'The greatest musical of the twentieth century'. Walter Kerr wrote: '*My Fair Lady* is wise, witty and winning. In short, a miraculous musical.' The *Daily Mirror*: '*My Fair Lady* is a felicitous blend of intellect, wit, rhyme and high spirits. A masterpiece of musical comedy legerdemain. A new landmark in the genre fathered by Rodgers and Hammerstein.' That payment was due Dick and Oscar, there is no doubt. Everyone driven towards the goal of a cohesive blending of book, words and music owes his vision and ambition to the origins they provided.

My Fair Lady won the Drama Critics' Award and the Tony. It ran for six and a half years in New York and almost six years in London, and was

translated into over twelve languages. (I am not counting the countries behind the Iron Curtain, though I do know that it has appeared in Polish and in Russian.) The film version won the Academy Award. It is performed and revived repeatedly, most prominently in recent years by Rex Harrison himself in America, and in the West End where it ran over two years, starring Tony Britton and Liz Robertson. Why do I mention them? Two reasons. They were both critically acclaimed and one of them is now my wife.

During the decade, Leonard Bernstein had written two and one-third musicals before the ultimate triumph of his theatrical career, *West Side Story*. In 1953 his collaborators on *On the Town*, Betty Comden and Adolph Green, had begun work on a musical adaptation of a popular comedy of earlier years, *My Sister Eileen*, by Chodorov and Fields. The music was to be written by Leroy Anderson, the composer of numerous popular orchestral works. When Anderson found the theatre too foreign for him, Betty and Adolph turned to Lenny, and in six weeks they wrote a jubilant, satiric and melodic score. Rosalind Russell, who had played in the screen version of *My Sister Eileen*, made her musical debut on Broadway with delightful results. Rechristened *Wonderful Town*, it ran well over a year. The success of the score in the theatre, however, was not duplicated in the music and record shops across the country. I was rather surprised. There was one song, a tuneful but tongue-in-cheek anthem to Ohio called 'Ohio' that I thought especially catchy. I was having lunch with Max Dreyfus shortly after the opening and I said to him that I thought he had a hit with 'Ohio'. Max shook his head. 'Why not?' I asked. Said Max: 'The public knows they're kidding.'

Two years later came his one-third of a musical. *All in One* was a diversified evening consisting of a one-act play by Tennessee Williams, a dance performance by Paul Draper, a popular artiste of the time who combined tap and ballet with movement of his own creation, and Bernstein's one-act opera of suburban life, *Trouble in Tahiti*, for which he also supplied the libretto. *All in One* could not find an audience.

In December 1956 Bernstein opened *Candide* on Broadway. Obviously based on Voltaire's picaresque novel, it was adapted by that most famous and respected playwright, Lillian Hellman, and three extraordinarily talented lyricists, only one of whom owed his roots to the theatre. He was John LaTouche, who tragically died suddenly at the age of thirty-eight before the show opened. The other two were the Pulitzer Prize-winning poet, Richard Wilbur, and Dorothy Parker. In style, *Candide* ran the gamut from light opera to Bernstein's version of musical comedy, and with Hellman's book very much in evidence, it was a *mélange* of *opéra-bouffe* and musical play. The most enduring music in *Candide* was the overture which was a work unto itself, and in the concert hall it is one of the most frequently performed orchestral works of the contemporary theatre.

Thornton Wilder once wrote that more plays fail because of a breach in

West Side Story

style than for any other reason. *Candide* moved from scintillating moment to scintillating moment, but the moments too often seemed too stylistically unrelated, and the play paid for its sins.

In 1974 *Candide* was revised, revived and directed by Hal Prince with some additional lyrics by Sondheim. Although Lenny Bernstein was far from pleased with the deletions and changes, Prince managed to make the variety of styles an asset. Both critics and public fell under its spell with such enthusiasm that an event unparalleled in the history of the theatre occurred. *Candide*, fundamentally a revival, won the Drama Critics' Award for the Best Musical of the season.

One of the early openings of the 1957–8 season was *West Side Story*, a musical of remarkable originality, pulsating excitement, dynamic and passionately beautiful music, and choreography that has never been equalled in any musical from that day to the present. It was a collaboration of Bernstein's music, Arthur Laurents' book, Stephen Sondheim's lyrics (his first Broadway show) and choreography by Jerome Robbins. It was a modern retelling of *Romeo and Juliet* with the Montagues and the Capulets converted into two warring street gangs, one Puerto Rican and the other a potpourri of various strains of American, which took place in the slums on the Hispanic borders of uptown New York. Laurents skilfully told the story with sufficiently broad and precise strokes to enable the action to be whipped forward by the score and Robbins' feverish and breathtaking choreography.

Lyrically it was quite a debut, but I have often been told that Steve Sondheim grew to hate his work for *West Side Story*, for what seemed to him its moments of operetta sentimentality. Although here and there his lyrics may not have had the amazing polish and wizardry of his later work, I, for one,

wish he could have achieved it without the loss of some of the honest emotion that was in *West Side Story*.

West Side Story, with one exception, received superb reviews. It ran for almost two years in New York and even longer in London. As for the music, it was the success of the film, which won the Academy Award, that gave it the universal recognition it deserved. Its popularity has grown through the years, and despite the impact of Robbins' choreography in the original show, it is the music that has taken *West Side Story* into the next generation and is reponsible for the continuing appetite of audiences to see it on the stage.

In the world of musical comedy during the 1950s, Betty Comden and Adolph Green, besides *Wonderful Town*, collaborated with Jule Styne on four musicals. The first, in 1951, was *Two on the Aisle*, a revue for Bert Lahr and Dolores Gray (*Annie Get Your Gun* in London) that fell far short of the great revues in which Lahr had starred in the thirties, but which was good enough to run the season. Their second in 1954 was a musical version of *Peter Pan* for Mary Martin, which had begun its career as part of a Los Angeles light opera summer season before flying East. The original score had been written by

MUSICAL
COMEDY

BELOW: Judy Holliday, the star of
Bells Are Ringing

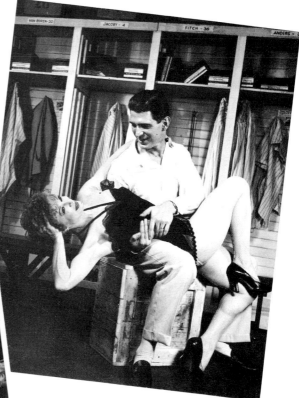

ABOVE: Gwen Verdon and Stephen Douglass
starring in *Damn Yankees*, 1950

Mark Charlap and Carolyn Leigh, an expert and unappreciated craftsman, but only two of their songs remained by the time the show reached Broadway. *Peter Pan* was less successful on the stage than when it was televised. So successful a television show was it, in fact, that it was later repeated.

In 1956 they wrote their most smashing hit of the fifties, *Bells Are Ringing*, for that most beguiling of stars, Judy Holliday, who had begun her career performing with Comden and Green when they were in cabaret. *Bells Are Ringing* was by far the most popular score Comden and Green had written or have written since. Two songs in particular, 'Just in Time' and 'The Party's Over', are still heard today. (Yes, Noel Coward also wrote a song called 'The Party's Over'. There is no copyright on titles.) The show ran over two years and later became an equally successful film.

In the spring of 1958 they wrote *Say, Darling*, a musical about the making of a musical in which all the characters had their living counterparts in the theatre – what one might calle a *pièce à clef*. The show, brightened at times by Comden and Green's irrepressible humour and Jule Styne's ever-attractive music, was enjoyable but perhaps too special in its appeal, and *Say, Darling* failed to go the distance.

During the fifties, three more teams and one composer/lyricist stepped into the theatre with rousing results. The first team was Richard Adler and Jerry Ross, who, after contributing a few songs to a revue in 1953, in the following two years wrote *The Pajama Game* and *Damn Yankees*, musical comedies which the critics and public alike feverishly embraced and which established them as major lyricists and composers. I use the plural because they each did both. *The Pajama Game* also launched the career of Bob Fosse, whose choreography was one of the highlights, as it was again in *Damn Yankees*. The future of Adler and Ross, which seemed infinite, was sadly halted by the death of Jerry Ross a few months after the opening of *Damn Yankees*. He was twenty-nine years old.

In the season of 1955–6, one of the earlier shows to open – and close – was an intimate revue called *Catch a Star*. A few of the songs were the work of a new composer on the scene, Jerry Bock. Shortly after the opening of *My Fair Lady*, Sammy Davis Jr took a musical to Broadway, *Mr Wonderful*, which was primarily his cabaret act featuring himself, his father and uncle, who were known as the Will Mastin Trio. One of the composers was Jerry Bock. And during those early years of the fifties, a lyricist and part-time composer named Sheldon Harnick was contributing material to revues. Then in 1958 Bock and Harnick joined forces, with historical results. Their first effort together, *The Body Beautiful*, indicated little of the talent that emerged the following year in *Fiorello!*, based on episodes in the life of New York's greatest and most endearing mayor, Fiorello La Guardia, which was so good and possessed of such witty and winning music.and lyrics that it proceeded to be the third time

the Pulitzer Prize Committee gave the award for drama to a musical. When the time came for parcelling out the Drama Critics' Awards, Jerry Bock ended up in a tie with Richard Rodgers (for *The Sound of Music*) for Best Composer. One of the last songs they wrote for the score of *Fiorello!*, 'The Little Tin Box', is a memory cherished by everyone who was fortunate enough to have seen the show. And they were only beginning.

One of the last musicals of the 1959–60 season was a bright, breezy and bouncing hit called *Bye, Bye Birdie*, which was the work of the third new team of the fifties to enter the arena, composer Charles Strouse and lyricist Lee Adams. Strouse had studied at the Paris Conservatory under Nadia Boulanger and his primary ambition was operatic, but his natural talent for tunier tunes inevitably led him to the theatre where he bypassed 'promising' and went straight to 'smash'. *Bye, Bye Birdie* became the recipient of the Tony Award for Best Musical.

Story. The wisest man I have ever known in the theatre was Moss Hart. We were also very close and spoke on the phone every morning. One day he told me that Kermit Bloomgarten, one of Broadway's most respected producers, who seldom ventured into the hazardous waters of musical comedy, had asked him to listen that evening to a musical he intended to produce, for which he was hoping to obtain Moss's expert services as director. The following morning I asked Moss how the musical was. Moss told me he was in a dilemma.

Robert Preston and Barbara Cook in *The Music Man*

Should he simply tell Kermit, who was a good friend, that he did not feel the musical was for him, or should he tell him the truth which was that it was so bad he should drop it. Finally he decided simply to exclude himself as director. The musical was *The Music Man* (!), one of the great hits of the fifties for which the book, music and lyrics had been written by a neophyte to Broadway, Meredith Willson. I later told Moss that for a suitable share of his royalties as director of *My Fair Lady* he could seal my lips about that telephone conversation.

This kind of miscalculation is far from uncommon in the theatre. As I mentioned earlier, Rodgers and Hammerstein turned down *Pygmalion*, and I turned down *The Teahouse of the August Moon*, which Fritz wished to do, and which ran as a straight play for years and years.

The Music Man was born out of Willson's youth in Iowa and the period was 1912. Willson's style was completely his own. Songs like 'Trouble', which took the breath of a long-distance runner, and 'Seventy-Six Trombones', an echo of John Philip Sousa, had an innocence and humour that spread a smile of joy over the theatre. Robert Preston, who had never appeared in a musical before, performed with gusto and charm and the audience began a love affair, which has lasted until today, with the leading lady, Barbara Cook. When spring came and the sound of the Tony was heard in the land, *The Music Man* and not *West Side Story* won the Award for Best Musical. As an indication of the slow appreciation of Bernstein's score, Meredith Willson also won the Award for Best Composer. Even the Drama Critics crowned *The Music Man* as Best Musical.

WORDS
AND
MUSIC

Following *Guys and Dolls*, Frank Loesser, always a man of vaulting ambition, disappeared for five years and devoted himself to writing the music, lyrics and adaptation of Sidney Howard's celebrated drama of the mid-twenties, *They Knew What They Wanted*. Retitled *The Most Happy Fella*, it finally opened in May 1956. Being his first musical since *Guys and Dolls*, it was an eagerly awaited event and there was considerable surprise, some disappointment, but, in general, admiration for the distance he had travelled from 'the oldest established permanent floating crap game in New York'. The distance was not necessarily in quality but in substance. Consisting of over forty songs, *The Most Happy Fella* was almost a popular opera. A good deal of the music was moving and highly melodic, but when he needed variety and tempo he resorted to the popular idiom with which he was long associated, including one number clearly earmarked for 'hit' – which indeed it became – called 'Standing on the Corner'. The score was beautifully sung by Jo Sullivan, Robert Weede and Art Lund, but the style was too uneven to equal the grandeur of Loesser's conception. Nonetheless it was a noble effort and a successful one, running over a year and a half.

In *Greenwillow*, four years later, he again went in search of fresh pastures

Oliver! – 1979 revival

Eric Flynn and Lauren Bacall in *Applause*, and
Katharine Hepburn as Coco Chanel in *Coco*.

for expression, this time to a bucolic America of earlier days. It was a gentle tale and because he wrote appropriately gentle music and little of the Loesser humour found its way into the play, *Greenwillow* was received with more reservation than appreciation and lasted only three months.

In the 1954–5 season, Saint Subber came to town with *House of Flowers*, a promising musical set in the West Indies and magnificently mounted by the English scenic and costume designer, Oliver Messel. The book and lyrics were the first and only attempt at same by Truman Capote, the novelist and short story writer and self-appointed chronicler of the world of the rich and social, whose diminutive size provided more than adequate room for his soul. It was the first of three musicals that Harold Arlen wrote during the fifties and his fascinating songs again sounded better out of the play than in it. With a book that was minus both sentiment and wit, it obviously did not add up to a thrilling evening in the theatre.

Three years later in 1957, Harold paid another visit to the West Indies, this time with Yip Harburg writing the lyrics and with the book by Harburg and Fred Saidy, who had written *Finian's Rainbow*. It is an impossibility for Harold Arlen to write a bad song and *Jamaica*, aided by the one and only Lena Horne, remained where it was for over a year.

His final effort of the decade was more than merely disappointing because after it Harold returned to his house in Beverly Hills, where a thriving career writing for films awaited him – *The Wizard of Oz*, which he wrote some twenty years earlier, is one of the best film scores of all time – and he never again composed for Broadway.

This last show was *Saratoga*, based on a best-selling novel by Edna Ferber, and which as a film had starred Gary Cooper and Ingrid Bergman. The setting was, naturally, Saratoga, the horse-racing centre of the very, very, very rich. The period was the 1880s and the sets and costumes were provided by Cecil Beaton. The lyrics were by Johnny Mercer, but the plot was as heavy as a ton of oats which weighed Johnny and Harold down with it. It ran less than three months.

Two years before *Saratoga*, Johnny Mercer, the poet of pop, had his first genuine hit with the musical version of Al Capp's then wildly popular cartoon strip, Li'l Abner. I was all admiration for his work because I had laboured for a year trying to turn Li'l Abner into a hillbilly 'Good Soldier Schweik' and come up empty-handed. Johnny and his collaborators were wise enough to turn L'il Abner into *Li'l Abner*.

Giancarlo Menotti was not idle in the fifties and in December 1954 he presented a melodramatic opera, *The Saint of Bleecker Street*, replete with incest and murder. Although it won the Tony Award for Best Musical of the year, as the accent on comedy became more and more pronounced, the audience for pure musical drama diminished and *The Saint of Bleecker Street* became the least successful of his operas to date. Four years later, he adapted

Alfred Drake and Doretta Morrow in *Kismet*

for the theatre his opera *Maria Golvin* which had originally been presented on television. By this time the taste for musical drama had all but evaporated and *Maria Golvin* closed in a week.

Of passing interest in the 1958–9 season was *Goldilocks*, with book and lyrics by Jean and Walter Kerr and choreography by Agnes de Mille. Composer Leroy Anderson once again tried his hand at the theatre and this time completed the job. As talented as he was, his music lacked the inner drive and the ability to capture the variety of mood and emotion that constitute good theatre music, and the book could not overcome it.

Of considerable interest, however, was the kismet of *Kismet*, which opened in December 1953. The play upon which it was based was written before the First World War by a popular but pedestrian playwright named Edward Knoblock who, it seems, was famous for not being, shall we say, an invigorating companion. Sir John Gielgud, besides being one of the greatest actors of the twentieth century, has also an extraordinary talent for extraordinary gaffes which he himself relates with great glee, so I am not betraying a confidence when I reveal that one day Sir John was having lunch with the playwright and Knoblock asked if he knew a certain man. Sir John replied: 'Know him? Next to Edward Knoblock he's the dullest man in London.'

The original *Kismet*, with its Baghdad setting, was a huge success. Plays or musicals with Arabian nights or oriental ambience were much in favour at the time. In fact one musical, *Chu Chin Chow*, which opened in 1916, was one of the longest running musicals in the history of the British theatre. *Kismet* had

twice been a motion picture and it was inevitable that it would eventually find its way to the musical stage.

The book and lyrics were written by Robert Wright and George Forrest, who had adapted Grieg so successfully in *Song of Norway*. This time the score was taken from the works of Borodin, and lovely songs they became. The performance of Alfred Drake was a textbook of musical theatre artistry. But the book – ah, the book – was not only operetta, but the kind of operetta that awakens the primaeval savage in every critic. But they could not review it! Why, you may ask? Because there was a newspaper strike that lasted for weeks and weeks. The audiences, on the other hand, adored it and by the time the strike was over and the critical claws could get at it, *Kismet* had gathered such popular momentum that nothing short of armed attack could have stopped it. It not only became a resounding hit, but, to the collective critical despair, won the Tony Award for the Best Musical of the year.

I can already hear you wondering to yourself: how many other pleasurable evenings in the theatre have those damned critics denied us? But that, dear reader, is not the point. The point is: why do you listen to them so avidly, follow their advice so unquestioningly, and allow yourself to become sheep to their shepherding? Wretched as the reviews eventually were, there was universal high praise for Alfred Drake's performance. Would not that alone have piqued your curiosity? I doubt it. No, I am afraid the fault, dear Brutus, lies not in the *Morning Star* but in yourself.

In fairness, I must add that this sort of critical demolition was far more characteristic of New York than London. Over the years the situation, instead of improving, has deteriorated to such an alarming degree that, coupled with other dangerous factors, the contemporary New York theatre is in serious threat, all of which shall be discussed in detail at the proper time in this volume.

What shall be discussed at this moment is an opening that took place on Broadway on 21 May 1959 of one of the best musicals of the decade, that brought pure musical comedy across the border and into the fields where grazed such musical plays as *The King and I* and *My Fair Lady*. Called *Gypsy*, for once not of Himalayan extract, it was a tale, part fiction, taken from the memoirs of America's stripteuse supreme, Gypsy Rose Lee. The music by Jule Styne was the crowning achievement of his career, and the lyrics by Steve Sondheim were warm, witty and expert. The book and the choreography were by his other two collaborators from *West Side Story*, Arthur Laurents and Jerome Robbins. What made *Gypsy* a break with the past was that where previously musical plays were written in the post-*Oklahoma!* modern operetta style, *Gypsy* told a realistic and emotional story to the beat of the musical and lyrical language of pure musical comedy. Despite the title, the main character was Gypsy's mother, played by Ethel Merman who gave a dramatic performance of hitherto unrevealed power. Her last soliloquy,

'Rose's Turn', was without question one of the most moving moments ever seen in a musical.

Ethel Merman later starred in a revival of *Annie Get Your Gun*, and for a brief period succeeded Carol Channing in *Hello Dolly*, but *Gypsy* was the last role she created on Broadway and in it she reached her peak – and she knew it. Thereafter, she always said that of all the musicals, whether great or made great by her presence, her role in *Gypsy* was her favourite.

The score not only characterized and dramatized but did what all good music and lyrics should do: they gave a universality to each situation. One song in particular, 'Everything's Coming Up Roses', passed quickly on to the shelf where standards for ever lie. Unfortunately, because it opened so late in the season and after the balloting had closed, the Award for Best Musical went instead to a rather run-of-the-mill show called *Redhead* that derived its distinction from Gwen Verdon, and Bob Fosse's choreography.

Composer/lyricist Harold Rome had three entries in the decade's sweepstakes, none of which was a critical success but two of which enjoyed sufficient popular success to be classified as hits. The two that were winners were directed and co-authored by Joshua Logan, and there was a feeling shared by those who knew Harold that Josh, after *South Pacific*, had become so indoctrinated by Rodgers and Hammerstein that he had consciously or unconsciously led Harold away from his natural expression, which was comedic, and into sentiment. That may not have been the reason, but there was most definitely a change in Harold's style.

Their first effort was an adaptation of Arthur Kober's comedy of earlier years about life in a Jewish summer camp in the Catskills. Originally called *Having a Wonderful Time*, the musical became *Wish You Were Here*. Unfortunately, it could not enjoy the benefits of the usual Broadway try-out because the action took place around a real, live swimming pool, diving board and all, and the country that split the atom was unable to find engineers capable of inventing a travelling swimming pool. So *Wish You Were Here* filled the tank at the Imperial Theatre, where it had a longer run of previews than most shows have after they have opened. After repeated changes and delays, *Wish You Were Here* finally opened to a press that did not wish they were there.

There were a few of the comedy songs one expected from Harold Rome, but the score had more than its share of ballads, one of which single-handedly turned *Wish You Were Here* into a hit. The most popular singer of the day was Eddie Fisher, and his recording of the title song not only swept the country but audiences into the theatre.

Wish You Were Here was followed in 1954 by *Fanny*, an attempted musicalization of Marcel Pagnol's trio of film masterpieces, *Marius*, *Fanny* and *Cesar*. When I learned of it, I must confess it was one of the few times in my life that I was paralyzed with envy. There was no doubt in my mind, and there still is none, that those three films were the finest subject matter for a

musical invented by man. But, as all too often happens in the theatre, some-where along the line a step was taken on to the wrong road, and the further they went the dimmer became the original goal. When *Fanny* opened it no longer bubbled with touching and humorous antics of character, either in book or song, and Harold's score pendulumed back and forth between sentiment and sentimentality. (My initial reaction to the title song was that it was pretentious, but during the passing years whenever I hear it played I realize how wrong I was, and what a truly beautiful song it is.) With the box office assistance of Ezio Pinza in his first musical since *South Pacific*, *Fanny* overcame a mixed bag of reviews and ran over two years.

In 1959 Harold did a musical version of the famous Western film comedy, *Destry Rides Again*. It was the least attractive of the three scores, but Michael Kidd again came to the rescue and *Destry* ran a full calendar and then some. But despite the length of the run, the ominous cloud of rising costs that would eventually turn to a steady downpour prevented *Destry* from being a commer-cial success.

Four other musicals must be mentioned before leaving the decade. Open-ing shortly after *Destry* came *Once Upon a Mattress*, which not only intro-duced Carol Burnett but the music of Richard Rodgers' daughter, Mary. It was an amusing frolic with a score that was attractive but no threat to Daddy.

The second was *Plain and Fancy*, which took a sympathetic and polished look at the Amish society in Pennsylvania. The book was the work of Will Glickman and Joseph Stein, the latter of whom was to make such an illustrious contribution to the theatre in the sixties, and the melodic score and appropri-ate lyrics were by Albert Hague and Arnold Horwitt. *Plain and Fancy* received good notices and ran over a year, again aided by Eddie Fisher's recording of the show's ballad, 'Young and Foolish'.

The third show of interest was *The Golden Apple*, an adventurous musicalization and condensation of *The Iliad* and *The Odyssey*, which opened off-Broadway in 1954. The score by Jerome Moross and John LaTouche, which left little room for dialogue, was filled with melody and ideas, and lyrically was one of LaTouche's finest. Hanya Holm's choreography was a treat unto itself; in fact, it was her work in *The Golden Apple* that led Fritz, Moss and me to her door for the choreography of *My Fair Lady*. *The Golden Apple* won the Drama Critics' Award for the Best Musical.

The last of the quartet which opened at the end of the 1959–60 season is still running! Called *The Fantasticks*, it opened at a Greenwich Village theatre called the Sullivan Street Playhouse, which has a seating capacity of one hundred. (Shades of the Théâtre des Bouffes-Parisiens.) Based on Edmond Rostand's one-act play *Les Romantiques*, it was expanded into a full evening by author and lyricist Tom Jones, who, with his composer Harvey Schmidt, created a genuinely integrated little musical play, and 'Try to Remember' became an immediate and lasting hit song.

LONDON

The 1950s saw the musical theatre in London, undoubtedly stimulated by the rash of American importations, slowly begin to rub its eyes, go to the piano and write new music, pick up the pen and write new lyrics, and in general join the times.

The rash of American musicals was indeed a rash. In 1953 alone, three invaded the West End, all with immense success: *The King and I* starring Herbert Lom and Valerie Hobson; *Guys and Dolls* with almost the entire New York cast intact; and *Paint Your Wagon*, in which the famous English musical star Bobby Howes played the father of his own daughter, Sally Ann, the first and only time they appeared together. After *Paint Your Wagon*, Sally Ann, as beautiful as her voice and an accomplished actress, via films, television and stage followed her father into the firmament.

During the next six years the American visitors included *Kismet* with Alfred Drake (result: smash); *Wonderful Town* (fair); *The Pajama Game* (smash); *Damn Yankees* (fair); *Bells Are Ringing* (fair plus); *West Side Story* (smash plus); *Flower Drum Song* (smash); *Candide* (poor); and the greatest American success ever to go to London, *My Fair Lady*. For the theatrical record and for the pleasure it gives me to report it, no musical in history was preceded by so much furore. It had been the intention of the publisher and the management to prevent the sale of the cast album before the London premiere. But British visitors to American shores brought back albums for their friends, pursers and stewards on trans-Atlantic ocean liners and aeroplanes did a thriving trade in illicit records, and between fifty and one hundred thousand were in circulation before the opening. For five days before that premiere, one of the evening newspapers ran a headline 'Five More Days', 'Four More Days', 'Three More Days', etc. On the opening night itself there were crowds on either side of the street from the Strand all the way to the Drury Lane Theatre, I suppose to see who was in each passing limousine and taxi. The entire exercise was an event without precedent and far too overwhelming an experience for any man, especially an author, to absorb.

The initial signs of change in the English musical came in the subject matter. For the first time it became normal practice for musicals to be based on former plays, which could offer a firm structure and something more than cardboard characters. Some were successful, some were not, but it was the awakening that mattered.

Among the successes were *Zip Goes a Million*, based on that popular warhorse *Brewster's Millions*, and *Love From Judy*, taken from *Daddy Long Legs*. Among those that did not fare so well were Noel Coward's adaptation of *Lady Windermere's Fan*, which he called *After the Ball* and which the critics found too old-fashioned, and *Dear Miss Phoebe* taken from James Barrie's *Quality Street*, which suffered the same fate and for the same reasons.

Then, in 1954, came two musicals of original conception that had London throwing bowlers and top hats in the air. The first was the previously men-

tioned spoof of the twenties, *The Boy Friend*, with book, lyrics and music by Sandy Wilson. The music was a conscious caricature of Kern, Rodgers and Coward, 'A Room in Bloomsbury', for example, being obviously inspired by Noel's 'A Room with a View', and the title song being a memory of Rodgers and Hart's 'The Girl Friend'. But *The Boy Friend* miraculously managed to walk the fine line between camp and nostalgia with an unerring step, and the result was a work of delicious delight that graced the stage of Wyndham's Theatre for over two thousand performances. When a second company opened in New York that same year, the critics and public alike melted. Anne Rogers starred in the English production and when it was decided that she remain in the London cast, the American producers Feuer and Martin found another young girl whom they regarded as eminently suitable, Julie Andrews. Part of the reason New York melted was Miss Andrews. She certainly melted Fritz and me.

The other original smash of 1954 began inconspicuously and unambitiously as an end of season entertainment for the Bristol Old Vic. Two members of the Bristol company were Julian Slade and Dorothy Reynolds. Slade composed the music and collaborated with Reynolds on the book and lyrics. They called it *Salad Days* and fundamentally it was precisely that: a frothy, disarming little show about the joys and blushes of youth. Both Slade and Reynolds were astounded by London interest, and in August 1954 it tiptoed into the Vaudeville Theatre in the West End.

Without for a moment demeaning either the authors or the British public, the fact is there happens to be a certain type of theatrical offering that cannot be called amateurish, because at its best it is too adroit, but which, nevertheless, is so ingenuous that at times it seems so. It is home-grown, quintessentially British, and once this unique alchemy strikes a chord in the British heart, affection comes gushing forth. So it was with *Salad Days*, which once opened ran even longer than *The Boy Friend*. But whereas *The Boy Friend* was transportable to other lands, *Salad Days* was not. Neither one could be accused of moving the musical theatre forward, but Sandy Wilson proved to be a talent to be reckoned with.

In 1958 he not only attempted the impossible, but, in the minds of many, he achieved it. The impossible was a musical adaptation of the novel *Valmouth*, written by Ronald Firbank, an English author who had died at the age of forty back in the mid-twenties, and who had written a handful of fiction so bizarre in humour and esoteric in subject matter as to give *recherché* a new meaning. His style was as light as a feather on a Beaton chapeau, but under that hat a complex mind was at work.

One of the reasons F. Scott Fitzgerald has always proven veritably impossible to dramatize is because although the plot could be told, his style could not be captured. To try and bring Firbank's feathers to the stage was no less difficult, but somehow Wilson caught Firbank's *soignée* decadence and mis-

chievous sexual variations in mid-air and wrote a fascinating score, which though not distinguished for popularity, remained faithful to his subject. *Valmouth* had just begun to find its audience when it was forced to close because the theatre had made a previous commitment. Double the pity, for the commitment was to Bernstein's *Candide* which only lasted a few weeks.

But the most important musical and lyrical talent England was to produce in the decade was Lionel Bart, who emerged in 1959. He had not attended Harrow and Oxford, as had Sandy Wilson, or Eton and Cambridge, as had Julian Slade. He came from the East End of London and his first collaborator was an ex-convict.

One of the most vital and innovative forces in the British theatre at that time was Joan Littlewood. Although her talents were far from unappreciated, she preferred the free rein of working in a small theatre in the East End, called Stratford East. It was she who met Bart and encouraged him to write his first musical. The musical was *Fings Ain't Wot They Used t'Be*, the ex-convict who was the author of the book was Frank Norman, and it graphically but infectiously dramatized and musicalized the pimps, the crooked policemen (bent cops on the other side of the Atlantic), the gamblers and the tarts who populate the sleazy side of London life. Much closer to the knuckle than *Guys and Dolls*, it was, as they say, a bit of a shocker. Although that may have been part of its appeal, the true eye-opener was Bart's endless stream of tuneful music and the honesty, clothed in wit, of his lyrics. *Fings Ain't Wot They Used t'Be* played a short run at Stratford East and then a few months later transferred to the West End, where it proceeded to run for over two years.

In that same year Bart provided lyrics, laced with gutsy humour, for the

Salad Days: The Piano

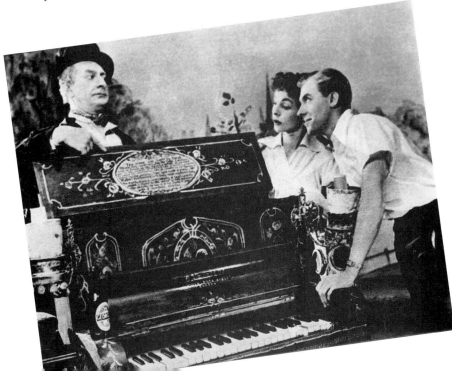

Mermaid Theatre production of *Lock Up Your Daughters*, which had a healthy run and which three years later was revived in, or belatedly transferred to, the West End, where it continued its success for a total of over six hundred performances.

Like *Salad Days*, but patently for different reasons, *Fings Ain't Wot They Used t'Be* was too English for foreign comprehension and Broadway never saw it.

One musical, however, did cross the Atlantic with gratifying results. It actually had to cross the Channel to get to London in the first place. It was *Irma La Douce*, which first saw the light of night in Paris, where it was presented in a small theatre on the Left Bank. To book and lyrics by Alexandre Breffort, Marguerite Monnot wrote what was virtually a small, cabaret operetta. Melodically it was as French as onion soup, but far above most of the popular French music of the period. In Paris it was not only a great success, but by way of being a novelty. The French had not involved themselves in the musical theatre since the operetta days of Reynaldo Hahn in the twenties.

The Wyndham's Theatre programme
cover for *The Boy Friend*

Among the British who came to see it was Peter Brook, a Francophile to his toes as his later career would prove. Engaging the services of Julian More, Monty Norman and David Heneker to adapt the book and lyrics, they were able to preserve its charm and appeal, and in 1958 *Irma La Douce* became an even greater success in London than it had been in Paris. Two years later it went to Broadway with the original British cast, where its acclaim was repeated but without as long a run. Three years later, to complete the journey, it was brought to the screen by Billy Wilder in a film starring Shirley MacLaine and Jack Lemmon – but without the songs. The music was only used thematically as background material. (The same fate was suffered by Harold Rome in Joshua Logan's film version of *Fanny* – in which Chevalier starred but never sang.)

The sum total of the decade was not the renaissance of the British musical theatre but the nascence. With Sandy Wilson and, more significantly, Lionel Bart, the West End had made a beginning that would see it eventually become a dominating force in the theatre.

23 The Great Rebellion: the Sixties

The 1960s in America was the scene of the greatest social upheaval of the century. The causes were partly historical and partly anatomical. To define the latter first, with the end of the Second World War in 1945, millions of young men returned to their homes and before the year was out the maternity hospital became the most thriving assembly line in the world, and remained so for years to come. With a more than normal backlog that began during the war years, it was computed in the mid-sixties that of all the people who were living on the planet Earth, over twenty-five per cent were under twenty-five years of age.

Historically, a major catastrophe to strike the United States – and the rest of the world – was the assassination of President John F. Kennedy in November 1963. The alleged assassin, Lee Harvey Oswald, was captured the same day but before he could be properly examined, to discover if he were acting alone or as part of a conspiracy, two days later he was gunned down in a Dallas jail by a seedy café owner and minor handyman of The Mob named Jack Ruby. Ruby's reason for his action was that he was trying to spare Mrs Kennedy the anguish of having to testify at Oswald's trial. To compound the shock and despair that settled over the land, a governmental commission determined that the assassination was the act of one man, and the newspapers from coast to coast cynically endorsed the decision of the commission – which meant that the Fourth Estate, in their wisdom and experience, believed that a cheap hoodlum shot Oswald to spare Mrs Kennedy further distress. They not only believed it then, but many still do, despite the fact that since 1963 over twenty people have been murdered who were later proven to be connected with, or had knowledge of, Ruby, Oswald or both. Many years later, as the result of the constant clamouring of some knowledgeable, investigative authorities, and, perhaps, because a public opinion poll showed that over eighty per cent of the American people disbelieved the findings of the commission, a congressional committee reopened the case and came to the conclusion that it was highly doubtful Oswald had acted alone.

At the time, incredulity touched all classes and ages, but it was most prevalent among the country's youth. Whether it was because of crushed hope by the assassination or an unexplained coincidence, a strange phenomenon occurred: within a year hair among the young grew to shoulder length, and beyond. When asked by a reporter the reason, one long-haired boy said that it was his way of demonstrating he was disavowing the society in which he lived. The rebellion had begun. A rebellion that was to influence popular art, fashion, culture, and even alter the course of history.

The death of Kennedy was followed by the calamitous escalation of the Vietnam War, during which the straining seams of the nation were ripped apart by the assassinations in one year of Martin Luther King and Senator Robert Kennedy. Both had been emissaries of peace: King making pacifism his weapon in the struggle for racial equality, and Kennedy running for President on a platform of an end to the war. Both were heroes of youth and again the cloud of dissatisfaction hung over the solution to each crime.

In the world of popular music, rock became the rhythm of rebellion. Even in Poland and Russia rock concerts were recognized as such and were censored. In Poland, however, the government finally decided it was better to join in than fight and eventually sponsored them. In the musical theatre, as had happened at the beginning of the century with the birth of jazz, it was well into the decade before a rock musical appeared on Broadway.

BROADWAY 1960–1

In the Broadway season of 1960–1, while the social Vesuvius still slept, there were only ten musicals, but three were hits and one of the three joined the ranks of the perennials. Bock and Harnick continued their collaboration with *Tenderloin*, which proved a disappointment after *Fiorello!* Nevertheless, as was to be expected, there were some lovely melodies and moments when Harnick's inimitable humour shone through.

Meredith Willson returned to Broadway with *The Unsinkable Molly Brown*, which did not equal *The Music Man* as a unified piece of work but did provide a handful of good songs, some fine singing and enough good fun to run a year and a half. Hit number one.

The highest expectations of the season, however, were reserved for *Camelot*, the first show by Fritz and me since *My Fair Lady*, with several former associates, namely director Moss Hart, choreographer Hanya Holm, and starring Julie Andrews. Her co-star was Richard Burton.

Fritz and I had been away from the theatre for four years, during which time we had written the screenplay, music and lyrics for the film *Gigi*. Because *Gigi* was not only successful, but won more Oscars than any film in history up to that time, and because of *My Fair Lady*, the advance sale for *Camelot* was monumental. But from the first day that pen was set to paper, *Camelot* was plagued by enough misfortunes to send all connected with it into the desert for forty years. Adrian, the famous motion picture costume designer, came out of

ABOVE: Julie Andrews in *Camelot*
BELOW: The first rehearsal for *Camelot*

retirement, and when he had completed only half of his work died of a heart attack. Two months before rehearsal, I became ill. When the play opened in Toronto, the running time was over four hours. The day after it opened, I went into hospital for ten days and the day I returned to work, Moss Hart suffered a serious heart attack and never saw the play again until four months after its New York opening. *Camelot* on Broadway became known as a 'medical' more than a 'musical'. Thanks to the high degree of professionalism of Richard Burton, Julie Andrews and dear Roddy McDowell, who held the company together while the play was being rewritten and restaged, *Camelot* opened only a week late on 3 December 1960, to the most star-studded audience in memory. People literally flew trans-continentally and trans-Atlantically to attend the premiere. I remember the last person to rush to his seat before the curtain rose was Noel Coward, who had arrived from London late that afternoon.

It was not a warm audience and the play was still too long, barely under three hours. The reviews ran the gamut from 'magnificent' in the *Daily News*, admiration but fault-finding in the *New York Times*, 'not another *My Fair Lady*' in the *Mirror*, to good or less than good in some of the evening papers. But the score was unanimously singled out for praise, and Richard Burton's performance earned him a Tony – as well he deserved.

The huge advance began to dwindle. Then in March, Moss returned and, viewing the play with a fresh eye, guided me into cutting twenty minutes. Simultaneously, there was a television show in tribute to Fritz and me to honour the fifth anniversary of *My Fair Lady*, and fifteen minutes of *Camelot* were included in the programme. The following day, the pre-opening line returned to the box office and *Camelot* ran over two years, almost that again on tour, and its success was repeated across the Pacific and Atlantic.

When President Kennedy died, two quatrains of the song 'Camelot' became associated with his thousand days in office:

> Ask every person if he's heard the story,
> And tell it strong and clear if he has not;
> That once there was a fleeting wisp of glory
> Called Camelot . . .
>
> Don't let it be forgot
> That once there was a spot
> For one brief shining moment that was known
> As Camelot.

One of the first books to appear after the assassination was entitled *A Fleeting Wisp of Glory*, and in the early eighties, William Manchester, Kennedy's official biographer, brought out a book of reminiscences called *One Brief Shining Moment*. *Camelot* became synonymous with the Kennedy years,

and in the late sixties when the *Oxford History of the American People.* was published, it ended with Kennedy, and the lyric of *Camelot* is printed on the last page.

Over the years the popularity of *Camelot* has grown. It is constantly being performed somewhere, and in 1981 it was revived in all its mediaeval splendour by Richard Burton – and there was a decided improvement in the reviews when it visited New York. When Burton became ill, Richard Harris, who had played King Arthur in the film, replaced him and, except for short vacations, is still playing him.

Sadly, both for music and for me, Fritz, who had had a coronary himself two years before *Camelot*, decided it was time to retire, and in the autumn following the opening, Moss Hart died at the age of fifty-seven – an irreplaceable loss to the theatre he loved, and to those in it and out of it who loved him.

That season saw the queen of television, Lucille Ball, come to Broadway with a fast-moving, good-natured musical, *Wildcat*, which had a better than average score by Cy Coleman and Carolyn Leigh. One song in particular, 'Hey, Look Me Over', became a minor standard. But *Wildcat* left its investors with a tax deduction.

Do Re Mi, with a book by Garson Kanin and a score by Jule Styne and Comden and Green, and a lovely song, 'Make Someone Happy', was good enough to run over four hundred performances, but not good enough to overcome the rising costs of production.

Three other musicals lasted various degrees of brevity, and then in April came the third hit of the year, *Carnival*, with music and lyrics by Bob Merrill. After two promising efforts, *Take Me Along* and *New Girl in Town*, both based on O'Neill – the first, *Ah, Wilderness* and the second, *Anna Christie* – Merrill came into his own with an accomplished score. *Carnival*, taken from the popular film *Lili* and with a circus background, was imaginatively directed and choreographed by Gower Champion, and won the Drama Critics' Award for the Best Musical.

In the following season, after three off-Broadway warm-ups, composer and lyricist Jerry Herman finally was heard uptown in *Milk and Honey*. It was a fine score of sound melody and honest lyrics, but shorn of the zippy Broadway show tunes that were to identify his later work. It was a creditable beginning for a man who for the next twenty-five years (and many more, I am certain) was to provide Broadway with some of its most solid hits. Not necessarily with an ambition to change the direction of the theatre, but, at his best, a source of pure enjoyment. BROADWAY 1961–2

The major event that season was the fourth musical to be awarded the Pulitzer Prize in the theatre. Once again, Feuer and Martin brought Abe Burrows and Frank Loesser together with splendiferous results. Called *How*

Barbra Streisand in *Funny Girl*

to Succeed in Business Without Really Trying, it was a satire of such perfection in all departments that it became lovable.

As the years pass, the list of obituary notices of the great talents of the musical theatre grows longer. A few months after *How to Succeed* opened, Frank Loesser died at the age of fifty-nine.

There were eleven other musicals that year, nine of which were authored by some very impressive names, but only two of the eleven succeeded. A quick rundown: *Sail Away* by Noel Coward; *Kwamina*, Richard Adler's first attempt without his late partner Jerry Ross; *The Gay Life* by Dietz and Schwartz; *Subways Are for Sleeping* by Comden, Green and Styne; *A Family Affair* with music by John Kander, his first Broadway show; *Kean* by Wright and Forrest and starring Alfred Drake; *All American* with a score by Strouse and Adams that included 'Once Upon a Time', in my opinion the most beautiful song they ever wrote, and with a book by Mel Brooks; *I Can Get It for You Wholesale* by Harold Rome, in which the table-talking moment of the evening was a song called 'Miss Marmelstein', sung by Barbra Streisand making her Broadway debut; and *Bravo Giovanni*, which starred the Metropolitan Opera's handsome basso, Cesare Siepi.

The two that went home happy were Richard Rodgers and Steve Sondheim. With *No Strings*, Dick Rodgers, in his first outing without Hammerstein, provided his own lyrics to some lovely melodies, splendidly sung by Diahann Carroll and Richard Kiley. Always restless for change, *No Strings* was the first show where the orchestra was not in the pit but offstage, and, at times, on. The instrumentation excluded strings, hence the title. The funniest moment occurred only once on a night well into the run, when one of the characters sang a song called 'The Man Who Has Everything' with his fly open.

In *A Funny Thing Happened on the Way to the Forum*, Steve Sondheim reversed Dick Rodgers and, for the first time, composed his own music. Suggested by the works of Plautus, it was set in Ancient Rome and starred one of America's most original comic actors, Zero Mostel. The book was by Burt Shevelove and Larry Gelbart, an extremely funny writer. (It was he who said one day: 'I hope Hitler is alive and on the road with a musical.') The music was serviceable, but the lyrics were funny, clever and rhymed with the ingenuity that was to become one of Sondheim's trademarks. When they were out of town, they had considerable difficulty in involving the audience with the play. Jerome Robbins came up to see it and said that in his opinion it took too long fot the audience to know what to expect. So an opening number was added called 'Comedy Tonight'. From that moment on, the play was a hit. *A Funny Thing* opened on Broadway, ran for almost two years, and went home with a basketful of Tonys.

ABOVE FAR LEFT: Mary Martin as Dolly in *Hello Dolly*
ABOVE LEFT: *How to Succeed in Business Without Really Trying*:
Rudy Vallee, Virginia Martin and Robert Morse

BROADWAY
1962–3

The rise of the British musical that had begun in the previous decade continued into the sixties, and in the season of 1962–3 two musicals that had scored heavily in the West End went to Broadway with impressive results. By far the greater was Lionel Bart's *Oliver!* Successful, but a trifle thin, was *Stop the World – I Want to Get Off*, the first collaboration of Leslie Bricusse and Anthony Newley who also starred in it. In later years Newley made his career more as an actor and entertainer than a writer. Both shows deserve more exploration, which they will receive when we return to the land of their birth.

Irving Berlin's *Mr President* did not have a successful term in office, but Bock and Harnick wrote a score for an enchanting musical called *She Loves Me*, which was as witty, melodic and irresistible as any to have been heard in years. Based on an Hungarian play which had become a successful and adorable film many years earlier, *The Shop around the Corner*, with James Stewart and Margaret Sullavan, it later became a film musical for Judy Garland (not with the Bock-Harnick score), and finally reached Broadway directed by Harold Prince and with Daniel Massey and Barbara Cook giving two captivating performances. *She Loves Me* ran only eight months and, harking back to Moss Hart, if ever a show received less than it deserved, *She Loves Me* was it. It also deserves a revival. (Just for me.) In that same year, Neil Simon wrote his first musical, *Little Me*, with a score by Cy Coleman and Carolyn Leigh (*Real Live Girl*). The main attraction was the first appearance on Broadway since he had become a television star of Sid Caesar.

BROADWAY
1963–4

While the Beatles, Bob Dylan, rock groups, guitars, flower children and dropouts were creating and screaming to music that was growing further and further away from Broadway and traditional popular music, the theatre was still able, from time to time, to produce a hit capable of keeping the musical theatre alive. There were two in 1963–4. One was *Hello, Dolly!* with a solid Broadway score by Jerry Herman and a title song, sung by Carol Channing, that was one of the most exciting examples of Broadway know-how in memory. *Hello, Dolly!* squeezed past *My Fair Lady* and for a short time became the longest running musical on Broadway.

The second hit was *Funny Girl*, with music by Jule Styne, lyrics by Bob Merrill, and a magnetic performance by Barbra Streisand which launched her spectacular career. In a theatre growing more and more bereft of stars, she, as had Julie Andrews after *Camelot*, left Broadway for motion pictures and never returned.

Another marquee casualty was Carol Burnett, who starred in Jule Styne's second musical of the year, *Fade Out – Fade In*. With book and lyrics by Comden and Green, there was a definite audience for it, but its run was foreshortened when Carol Burnett grew weary and departed – also never to appear on Broadway again.

Bea Lillie gave an uproarious performance as Madame Arcady in a musical

version of Noel Coward's *Blithe Spirit*. Called *High Spirits*, it played for almost a year, but became another victim to the high cost of operation.

Amid the wreckage of the year was *Anyone Can Whistle*, an interesting musical by Stephen Sondheim and Arthur Laurents. The critics were not intrigued, however, and although it had its fans the costs were becoming too high to play and pray, and it lasted less than two weeks.

On 22 September 1964, the *belle époque* of the musical theatre came to an end, but the finale was a triumph. It was the show that was to surpass *Hello, Dolly!* to become the longest running musical in history. The idea began with Joseph Stein's adaptation of some of the works of the great Yiddish author, Sholom Aleichem. Jerry Robbins undertook the direction and choreography, Sheldon Harnick and Jerry Bock provided the score, Zero Mostel starred, and to the smallest detail *Fiddler on the Roof* became a work of perfection – compassionate, moving, imaginative and humorous. It won every award the theatre can give, and I am certain that as I write, *Fiddler on the Roof* is being performed somewhere in the world.

From England that year came Joan Littlewood's stunningly conceived, satiric revue *Oh, What a Lovely War!*, a bitter view of the First World War which America, with all it had on its hands, was not in the mood for. Bricusse and Newley produced a successor to *Stop the World* with *The Roar of the Greasepaint – The Smell of the Crowd*, which instead of opening in London first, opened in New York. There was a hit song, 'Who Can I Turn To?' (which I think would have been just as big a hit if it were 'Whom Can I Turn To?'), but the New York reaction was so negative that London never saw it. There was, however, one English importation that equalled its success in London. It was *Half a Sixpence*, a musical version of H. G. Wells' *Kipps*, which starred one of London's favourites, Tommy Steele. There was nothing new or adventuresome about *Half a Sixpence*, but the audiences loved Tommy Steele and it did jolly well.

The most eagerly awaited musical went the way of so many eagerly awaited musicals. As usual the credits were impeccable: music by Richard Rodgers, lyrics by Stephen Sondheim and a book by Arthur Laurents based on his play *The Time of the Cuckoo*, which as *Summertime* had been brought to the screen by David Lean, starring Katharine Hepburn, and now as a musical was called *Do I Hear a Waltz?* Not only was there a sharp division of approach between Dick Rodgers on the one hand and Laurents and Sondheim on the other, but the professional division soon turned to personal acrimony. And a very unhappy time was had by all. Many years later in an interview with *Newsweek*, when asked about Rodgers and Hammerstein, Sondheim said that Hammerstein was a man of limited talent but infinite soul, and Rodgers, a man of infinite talent but limited soul.

BROADWAY
1965–6

The following year Dick and I tried collaborating and we, too, did not have an easy time. I cannot pass judgement on his soul because we were not together long enough for me to measure it. Dick regarded my work habits as erratic, which indeed they seemed. I was experiencing a great deal of personal difficulty at the time, over a matter not pertinent to the history of the musical

Rosalind Russell as Auntie Mame

theatre, and it pushed my creative hours into the night and early dawn. Further, the work was an original story about the paranormal (eventually *On a Clear Day You Can See Forever*), which like most original stories presented innumerable dramatic problems. I know that Dick did not have many kind words to say about me later, but I am quite certain that had we been engaged on an adaptation of an existing work, our collaboration might have succeeded.

The score for *On a Clear Day* was eventually composed by Burton Lane, and the show opened in 1965. Although the reviews were mixed, over the years the score, especially the title song, has become one of the most performed I have ever written, and I am – if I may be forgiven for saying so – rather proud of it. Burton's music, his first score since *Finian's Rainbow*, was justifiably praised and *On a Clear Day* ran long enough almost to see the sun.

It later became a film starring Barbra Streisand and Yves Montand – with Jack Nicholson in a small part.

There were only three hits in 1965–6. One was Jerry Herman's *Mame*, a musical version of Rosalind Russell's great success of many years before, *Auntie Mame*. Herman again produced a rip-roaring show-stopper in the title song and *Mame*, despite critical quibbling, eventually joined the golden dozen of the longest running musicals. The second was *Man of La Mancha*, which travelled a long and circuitous route before it reached Broadway. It began its life in regional theatre in Connecticut, moved to downtown New York into the Washington Square Theatre, and by the time it had played its run on Broadway at the Martin Beck Theatre it had become the fourth longest running musical. The music was by Mitch Leigh, who until that time had devoted his talent to commercial jingles, and the lyrics were by Joe Darion, who had written one failure in the late fifties. The author, Dale Wasserman, had originally written it for television, and combining Cervantes' book with Cervantes' life, *Man of La Mancha* was propelled by the idealism expressed most notably in 'The Impossible Dream'. Richard Kiley gave one of the finest performances of the decade, and the use of a divided orchestra in either wing, the staging of Albert Marre, and the theatricality without loss of feeling with which Wasserman told the story, made *Man of La Mancha* a moving and exciting experience.

Sweet Charity was the third hit, and besides Bob Fosse's brilliant choreography which was magnificently performed, as usual, by Gwen Verdon, Dorothy Fields crossed the generation gap to collaborate with Cy Coleman on a score that proved it was possible for 'the old school' to be impudent, clever and timely.

During the 1966–7 season, Jule Styne and Comden and Green wrote one of their best scores for a black cavalcade, *Hallelujah, Baby!*, and an off-Broadway musical based on the popular comic strip, *You're a Good Man,*

BROADWAY
1966–7

Charlie Brown, ran fifteen hundred performances and hundreds and hundreds more on tour.

But the most unusual and successful musical of the year was *Cabaret*, which was another case of a musical based on a based on a. The original was Christopher Isherwood's stories of life in Berlin in the twenties, *I Am a Camera*, upon which John van Druten had written a successful play with the same title. John Kander and Fred Ebb, who had made their collaborative debut the previous year on a so-so musical, *Flora, the Red Menace*, came very much into their own with a brilliant, atmospheric score, consciously reminiscent of Kurt Weill. In fact, Kurt's widow Lotte Lenya appeared in one of the roles. The book by Joe Masteroff honestly and realistically remained true to its origins, and Hal Prince's direction captured the exact mood of the period. *Cabaret* ran over eleven hundred performances and, despite its riches, when it reached the screen it became the only successful musical to improve in transition. The film, produced by Feuer and Martin, was one of the greatest musical films ever made and Bob Fosse, directing in motion pictures for the first time, won the Academy Award, as did the film.

BROADWAY 1967–8

The following season, Kander and Ebb continued their collaboration, but with less fruitful results, in an almost charming musical, *The Happy Time*. Its French-Canadian setting was too gentle for the solid strength and lyrical humour of their basic style. Robert Goulet, who had become an overnight star as Lancelot in *Camelot*, gave an expert performance, but despite Gower Champion's gift for directorial surprise *The Happy Time* did not have a happy time.

A most interesting and, I might add, successful musical came to town shortly after *Cabaret* which was based on an earlier two-character play called *The Fourposter*. The original play took place entirely in a bedroom and spanned the life of a married couple. Musicalized by Harvey Schmidt and Tom Jones (*The Fantasticks*), it was called *I Do! I Do!* and retained the original setting and personnel – in short, a two-character, one-set musical. But – and a large 'but' it is – the husband and wife were played by Mary Martin and Robert Preston, and it was ingeniously directed and choreographed – yes, choreographed – by Gower Champion. The score was tasteful without necessarily being inspired, and one song, 'My Cup Runneth Over', enjoyed great popularity.

In downtown Manhattan, generically known as Greenwich Village which is actually but a small part, there were and still are a string of theatres of various sizes, and they suddenly began to thrive with the kind of theatrical activity that was too daring for the high-cost commerical theatre of Broadway. In January 1968, the Village Gate opened its doors to a small revue devoted to the music and translated lyrics of a brilliantly talented Belgian songwriter and per-

former, Jacques Brel. Called *Jacques Brel Is Alive and Well and Living in Paris*, its songs had a vitality, earthiness, anger and bitter romanticism that reached out and demanded attention. And attention they received. For over eighteen hundred performances.

Not far from the Village Gate was the Orpheum Theatre, and it was there, in that same month of January 1968, that the musical revolution that was taking place outside the theatre finally set its foot on the stage. It was a rock adaptation of Shakespeare's *Twelfth Night*, with music and lyrics by Hal Hester and Danny Apolinar (both did both) – who have never been heard from since. Called *Your Own Thing*, a contemporary expression that soon became a bromide, New Yorkers flocked to it and it even won the Drama Critics' Award for the Best Musical. Clever and contemporary as it was – so contemporary, in fact, it included slides of prominent figures of the time – its significance is purely historical. Nothing in the score survived and its very topicality made it soon out of date. But it was a preparation for what was to come.

What was to come came in April, when *Hair* opened on Broadway. It, too, had begun downtown, but its influence reached further than any musical of its time. The music was by Galt MacDermot, a trained musician who wrote a score that used rock rather than merely being rock. The lyrics by James Rado and Gerome Ragni were not the familiar medley of repetitious lines so prevalent in all those millions of rock albums, but were lyrics with fresh ideas ('Aquarius'), were fresh and funny ('Frank Mills'), and fresh and touching ('Good Morning, Starshine'). *Hair* called itself an 'American tribal love-rock musical', and the book, hardly a piece of coherent, dramatic story-telling, celebrated the long-haired dropouts and opponents to the Vietnam War. For the first time a director, Tom O'Horgan, did more than merely present a play imaginatively. He simply ran riot. By so doing, he thrust the role of director into a position that others, less bizarre and genuinely theatrical, were to follow. In future years, producers and customary investors became more concerned with who would be directing than the play itself. The producer who took *Hair* to Broadway was Michael Butler, and it was he who engaged the services of Tom O'Horgan. The original producer downtown was Joseph Papp, founder of the New York Shakespeare Festival Theatre and the only serious American producer to emerge in the last twenty years. *Hair* played over 1,700 performances. In London, at the Shaftesbury Theatre, in ran 1,998 performances – and only failed to reach 2,000 because the theatre roof fell in. Literally.

Returning to Broadway, the 1968–9 season brought to the theatre from the pop music world the team of Burt Bacharach and Hal David. Although they did not write in the rock idiom but in a style entirely their own – a style

more dictated by the music than the lyrics – they nevertheless were among the most consistent producers of hit songs extant. Not only that, but Bacharach further departed from the norm by being a trained musician, composer and orchestrator. He and David were known and appreciated as expert exponents of contemporary music and their theatrical debut was one of those eagerly awaited events that, for once, was well worth being eagerly awaited. Neil Simon adapted the book from Billy Wilder's Academy Award-winning film *The Apartment*, and its young choreographer was Michael Bennett. Retitling it *Promises, Promises*, Bacharach and David remained in their own vernacular, making no 'grand' concessions because it was the theatre, and produced the most exciting musical since *Hair* – although in no way comparable. The fact that it was their first musical had much to do with its success. *The Apartment* was fundamentally a bitter yarn, but in their innocent hands it became innocent. The critics were unanimous in their praise, the public loved it and the regular theatre-goers were pleased with themselves for appreciating contemporary music. *Promises, Promises* enjoyed a run of over twelve hundred performances. The only misfortune was that the one person who did not enjoy it was Burt Bacharach! Accustomed to the recording studio where once he had 'a take' to his satisfaction it remained that way for ever, he found the minor irregularities that occur in theatrical performances extremely nerve-racking. Being an old and admiring friend of his, there have been many occasions since *Promises, Promises* when I have tried to inveigle him into collaborating. I have even suggested that once a play opens, he need never see it again. But he would have none of it. And so, to the theatre's loss, *Promises, Promises* is the only score Broadway has heard by that amazingly talented man.

Two other musicals of distinction that season were *Zorba* and *1776*. *Zorba* was a musical version of Kazantzakis' novel *Zorba the Greek*, an earthy and beautifully written panoply of his native land. The adaptor was Joseph Stein, the score was by Kander and Ebb, the entire production was masterfully directed by Hal Prince, and there was enough pride of endeavour to be shared by all. *Zorba* has recently been revived with Anthony Quinn repeating his film role with equal vigour and magnetism. Tony Quinn, a joyous, life-giving and wonderful man, as of this writing seems to be following the path hewn by Yul Brynner in *The King and I* and Richard Harris in *Camelot*, and may be 'Zorba' for ever. He and I have been friends since the Boer War, in fact I rented his house when I first went to California to write a film. Some twenty years ago when he was appearing in a play in New York, he dragged me to a retrospective exhibit of Kandinsky's paintings. When he tried to buy one and heard the price, he decided to go home and paint his own Kandinskys. To his amazement, or perhaps not, he discovered a buried talent. He recently had a sell-out exhibition of his own works which fetched over two million dollars.

Godspell – The Chorus, and 'The Tribe' from *Hair*

A Little Night Music. Left to right: Laurence Guittard, Glynis Johns, Len Cariou, Victoria Mallory

Mandy Patinkin as George the artist in
Sunday in the Park With George

Joseph and the Amazing Technicolor Dreamcoat: Jess Conrad

'Les Cagelles' – the Chorus from *La Cage aux Folles*, and Anita
Morris as Carla in *Nine*

217

1776 was the one and only score of composer-lyricist Sherman Edwards. It was his life's work as he laboured almost ten years before it was produced. With an admirable book by Peter Stone, it depicted the events leading up to the signing of the Declaration of Independence. What was extraordinary about *1776* was that although everyone knew the ending when he walked into the theatre, the tension and conflict that preceded its eventual signing was so dramatically written that when agreement was finally reached, and the quill touched the document, it was a rare moment in the theatre. Perhaps because it was a declaration primarily asserting the independence of America from Great Britain, it had a patriotically short run in London.

In the season of 1969–70 there were two commercial hits, one of which was critically approved and the other was not. The latter was *Coco*, taken from the life of the famous couturier Coco Chanel who invented the clothes of the emancipated woman of the twentieth century. The score was by André Previn and the author of this book. The star was the last great *monstre sacré* of the American theatre, Katharine Hepburn, making her debut in a musical. The lyrics were the most intricately rhymed I had ever attempted, and working with André was a delight. He is a man of extraordinary facility, knowledge and great good humour. Kate was Kate, which gave the theatre a little well-needed glamour. Besides her talent, which is prodigious – she is the only woman to have won four Academy Awards, and the last time she won, when I called to congratulate her, she said: 'They can't stop giving me the goddam things, can they?' – she is the only genuinely beloved performer in America today. She never reads reviews because first, she is not interested, and second, any play in which she appears is immune. She is also what is commonly known as a 'character'. Example: *Coco* was playing at the Mark Hellinger Theatre on 51st Street. Across the street they were building what is now the Gershwin Theatre, and on matinee days the noise was horrendous. John Lindsay, vastly unappreciated, was then Mayor of New York and not only a friend of mine, but when he was in Congress one of the best friends the Arts ever had. I called him as well as the builders to see if the noise could be reduced in decibels during the matinee. Nothing could be done. Finally, one matinee day Kate appeared on 51st Street around noon and sat on one of the girders. With that unique voice of hers which could be heard for four blocks, she shouted up to the workers to come down. When they realized it was Katharine Hepburn, they dropped everything and assembled around her. In paraphrase, what she said to them was: Now look here. You're the stingiest bunch I've ever encountered. I know you have a strong union and you're making a damn good salary. But not one of you has the decency to come into the theatre one night, stand at the back – which doesn't cost very much – and see the play you're ruining every Wednesday and Saturday afternoon. She then proceeded to tell them the story of the play. In the middle of the first act, said she, I have to sing a

BROADWAY
1969–70

very tender song called 'Coco'. Now you all known damn well that I can't sing. But whatever sound I can produce is drowned by the racket you lot are making. That song goes on at 3.20. If you can't do anything else, for heaven's sake at 3.20 have a little decency and shut up! Well, from that moment on, on Wednesday and Saturday afternoons, 51st Street became the quietest thoroughfare in the city of New York. One day there was a break in the gas main under the street, and when the servicemen came to repair it, they were mobbed by the builders who told them Kate was singing in there and to come back in the morning. Which they did. She is a magnificent lady and working with her was one of the joys of my professional life.

To complete the statistics, Cecil Beaton designed the sets and costumes, and that young choreographer Michael Bennett supplied the dances. It has been frequently quoted that *Coco* was a financial failure. Let me assure all future historians that nothing could be further from the truth. It made a sizeable profit and the accounting department of Paramount Pictures, who financed the play, totted up the final figures with black ink.

The other commercial success was *Applause*, which starred Lauren Bacall in her first musical and was possessed of a solid Broadway score by Strouse and Adams. The play, written by Comden and Green and based on the Academy Award-winning film *All About Eve*, the performance of Betty Bacall, and the slick professionalism were rewarded with good reviews and the Tony for Best Musical.

The winner of the Drama Critics' Award, however, was Stephen Sondheim's *Company*. *Company*, with a book by George Firth, concerned itself with a handful of Manhattan couples whose marriages would have been unbearable without the company of their bachelor friend Bobby. But it was about more than it was about. Fundamentally it was a disenchanted and acid view of the cocktail party belt of urban society. Although written in a musical comedy style with wit and humour aplenty, there were no rainbows, no joy, no hope, no melody aimed at the symbolic heart; none of the ingredients that had previously distinguished the best of the genre. The critical reaction for the most part bordered on the orgasmic. The feeling was that it was so new in concept and execution that it defied comparison. Jack Kroll of *Newsweek*, one of America's most sensitive and knowledgeable theatre critics, called it 'a landmark'. Walter Kerr, however, seemed to sum up both the critical and public reaction: 'Original and uncompromising,' he wrote, 'it is brilliantly designed, beautifully staged, sizzlingly performed, inventively scored, and it gets down to brass tacks and brass knuckles without a moment's hesitation, staring contemporary society straight in the eye before spitting in it . . .' Words of high praise for Sondheim, director Hal Prince and choreographer Michael Bennett, and then: 'Now ask me if I liked the show. I didn't like the show. I admired it.' Kerr's professional appraisal was reflected in popular attendance. Notices such as *Company* received ordinarily would have guaranteed the

The author, sitting in the alcove
where he reworked *Coco*

around the block for the foreseeable future, but after a few
ıny began to struggle. There was definite audience resistance. It
: a year and returned the cost of production with a bit to spare.
ity between critical and public reaction was even more pro-
ndon. Reviewing it for *The Sunday Times*, the famous British
Hobson wrote: 'It is extraordinary that a musical, the most
rical forms, should be able to plunge, as *Company* does, with
ity into the profound depths of human perplexity and misery.'
ıd, *Company* ran six months and lost its entire investment.

The biggest achievement in London in 1960 was without question Lionel
Bart's *Oliver!*, an adaptation of *Oliver Twist*, dealing with a background with
which he was well familiar. Bart wrote a score that could not have been
improved upon, from his children's chorus of 'Food, Glorious Food' to the

immensely touching 'As Long as He Needs Me', passionately sung by Georgia Brown. Ron Moody gave a magical performance as Fagin, and *Oliver!* became the longest running West End musical until *Jesus Christ Superstar* some twenty years later. In 1963, when it came to Broadway, its virtues were not critically appreciated, but, nevertheless, it caught the public where it lived and had a healthy run. The role of Sowerberry, incidentally, was played in both London and New York by Barry Humphries, the future Dame Edna Everage, and one of the funniest entertainers now on the boards, a favourite in London but unappreciated in the colonies.

The other major success of the 1960 season in London was *Stop the World – I Want to Get Off*, with book, music and lyrics by Leslie Bricusse and Anthony Newley, directed by Newley and starring Newley.

(*Non sequitur*. Tony Newley's multiple participation reminds me of an ill-fated musical that passed in the night in the early forties called *My Dear Public*. It was produced by Irving Caesar, co-authored by Irving Caesar, had lyrics by Irving Caesar and was co-composed by Irving Caesar. The notices were dreadful. The following day, Caesar called Oscar Hammerstein and said: 'All right! So they didn't like it! But why pick on me?')

Stop the World was the story of an Everyman called Littlechap, a character dear to Newley's heart, set in a circus arena and with an excellent score and a very big hit song, 'What Kind of Fool Am I?' It was well received by the press and the public enjoyed it 478 times. It ran even longer on Broadway.

Leslie, after much successful film work, collaborated once more with Newley in 1972 on a show called *The Good Old Bad Old Days*, in which Newley again starred as a version of Littlechap who travels from Roman times to the present. The book was a bit of mish-mash but the score contained some good numbers, and, with the drawing power of Newley, it ran for a year.

In 1962 Lionel Bart wrote an ambitious musical called *Blitz*, in which he recalled his youthful days in the East End during the war. There were touching moments, such as the children marching off to be evacuated and singing 'We're Off to See the Country', but the critics in general did not treat it kindly. His next effort, two years later, fared better. Called *Maggie May*, it had a book by the extremely talented writer Alun Owen, and took place in and around the Liverpool docks. Again the score was criticized, but it managed to run over a year. The following year he tried again, with a musical based on Robin Hood called *Twang*. With Joan Littlewood directing, the future looked promising – but not for long. Divergences of opinion became violent and Littlewood walked away before the opening night out of town. It did, however, go to London where the notices were ghastly. Bart never again was represented in the West End – except by the repeated revivals of *Oliver!* He went to America in 1969 and wrote the score for a musical version of Fellini's popular film *La Strada*. It also failed. In 1972, returning to his original home at Stratford East and working with his collaborator of earlier days Frank Norman, he wrote a

musical called *Costa Packet*, a satire on package holidays which, despite Joan Littlewood's direction, never reached the West End. And there his career ended.

It is difficult to believe that talent such as Lionel Bart's could simply disappear. Max Gordon, the famous Broadway producer, once said to me years ago: 'My boy, the only difference between you and a hit is the subject.' Could that have been it? And then can failure literally produce such paralysis that one ceases to function, and by not functioning ceases to grow, and by not growing loses touch with one's times? On a grander level, Rossini stopped composing at forty-four and never wrote another bar of music until his death eleven years later, and Arthur Rimbaud tore up his manuscripts and never wrote another line of poetry after the age of nineteen.

In 1963 British composer David Heneker, who had served twenty years in the army before retiring from military service to devote his life to music, began civilian life with another hit, the aforementioned *Half a Sixpence* starring Tommy Steele. Again, nothing new, but everything in its place. While still in uniform, and a few months before *Irma La Douce*, he had again collaborated with Norman and More on *Expresso Bongo*, a show about the world of pop music which, perforce, introduced pop music to the British stage. It starred Paul Scofield, and to this day I keep cudgelling my brain for an idea that might entice him back on to the musical stage. But Heneker's most profitable effort of the sixties was *Charlie Girl*, another of those 'quintessential, British musicals', which starred Anna Neagle, one of Britain's most beloved performers, in top form. *Charlie Girl* was not admired by the critics but it was one of those rare occasions when they might as well have written a letter home to mother. The audiences oozed with pleasure and before it was finished, *Charlie Girl* had racked up over two thousand performances.

The male counterpart of Anna Neagle in British affection is Harry Secombe who, besides being one of the dearest of men, has a smile like Chevalier's that is a veritable sunburst, a laugh that could turn a funeral into a comedy, and an absolutely glorious tenor voice. All of this he put on display twice in the sixties. In 1963 he played the title role in *Pickwick*, another Dickens original undoubtedly inspired by *Oliver!*, with a very good score by Cyril Ornadel ('If I Ruled the World'), and in 1967 he lit up the Drury Lane with *The Four Musketeers*.

Another British bonanza of the decade was *Robert and Elizabeth* which opened in 1964. Based by author Ronald Millar on the popular play of the thirties, *The Barretts of Wimpole Street*, *Robert and Elizabeth* had a better than serviceable score by Ron Grainer and three fine performances by June Bronhill, Keith Michell and John Clements.

The main contributions from Broadway to the West End were *A Funny Thing Happened on the Way to the Forum*, *Hello, Dolly!*, *Funny Girl* with Barbra Streisand (for a short time), *Fiddler on the Roof*, *Man of La Mancha*, *Carbaret* (blessed with the performance of Judi Dench), *I Do! I Do!* and *Hair*.

24 Sound and Fury: the Seventies to the Present

With the dawn of 1970 it is necessary to rise above the rubbish-strewn streets of Broadway and gaze not only about it, but at the decade that followed. The public clamour against Vietnam, led by the youth of the country, continued to mount unabated until it became a force that invaded all segments of society. Finally, in 1972, the United States buried the last of its more than fifty thousand young men who had, simply put, died for precisely nothing – despite the hollow, patriotic sophistry of Henry Kissinger and, before him, the megalomaniacal Lyndon B. Johnson to the contrary (Woodstock Rock Festival: 'Hey, hey LBJ, how many kids did you kill today?'). After strategically decimating the innocent country of Cambodia and dropping more bombs per acre than had ever been achieved in the history of bombery, President Richard Nixon decided it was of no consequence to mention that America had lost the war and proudly proclaimed 'peace with honour'. He managed to squeeze this in a few months before the domestic chagrin of Watergate, the conclusion of which was his decision to resign before he was impeached. During his term in office his Vice President, Spiro Agnew, was also forced to resign because of financial transactions concealed by the tablecloth. Nixon chose Congressman Gerald Ford to succeed Agnew as Vice President. In 1974, following Nixon's retirement from governmental duties, Ford succeeded Nixon as President. A few months after assuming office, in order to spare the American people and the world the unappetizing spectacle of an ex-President standing trial, and so that the country could then go forward pure in heart and face the bright future in a state of amnesia, Ford granted Nixon full pardon. Thus a decade plus one year, which could hardly be considered America's finest hour, came to an untidy end.

With the book closed on Watergate and Vietnam, the tonsorial industry registered a sharp rise in business. Hair became shorter and shorter, calm returned to the campus, youth became more and more conservative, and by the end of the seventies not only was the country eager for another Republican

David Essex and
Jeremy Irons in *Godspell*

Dean Jones as Robert and
Susan Browning as April
in *Company*

president – which it got – but money and the acquisition of same resumed its
traditional role as the primary preoccupation of those who needed it, and the
reason for living for those who did not.

Pleasure and permissiveness became the manhole cover of a growing emptiness in the social soul, and lack of unhappiness more and more became the definition of happiness. Britain, too, took a right turn to Toryville, and the gentility of the British character gradually melted into placidity and accepted governmental insensitivity in the name of economic stability.

In the musical theatre, the generation of composers and lyricists that should have replenished the gradual loss of the first and second generations who had created the modern musical theatre did not appear. In the sixties, the musical theatre was regarded as the establishment and musical expression became the exclusive property of rock and deafening amplification, which made unintelligible lyrics beneficially more unintelligible. Genuine talents, such as Paul Simon, who in another age might have glorified the theatre, eschewed it. When I was growing up in the thirties, my heroes were Larry Hart, Cole Porter, Ira Gershwin and Howard Dietz. In the sixties, neither Oscar Hammerstein nor I, for example, was a hero of the generation behind us. Even Stephen Sondheim, who became the cheer leader of alienation in the seventies and who had been a pupil of Oscar Hammerstein, regarded him, as you may remember, as a man 'of limited talent', and wrote of Larry Hart: '[his] work has always struck me as being occasionally graceful, touching, but mostly technically sloppy, unfelt and silly.'

ROCK AND SONDHEIM

The flower children, who began blooming in the sixties, planted themselves on the stage in Stephen Schwartz's *Godspell*, a part rock, part revival-singing version of the Gospel according to St Matthew, which opened off-Broadway in 1970 and stayed open for over twelve hundred performances. Its success was repeated, and then some, in London, where the rule of Judas was played by Jeremy Irons, who had begun his career as a member of a teenage pop group.

In that same season Stephen Sondheim followed *Company* with an extraordinary endeavour, *Follies*, in which, in Steve's words, 'we deliberately decided not to create characters with warts and all. Everybody would be not a type but an essence.' According to director Hal Prince's definition, the intention was to use the Ziegfeld Follies form as a metaphor of shredded dreams. To most people, however, it still seemed what critic Clive Barnes called another 'torn marriage manual'. The reviews were decidedly mixed, ranging from 'so brilliant as to be breathtaking at times' (Douglas Watt in the *Daily News*) to '*Follies* is intermissionless and exhausting, an extravaganza that becomes tedious' (Walter Kerr). It is quite true that it was intermissionless. During the previews so many people did not return for the second act that when the cuts were being made, one of them was the intermission.

Whatever may have been unsatisfactory about *Follies*, it contained some of the most remarkable lyrics in the modern musical theatre, and even though

it failed commercially, it received the Drama Critics' Award for the Best Musical of the season.

Another musical that year that must be mentioned was *The Rothschilds*, a musical that produced an off-stage tragedy. Composed by Sheldon Harnick and Jerry Bock, it missed the mark by a centimetre, and in so doing it brought that great collaboration to an abrupt halt. Not only did they never work together again, Jerry Bock walked away from the theatre and did not return. A loss of talent the theatre can ill afford.

On to the Broadway stage the following season came *Jesus Christ Superstar*, the work of two young Englishmen, Andrew Lloyd Webber and Tim Rice, who, with Sondheim, were to dominate the musical theatre from that day to the present. In form it was rather like adding a plot to a rock concert. Whereas Sondheim expressed himself within the existing theatrical framework, Webber and Rice simply wrote their own rules.

How *Jesus Christ Superstar* arrived on Broadway is a labyrinthine tale. Webber's father was the Dean of Music at London University. Young Webber's childhood was steeped in the classics, which becomes more and more apparent the more one listens to his music. Influences abound but they are filtered through a very distinctive musical personality, which gives his music a sound of its own. He and Rice began their collaboration at the suggestion of the choirmaster at St Paul's. Using the story of Joseph from the Old Testament, they wrote a few songs which came to the attention of a London manager, David Land. Impressed with their work, he suggested they further explore the Bible for source material, and after toying with the story of David, then Daniel in the lion's den, they flipped the pages to the New Testament and found Jesus waiting for them. Land was terrified at the prospect of 'rocking' Jesus, but after seeking and receiving the approval of a trendy archbishop, they wrote most of the score, which, first refused by RCA (who had also rejected *My Fair Lady* several years earlier), was recorded by MCA. For reasons that defy reason, the album first became a hit in Holland and Brazil, and then proceeded to sell into the millions in the English-speaking countries. Encouraged by the reception, they decided to put it on the stage. Rejecting Hal Prince as being too conservative, they enlisted the services of Tom O'Horgan, who strung a book together and directed it with his customary flair. In October 1971, *Jesus Christ Superstar*, hand-microphones, amplification and all, opened on Broadway to reviews that varied from less than cordial to consternation. It was regarded more as a novelty than an innovation, but with the success of the album preceding it, it ran a year and a half. When it opened in London the reception was infinitely more gratifying, and the show went on to pass *Oliver!* as the longest running musical in British theatrical history.

There were two other rock and rollers that season, *Two Gentlemen of Verona* and *Grease*. *Two Gentlemen of Verona* was delightfully modernized by John Guare and Mel Shapiro who also directed and directed beautifully.

The adequate lyrics were by John Guare, and the music – a wonderful score – was Galt MacDermot's first effort since *Hair*. It opened at Joseph Papp's outdoor Shakespeare Festival in Central Park as free entertainment – a festival subsidized by the city. When the weather became inclement, it moved indoors where it completed a lovely run of over six hundred performances. And Galt MacDermot won the Tony Award for the Best Music.

Grease harked back to the fifties and the teenagers who were bopping up and down. To the intellectual embarrassment of the community at large, *Grease*, which was received as a nice little show, proceeded to become one of the longest running musicals in history with almost as many road companies as *Blossom Time*. The British, however, did not find it so adorable and its visit to the West End was brief.

The same fate awaited *Pippin*, a run-of-the-mill musical which, for the first time, proved to the producing hierarchy the efficacy of television advertising. *Pippin*, with the first score by Stephen Schwartz since *Godspell*, and flashingly directed and choreographed by Bob Fosse, was hardly a musical to preserve in the scrapbook of memory. Outside of Fosse's work and some imaginative scenery, which included a handful of luscious ladies, a definite cloud of mediocrity hung over the proceedings. But Fosse went into the television studio and created a commercial so enticing that *Pippin* took a sharp turn towards the stars. Opening in October 1972, it went on and on and on for almost five years. In London it only went on, and closed after eighty-five performances.

The most popular and successful Sondheim musical, *A Little Night Music*, decorated Broadway that season. Again directed by Hal Prince, its book by Hugh Wheeler was based on Ingmar Bergman's film *Smiles of a Summer Night*. As *Follies* had used the old Ziegfeld Follies as a conceptual frame, so *A*

Glynis Johns and Len Cariou in *A Little Night Music*

Little Night Music used operetta. The entire score was written in variations of three-quarter time, and, besides the usual lyrical string of Sondheim pearls, there appeared in the second act the best and most memorable song he has ever written, 'Send in the Clowns'.

A Little Night Music ran well over a year in New York and a little less in London, where it was also warmly received. Needless to say it won thé Drama Critics' Award.

The next two seasons were too embarrassing to discuss at the dinner table, but in 1975–6 came one of the great glories of the modern musical theatre, *A Chorus Line*. Composed by Marvin Hamlisch and with touching and funny lyrics by another newcomer, Edward Kleban, and a book by James Kirkwood and Nick Dante, it was conceived and magnificently directed by Michael Bennett. The subject of *A Chorus Line* deals with one of the most basic emotions in human experience: who will be the winner? – in this case, who will be selected for the chorus line? Members of ensembles in the theatre are known as gypsies. This was a musical that only Michael Bennett, a former gypsy himself, could have understood. The hopes, the fears, the camaraderie despite the competition, the heartbreaks and the victories. Produced, naturally, by Joseph Papp, it began downtown where, from the first performance, there was no doubt a rare theatrical experience had opened. The audience readily accepted the unreal notion of a director asking the type of questions usually reserved for a psychiatrist's office, and in relatively brief patches of book, music and lyrics, we come to know each of the gypsies whose life seems to depend on being chosen by the director to make up the chorus line. The ultimate choice shows how closely tears and smiles walk together. The *finale ultimo* of the selected ensemble in costume doing their stuff is theatrical magic. *A Chorus Line* is still running and deserves to run for ever. It was the recipient of the Pulitzer Prize for Drama and every award in the book of acclaim, and if there be anyone who disdains it, he should immediately return to the sea and spend the rest of his life among the crustaceans.

Marvin Hamlisch wrote another musical four years later, *They're Playing Our Song*, which, although successful, was truly beneath his talent. The lyrics were by Carole Bayer Sager, christened by a well-known British disc jockey as 'the singing aspirin', and the genuinely good book was by Neil Simon. It was a hit in New York. It was a hit in London. And God bless them all.

Steve Sondheim had one of his rare critical failures in that season of 1975–6, *Pacific Overtures*. The goal was, again according to Steve, 'to tell a story that has no characters at all'. Without characters but only attitudes, there was little to entertain the troops. A plot without living people can only be found in a cemetery. *Pacific Overtures* ran but a few months.

Bob Fosse added another glittering evening to the theatre with *Chicago*, a musical version of a hit comedy of the mid-twenties, which recounted the rowdy and raunchy tale of a lady named Roxy Hart (Gwen Verdon) who kills

her lover and is acquitted by the legal chicanery of a shifty lawyer. The score by John Kander and Fred Ebb was, in a word, marvellous. Their finest effort since *Cabaret*, it included some of the outright funniest and most engaging songs in the musical comedy archives, 'Class' being in one by itself. Remaining in period, Fosse and the authors sprinkled it with rhythms of the twenties, and *Chicago* cakewalked and charlestoned for over nine hundred performances. Fosse, a man with a misanthropic view of life, could not have chosen a better subject.

LLOYD
WEBBER

Meanwhile, back in London, Rice and Lloyd Webber unveiled *Evita*, based on a most unlikely subject for a musical, Eva Peron, a nasty piece of Argentine life. Between *Jesus Christ Superstar* and *Evita*, they had presented the completed *Joseph and the Amazing Technicolor Dreamcoat*, which was their first work and the only one to which the adjective charming could be ascribed. Although it did not have the typical life-without-end run of the rest of Lloyd Webber's work (excluding the one hiccup *Jeeves*), it has been revived and revived and finally reached Broadway in 1981, where it ran for almost two years. Webber's rock-based music breathed with melody and Rice's lyrics were disarming. As in the case of *Evita*, no author of the 'book' was mentioned. The credits simply said 'Lyrics by Tim Rice'. The reason was that the complete story, with minor interludes, was told in lyrics, a variation of *opéra-bouffe* that in Rice's hands (and to Webber's music) gave originality to the form.

Having decided that Hal Prince was not too conservative after all, they enlisted his services as director, and his contribution had much to do with the extraordinary success of *Evita*. Duplicating *Jesus Christ*, the album long preceded the play and again sold well into the seven figures. 'Don't Cry for Me, Argentina', whose lyric has never been entirely clear to me, was, nevertheless, clear to the more tuned-in hordes of record buyers, and was as resounding a hit before the play reached London as was 'Tea for Two' back in the twenties.

But with *Evita*, the Rice–Webber style, whether working together or apart, became official. As a clue to Webber's fundamental concept, he said to me one day that what interested him when he wrote was less the plot and more a visually exciting effect. In *Evita* the spectacle was terrific, with the stage design beginning well past the proscenium arch.

Evita went to New York in 1979 where its critical acceptance was much less enthusiastic. Walter Kerr in the *New York Times* wrote: 'The evening is not boring. Though the Rice–Webber score sometimes sounds as though Max Steiner had arranged it for Carmen Miranda, there are waltzes and polkas and threatening marches to keep us alert . . . if your curiosity stays alive at *Evita* . . . it is due to the authoritative crackle of ringmaster Prince's whip. Listen, the whip says. You listen.' Despite criticism such as this, *Evita* defied the gods and proceeded to win seven Tony Awards.

ABOVE: Elaine Page, *Evita*
BELOW: *A Chorus Line*

The 1976–7 season saw the opening of one of the most successful and popular musicals of the last two decades, *Annie*. From the day work began, it took *Annie* almost five years to reach Broadway. It started in regional theatre, was revised and reopened in Washington, where its future might have ended had not director Mike Nichols been paid an enormous royalty to step in as nominal producer – with the benefit of his theatrical acumen – which attracted sufficient funding to bring *Annie* to Broadway. Nichols himself admits that his contribution was more of a counsellor, but his name was indispensable.

The idea of adapting the comic strip to the stage was Martin Charnin's, a theatreman of hitherto unappreciated talent. He provided the lyrics and the smooth, professional direction. The adaptation was the work of Thomas Meehan and the score was by Charles Strouse, who periodically erupted with a resounding hit. *Annie* was his third. Soon there were versions of the 'little redhaired tyke' running all over the country.

I Love My Wife was another hit launched that season. With delightful music by Cy Coleman, it was ingeniously staged by Gene Saks and equally well choreographed by Onna White.

The following year saw Bob Fosse return with an all-dance revue called, logically, *Dancin'*. Being a choreographer whose roots were in the theatre rather than ballet, the programme consisted of a series of production numbers danced to music from Bach to John Philip Sousa to George M. Cohan to Cat Stevens for an incredible number of performances.

Fortunately for composers and lyricists, Fosse has devoted most of his time since to motion pictures. Had he continued he would have made us all redundant – which I think might have pleased him!

The following two seasons were dominated by two musicals, one of infinitesimal insignificance and the other of significant substance. The ridiculous was *The Best Little Whorehouse in Texas*, a modest endeavour that had much to be modest about, but which was made congenial by the directorial skill of Tommy Tune. The second musical was *Sweeny Todd*. In it, the passion that Stephen Sondheim had so assiduously sidestepped in all of his previous musicals finally emerged in 'one ferocious metaphor of revenge . . . a dazzling opera of cannibalism and gore' (John Lahr). Musically, it mixed opera and song in a fashion reminiscent of Kurt Weill's *Street Scene*, but without those moments when melody took flight. It was in Hugh Wheeler's adaptation of an old English play by Christopher Bond – which was in itself an old English play – and predominantly in the lyrics that passion came clothed in anger and vengeance. The tale of a barber who is deported by an iniquitous judge in order to acquire the barber's wife and her accompanying daughter, and who returns to wreak revenge on his judicial enemy, is told replete with blood and bloodthirsty detail and, surprisingly, sporadic humour. What Sondheim set out to achieve he 'goriously' achieved, and one felt the outrage and contempt of the outsider. It was overwhelmingly praised by the critics, and after a rocky

beginning with the public, when it received the Drama Critics' Award and the Tony it found a sufficient audience to run well over a year.

It did not travel well, however. When it opened in London at Drury Lane, where it did not belong – the Theatre Royal, Drury Lane, the best and most popular musical theatre extant, is nevertheless not the setting for experimental theatre – it was beheaded by the critics and disdained by the British public. Had it been produced in a more operatic atmosphere the results might not have been so disappointing.

The Broadway event of 1980 was *42nd Street*, a musical based on one of the most famous Warner Brothers' musical films of the early thirties with the same name, and with a score culled not only from the original film, but from other songs written by the Warner Brothers' in-house team of Harry Warren and Al Dubin. It was and still is an irresistible hit. The rendition of 'The Lullaby of Broadway' alone is worth the price of admission ($60 in New York). It was Gower Champion's triumph and he died a few hours before it opened. The information was kept from the company. Then, during the curtain calls, the standing ovation was interrupted by the entrance of producer David Merrick, who announced to the audience: 'Gower Champion died this afternoon.' There was no mention of his crowning achievement, nor of his contribution to musical comedy. The curtain descended on a sobbing cast and a shocked audience.

The following season was a disappointing one for Stephen Sondheim and a happy one for Michael Bennett and Andrew Lloyd Webber. Steve's entry was *Merrily We Roll Along*, which was based on a not very successful play of the same name written by Kaufman and Hart in the thirties. It was the story of the loss of innocence and idealism by a songwriter, and the action began in the present and journeyed back. Without the three-act formula of the original play, in which each significant period of the songwriter's life was explored more fully and dramatically, the musical, reduced to two acts, required dates to be printed on to the sets, and not only became too difficult to follow, but gave the entire proceedings an air of confusion and superficiality. *Merrily We Roll Along* became the last play of the Sondheim–Prince collaboration that had begun with *Company*.

SONDHEIM AND LLOYD WEBBER

Michael Bennett's reason for joy was the black musical *Dreamgirls*, which was brilliantly staged but of shallow content. Suggested by the story of The Supremes, the famous Motown group which spawned Diana Ross, its highlight came at the end of Act One when one of the girls who had been asked to leave the group screamed a powerful song, 'I Am Telling You I'm Not Going' – and then proceeded to go. The incongruity bothered no one. The cast was remarkable and *Dreamgirls* ran till the summer of 1985.

In London, in Andrew Lloyd Webber's next musical, Tim Rice was replaced by T. S. Eliot. Andrew has an amazing gift for selecting subject matter

that lends itself to his music and to the kind of spectacle he seeks. The three contemporary poets to whom I have always turned for 'a stay in the confusion' (Robert Frost) have been Frost, Yeats and Eliot. My least favourite work of the three was Eliot's 'Old Possum's Book of Practical Cats', which I always found arch and 'twee'. Not, however, A. Lloyd Webber. Setting those verses to music and adding the slenderest thread to provide a climax, he produced *Cats*, which will undoubtedly be the most profitable musical in history, and, perhaps, even the longest running. Astoundingly conceived by Trevor Nunn and with equally astounding sets and costumes by John Napier, it was (and is) a dance musical for which the energetic, feline choreography was the work of the most outstanding lady in her field in England, Gillian Lynne. *Cats* opened in May 1981 and, five years later, it is still a feat to get a seat. The score is remarkably theatrical with one absolutely beautiful song, 'Memory', the lyric for which was written by Trevor Nunn and suggested by lines from other Eliot poetry.

Again New York received it with more *froideur* than London when it opened there in October 1982. One morning paper said: 'Less than purr-fect.' However, proving the wisdom of Webber's theatrical instinct, the *New York Times* wrote: 'It is not that this collection of anthropomorphic variety turns is a brilliant musical or that it powerfully stirs the emotions or that it has an idea in its head . . . Whatever the other failings . . . even banalities of *Cats*, it believes

Bonnie Langford, Elaine Page and Finola Hughes in *Cats*

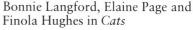

Starlight Express

in purely theatrical magic, and on that faith it unquestionably delivers.'

And it has continued to deliver to this day with no end in sight. There are at present more than a half-dozen productions of it being performed around the world, each with tremendous success.

Andrew's next work, *Song and Dance*, presented the following season, was as small in dimension as *Cats* was large – except in sound. It began its career as a one-hour television show, *Tell Me on a Sunday*. In it, one character sings twenty-two songs which chronicle the amorous adventures and misadventures of a young English girl in America. With lyrics by Don Black, the album again became a huge seller before the show opened. It was brought to the stage as the first act of an evening in which the second act consisted of pure dance, to the music of Webber's variations on the famous theme of Paganini which he had written for his brother, the celebrated cellist Julian Lloyd Webber. It was expected that *Song and Dance* might have a respectable run of a few months, but to the collective joy of all those concerned, the few months turned into two years and as of this writing is doing well on Broadway.

On Broadway, or off-Broadway to be exact, one of the hits of that season was *The Little Shop of Horrors*, an entertaining send-up of the old horror film, which was possessed of a sufficiently clever score, by composer Alan Menken and lyricist Howard Ashman, to keep audiences amused on both sides of the Atlantic for a long time.

But the most interesting musical of the season was *Nine*, based on Fellini's autobiographical film *8½*. The music and lyrics were by Maury Yeston, a newcomer to the big time, and his score was filled with talent, literate both musically and lyrically, and at times quite touching. The success of *Nine*, however, was due exclusively to the choreographic and directorial wizardry of Tommy Tune. It was not that he made what was unclear clear, he did something far more difficult. He directed it with such style that it did not matter.

In the 1982–3 season he gave another example of his touch and magic in *My One and Only*, with all-Gershwin music (and what ecstasy and relief to hear it) and starring himself and Twiggy. It was a show done twice. It opened out of town, closed out of town, and returned to New York where a new book was written by Peter Stone; it was re-rehearsed from page one, redirected, and finally opened in May 1983 to reviews that made all the work worthwhile.

The second winner that season was *La Cage aux Folles* which opened in August 1983. It was based on one of the most delicious, poignant and hilarious French films in memory about a middle-aged, 'married' couple who happens to be homosexual. Adapted for the stage by Harvey Fierstein and with an all-out Broadway score by Jerry Herman, which included two good romantic songs, a few rousers, a first-rate comedy number and a dramatic song of defiance, 'I Am What I Am', performed by George Hearn, *La Cage aux Folles* on the stage simplified the story almost to non-existence and replaced

sentiment with sentimentality. But in Arthur Laurents' show-wise hands it succeeded admirably on its own terms. Gene Barry returned to the stage from thousands of television shows and, with an immensely attractive voice and a winning performance, gave the play the emotional glue that held it together.

In 1984 there were two musicals that are perfect exhibits A and B of the difference of approach to the musical theatre by Sondheim and Lloyd Webber.

To Broadway in the spring came *Sunday in the Park with George*, with music and lyrics by Sondheim and book and direction by James Lapine, a relative newcomer to the scene. It was the story of the obsession of Georges Seurat to paint his pointillist masterpiece 'Un Dimanche d'été à la Grand Jatte'. It was also the story of the fanaticism required of any artist to achieve anything. The action carried over from Seurat's generation of the 1880s to the struggle of a fictitious contemporary descendant. No musical in recent memory ever aroused such controversy and divergence of opinion, both in the press and with the public, as did *Sunday in the Park*. One critic who felt it was a magnificent departure was the scribe of the *New York Times*. Hardly a Sunday went by when there was not a mention of it on the cultural pages of that most influential newspaper. This not only aroused the public, who proceeded to visit the Booth Theatre until August 1985, but the musical won the Pulitzer Prize for Drama. The story goes that at a meeting of the executives of the *New York Times* there was consternation that the paper had not won a single Pulitzer Prize that year. Someone said: 'But we did. For Drama.'

Although hardly distinguished for melody, *Sunday in the Park* was a small musical of infinite visual beauty. When Seurat finally finishes his painting and it comes to life on the stage, it is a rapturous moment – in fact two moments, because it happens twice.

In London, Lloyd Webber opened *Starlight Express*, a huge musical in which the cast instead of being 'anthropomorphic' cats are anthropomorphic trains, and the entire show is performed on roller skates. In a totally reconstructed theatre the performers go tearing around you, behind you, in front of and over you. There is again a wisp of a story which is family to *Cats* in theme, but the score was the first Webber offering without a hit. However, the spectacle is sufficient unto the day. For the audience, Webber's instinct for the colossal is spot on and *Starlight Express* is a smash.

In estimating the influence of Sondheim and Lloyd Webber, fundamentally Sondheim's contribution is to content and Webber's is to form. Sondheim is one of a kind. He cannot be imitated except by cloning. Webber, on the other hand, speaks in the popular musical language of the day, more literate but, nevertheless, contemporary through and through; and form, in these particular times, is apt to cast a longer shadow than content.

On Broadway, where the cost of a musical runs from $3 million on up, and the price of a ticket is as high as $60 per, the hit-loving as opposed to the theatre-loving public expects a lot for its money. Webber's concept of operatic spectacle fills the bill. With the exception of Joseph Papp and David Merrick, an empire unto himself, there are no producers in New York. The two organizations with sufficient funds to finance gargantuan extravaganzas are the two organizations that own and control the majority of theatres in the country – in other words, real estate operators. One is the Shubert Organization and the other is the Nederlander Company. Of the two the Shubert is the more affluent and more powerful. To bring *Cats* to New York, for example, cost over $3 million, but however long it took to recover its investment was of no consequence to the Shuberts. *Cats* productions were playing Shubert theatres throughout the country. They were reaping large dividends as landlords, and because the Shubert Organization is a trust, created by the original Shubert brothers for the preservation of their theatres, the lion's share of the profits goes straight back into the trust. So its resources are unlimited. Both organizations regard London as a workshop (said to me by a member of the Shubert Organization) and have even invaded the sacred halls of the National Theatre, where they finance at a third of the Broadway cost and have the extended rehearsal period which is permitted to the subsidized theatre. One of the Shubert investments was the musical *Jean* in 1983, which was directed by Sir Peter Hall, rehearsed for an endless number of weeks, and was an abysmal failure – which cost the Shuberts comparatively little but deprived the National and the British public of the opportunity to see the sort of play for which the National had been created. They also underwrote Peter Shaffer's *Amadeus* at the National and his next play, *Yonadab*.

Part of the reason for this open-door policy of the subsidized theatre has been the reduction of governmental grants, a destructive act in itself, but typical of the calculated indifference to the performing arts of conservative governments in general and the Thatcher one in particular.

The Nederlanders have recently purchased the Aldwych Theatre, and there is a growing movement afoot for more British theatres to become part of American real estate. In short, the altitudinous costs of the New York theatre have begun to play an unhealthy role in the life of the British theatre, which is one of the country's proudest and most glorious possessions. Further, this financial wheeling and dealing approach to the theatre has the subsidiary effect of inhibiting the development of young talent, without which the living theatre cannot survive.

History is replete with dire predictions about the future of the New York theatre. But the 'fabulous invalid', as Kaufman and Hart named it, has always recovered. This time the malaise may indeed be terminal. While the West End is booming and one cannot find an empty auditorium, half the theatres in New York are dark and with little prospect of future occupants. The financial crunch is on. With an occasional interloper, such as the recent musical version of *Huckleberry Finn*, only those musicals endowed by one of the two major organizations can enter the arena. Without the infusion of young talent, who is going to fill them? Cameron Mackintosh, England's wisest and most successful producer of musicals, said to me one day in jest: 'New York is becoming just a stop on the American tour.'

There are at present less than a dozen composers and lyricists who are consistent producers. Of that number only one, Andrew Lloyd Webber, is considered a blue chip investment. The bankable part of the theatrical team now is the director, with Michael Bennett, Trevor Nunn, Bob Fosse, Mike Nichols and Tommy Tune heading the list. This in itself is an unhealthy symptom. The theatre flourishes when it is a writer's theatre, as it has done since Offenbach arrived in Paris.

The year of 1985 marked the 100th anniversary of the birth of Jerome Kern and his music was played in appreciation throughout the world. In London there was a Kern celebration that ended with 'They Didn't Believe Me', written seventy-two years ago. As I listened I could not help but ask myself: is there any music being composed today that will be heard seventy-two years hence?

The truth is no one knows. The ultimate judgement lies in the hands of the clock. But whatever the judgement, we have sufficiently vast musical riches to keep us in pleasure and joy for years to come. And things will change. Somehow they always do. Broadway cannot live without the musical theatre, but the musical theatre can live without Broadway. After all, its first home was Paris and then Vienna and then London and then New York. So changes of address are not uncommon.

In the musical *42nd Street*, the director in the play says, in an ecstatic moment: 'The two most glorious words in the English language, musical comedy.'

Quite right.

BIBLIOGRAPHY

Bordman, Gerald, *The American Musical Theatre*, Oxford.

Bordman, Gerald, *Days To Be Happy, Years To Be Sad: The Life and Music of Vincent Youmans*, Oxford.

Brahms, Caryl, *Gilbert and Sullivan*, Little, Brown.

Dietz, Howard, *Dancing in the Dark: An Autobiography*, Bantam.

Eells, George, *Cole Porter: The Life That Late He Led*, Putnam.

Ewen, David, *The World of Jerome Kern*, Holt.

Ewen, David, *A Journey to Greatness: The Life and Music of George Gershwin*, Holt.

Faris, Alexander, *Jacques Offenbach*, Scribners.

Freedland, Michael, *Jerome Kern: A Biography*, Stein & Day.

Gammond, Peter, *Offenbach: His Life and Times*, Midas.

Green, Stanley, *Encyclopedia of the Musical Theatre*, Da Capo.

Green, Stanley, *The Rodgers and Hammerstein Story*, Da Capo.

Green, Stanley, *Ring Bells! Sing Songs! Broadway Musicals of the 1930's*, Galahad.

Hart, Dorothy, *Thou Swell, Thou Witty: The Life and Lyrics of Lorenz Hart*, Harper & Row.

Jablonski, Edward, and Lawrence D. Stewart, *The Gershwin Years*, Doubleday.

Jackson, Arthur, *The Book of Musicals: from Showboat to A Chorus Line*, Mitchell Beazley.

Kimball, Robert and Alfred Simon, *The Gershwins*, Bonanza.

Edited by Robert Kimball, *The Complete Lyrics of Cole Porter*, Hamish Hamilton.

Kreuger, Miles, *Showboat: The Story of A Classic American Musical*, Oxford.

Lahr, John, *Automatic Vaudeville*, Methuen.

Lesley, Cole, Graham Payn and Sheridan Morley, *Noel Coward and His Friends*, Weidenfeld & Nicolson.

Mander, Raymond and Joe Mitchenson, *Musical Comedy*, Peter Davies.

Marx, Samuel and Jan Clayton, *Rodgers and Hart*, Putnam.

Nolan, Frederick, *The Sound of Their Music: The Story of Rodgers and Hammerstein*, Walker.

Parker, Derek and Julia, *The Story and The Song: A Survey of English Musical Plays 1916–78*, Chappell.

Pearson, Hesketh, *Gilbert and Sullivan*, Hamish Hamilton.

Rodgers, Richard, *Musical Stages: His Autobiography*, W. H. Allen.

Rodgers and Hart Fact Book, The Lynn Farnol Group.

Schwartz, Charles, *Cole Porter: A Biography*, Da Capo.

Toll, Robert C., *Blacking Up*, Oxford University Press.

Taylor, Deems, *Some Enchanted Evenings: The Story of Rodgers and Hammerstein*, Harper.

Traubner, Richard, *Operetta: A Theatrical History*, Gollancz.

INDEX